Cross-Grained & Wily Waters

A Guide to the Piscataqua Maritime Region

South Berwick, Maine. Behind the boys sitting on the granite bulkhead of the old gundalow landing are buildings of the Portsmouth Manufacturing Company, and the bridge over the dam on what is today Route 4, or Portland Ave. The only building still standing is the Counting House (formerly the company's office), obscured by the tree in the distance. Much of this waterfront is currently being developed as a public park. Undated photograph. Courtesy of Old Berwick Historical Society, South Berwick, Maine.

Cross-Grained & Wily Waters

A Guide to the Piscataqua Maritime Region

W. Jeffrey Bolster, Editor

PETER E. RANDALL PUBLISHER
Portsmouth, New Hampshire
2002

"Atlantic Heights" was reprinted from Richard M. Candee, *Building Portsmouth: The Neighborhoods and Architecture of New Hampshire's Oldest City* (Portsmouth Advocates, Inc., 1992), with permission from Portsmouth Advocates, Inc.

"Guidebooks to the Piscataqua Region" was reprinted from *"A Noble and Dignified Stream": The Piscataqua Region in the Colonial Revival, 1860-1930,* eds. Sarah L. Giffen and Kevin D. Murphy (Old York Historical Society, 1992), with permission from the Old York Historical Society.

"Bud McIntosh, Piscataqua Boat Builder" was excerpted from *The Piscataqua Current: The Newsletter of the Piscataqua Gundalow Project.* Vol. XV (Spring, 1993), with permission.

Robert Dunn's poem "Some people say" was published in *quo, Musa, tendis?* and *Under the Legislature of Stars: 62 New Hampshire Poets,* 1999, and *Walking to Windward: I hear America Singing: sometimes it troubles me* (2001). It is reprinted with permission of Oyster River Press.

Esther Buffler's poem "May, June" is reprinted with permission of the author.

Excerpt from *Beachcombing for a Shipwrecked God* (copyright 1995) by Joe Coomer. Reprinted with the permission of Graywolf Press, Saint Paul, Minnesota.

Excerpt from *Harbor Lights* (copyright 2000) by Theodore Weesner. Reprinted with the permission of Grove/Atlantic, Inc.

Excerpts from *The Weight of Water* (copyright 1997) by Anita Shreve. Reprinted with the permission of Little, Brown and Company.

Cover Credits
Design: Brown & Co., Portsmouth, New Hampshire
Front cover photographs courtesy of Old York Historical Society and Milne Special Collections and Archives Department, University of New Hampshire.
Back cover photograph by Bill Finney, used with permission of the photographer.

Book Design: Grace Peirce

Peter E. Randall Publisher
Box 4726, Portsmouth NH 03802
www.PERPublisher.com

Distributed by University Press of New England
        Hanover and London

Library of Congress Cataloging-in-Publication Data
Cross-grained & wily waters : a guide to the Piscataqua maritime region / W. Jeffrey Bolster, editor.
        p. c.m.
    ISBN 0-914339-65-6
    1. Piscataqua River Valley (N.H. and Me.)—Description and travel. 2. Piscataqua River Valley (N.H. and Me.)—History, Local. 3. Piscataqua River Valley (N.H. and Me.)—Guidebooks. 4. Historic sites—Piscataqua River Valley (N.H. and Me.)—Guidebooks. I. Title: Cross-grained and wily waters. II. Bolster, W. Jeffrey.

F42. P4 C76 2002
917.42'6—dc21
                                                    2002017752

"Cross-Grained and Wily Waters." What a perfect phrase for Piscataqua waterways, where tidal currents surge up and down channels with fury, tipping buoys nearly on their sides, and spinning moored vessels with abandon. This book's title came indirectly from James L. Garvin, architectural historian at the New Hampshire Division of Historical Resources. Jim had used variations of the phrase to describe the river in several publications during the early 1970s. He, in turn, attributes the words, in other combinations, to William G. Saltonstall, historian and former principal of Phillips Exeter Academy. Mr. Saltonstall cruised Piscataqua by sailboat, racing shell, and kayak for many years, and wrote with care and authority of the area in his 1941 classic, Ports of Piscataqua. This title was chosen not only for its descriptive flavor, but as a tribute to both of these men, who, each in his own way, have educated so many by sharing their passion for Piscataqua.

Portsmouth Yacht Club, looking toward Four Tree Island. Portsmouth Harbor, circa 1900. The Yacht Club was located here before it moved to New Castle in 1938. Four Tree Island is now connected by a causeway to Peirce Island. Courtesy of Portsmouth Athenaeum.

LONG DEFINED BY ITS MARITIME COMMERCE, THEN BY
ITS WATER-DRIVEN MILLS, AND RECENTLY AS A MARINE
ECOSYSTEM WORTHY OF ATTENTION IN ITS OWN RIGHT,
THE PISCATAQUA REGION HAS A RICH AND ONGOING
ASSOCIATION WITH LOCAL WATERS.

Postcard view of schooners delivering coal to the Newmarket Mills, circa 1900. Courtesy of the Newmarket Historical Society.

Exploring the waters of Great Bay at Sandy Point Discovery Center in Stratham, New Hampshire. Photograph by Beth Heckman, 1998. Courtesy of the photographer.

CONTENTS

A Note to the Reader: This book is a sampler of sites, activities, and events that made, and continue to make, this region. It could have been arranged in many ways. Ultimately the table of contents was organized by town, as if approaching from the sea or the Isles of Shoals. The book proceeds to the seacoast towns of Seabrook, Hampton, and Rye, then upstream past New Castle and Portsmouth to the fall line of each river, before returning downstream to Kittery and York. This convention takes readers up the estuary and back to sea again, a generalized path followed by generations of gundalow men, and by the tide itself. Essays on various topics, some site-specific and some not, are interspersed with the towns.

BENEFACTORS

Cross-Grained and Wily Waters: A Guide to the Piscataqua Maritime Region

has been made possible by the vision and generous support of key institutions and individuals.

The Greater Piscataqua Community Foundation, including:

Winebaum Cultural and Environmental Fund

Paul and Mary Avery Charitable Fund

Elizabeth B. Carter Fund

Benjamin Allen Rowland Cultural and Environmental Fund

Mary Gaff Hinkle Fund

Julia's Fund

The University of New Hampshire's Office of Sustainability Programs

Great Bay Stewards

Ocean National Bank

Strawbery Banke Museum

Anonymous Friends

Martha Fuller Clark

Joseph C. Donnelly, Jr.

Jackie Eastwood and Mike McClurken

Cyrus B. and Barbara K. Sweet

This project was funded in part by a grant from the Office of State Planning, New Hampshire Coastal Program, as authorized by the National Oceanic and Atmospheric Administration (NOAA), Grant Number NA870Z0240.

The Bos'n Allen House, New Castle, New Hampshire, 1922. Allen served as boatswain (bos'n) with Captain John Paul Jones on the ship Ranger *during the American Revolution. Photograph by Paul Rubens Frost. Courtesy of the Portsmouth Athenaeum.*

ACKNOWLEDGMENTS

"COMMUNITY-BUILDING" IS THE TERM THAT BEST describes the production of *Cross-Grained and Wily Waters*. Individuals from many backgrounds and institutions worked in a genuinely collaborative fashion to create this book, and thanks are due to all who made it possible.

Early in 1998 a working group formed to discuss the feasibility of reaffirming the maritime identity of the Piscataqua River and Great Bay estuary. The initial idea was to develop coherent interpretive programs among the many historic sites and museums throughout the region, and to identify for the public other sites that would enhance understanding of the region's identity, social history, and environmental sensitivity. This book was born in those meetings. That visionary group consisted of Carol Walker Aten, then director of the American Independence Museum; W. Jeffrey Bolster, Associate Professor of History at the University of New Hampshire; Molly Bolster, director of the

Picnic at the beach in Rye, New Hampshire. Undated photograph. Courtesy of Milne Special Collections and Archives Department, University of New Hampshire.

Wentworth-Coolidge Mansion; Nicholas Brown, then at Strawbery Banke; James L. Garvin, the architectural historian at the New Hampshire Division of Historical Resources; Michael Gowell, then director and skipper of the Piscataqua Gundalow at Strawbery Banke; Thomas B. Johnson, curator of the Old York Historical Society; Wendy Lull, director of the Seacoast Science Center; Thomas C. Mansfield, the architect at the New Hampshire Department of Resources and Economic Development; Sharon Meeker, University of New Hampshire Marine Extension Specialist; Peter Michaud, a regional site manager for the Society for Preservation of New England Antiquities; Jeffrey H. Taylor, director of the New Hampshire Office of State Planning; Katie Vaillancourt, then a graduate student in Museum Studies at the University of New Hampshire; and Ursula Wright, then

with the Society for the Preservation of New England Antiquities.

Jim Garvin's wisdom and unmatched knowledge of the region was reflected in the initial proposal, which he wrote, and which became the basis for several successful bids for funding. Later, a streamlined steering committee consisting of Carol Aten, Jeff and Molly Bolster, Mike Gowell, and Jeff Taylor took charge of the project, and saw it through to completion.

Bethany S. Rutledge, a Museum Studies graduate student at UNH, and Nicholas B. Brown did yeoman service as researchers, combing local archives for information and images. Katie Vaillancourt became the graphics editor, energetically taking charge of finding, scanning, and arranging permissions for most of the art. Jennifer E. Merriam, an information technologist at UNH's Complex Systems' Research Center, graciously provided the fundamentals for the fold-out map accompanying the book. Laura Gowing, of the American Independence Museum, researched details for the map, and Tricia Miller, of Brown and Company in Portsmouth, enhanced it with decorative elements. The striking cover is the work of Scott Buchanan and Alicen Brown. Peter E. Randall did much more than publish the book. He was unfailingly helpful along the way with suggestions, photographs, and answers. Decades of publishing and writing Piscataqua-related books have made Peter an impressive authority, and he willingly shared his encyclopedic knowledge. Thanks also to Deidre Randall, and to Grace Peirce, at Peter E. Randall Publisher. Grace did a wonderful job with layout and design. Suzanne Guiod is an extraordinarily talented and dedicated copyeditor, and her sharp eye made *Cross-Grained and Wily Waters* a substantially better book from beginning to end.

The Greater Piscataqua Community Foundation is fortunate to have a man of the caliber of Peter Lamb at the helm. Peter backed this project from the beginning in many important ways, and we are grateful to him. Thanks also to Racheal Stuart and Maryellen Burke at GPCF. Terri Beyer arranged for crucial financial support from Ocean Bank. Tom Kelly thought it appropriate that the University of New Hampshire's Office of Sustainability Programs support the project. Without them and the project's other benefactors, this book never would have gotten off the ground. Thanks to all. Finances were capably managed by UNH's Office of Sponsored Research, and by the Wentworth Coolidge Commission, specifically Mary Griffin, treasurer, and Jennifer Croteau, bookkeeper.

Several archives provided the lion's share of the images in *Wily Waters*. We would like to thank the staffs at the Portsmouth Athenæum, the Milne Special Collections and Archives Department of the University of New Hampshire, the Old Berwick Historical Society, and the Old York Historical Society, all of whom were unfailingly helpful. The Computing and Information Services staff at UNH assisted in crucial ways, and we appreciate it. The work of many photographers is represented here, but we must single out contemporary photographers Ralph Morang, Peter E. Randall, Fred Pettigrew, and Scott Sulley for special thanks. Their evocative images are crucial pieces of this book.

The list of contributors reveals tremendous breadth and depth of knowledge. This was truly an interdisciplinary project, representing the complimentary perspectives of historians, anthropologists, journalists, museum professionals, science educators, scholars of literature, architects, economists, mariners, and others, all dedicated to understanding the essence of the Piscataqua region. A hearty thanks to each author.

The editor and steering committee also would like to acknowledge the inspiration of William G. Saltonstall's *Ports of Piscataqua* (1941), John P. Adams' *Drowned Valley: The Piscataqua River Basin* (1976), and Frederick T. Short's *The Ecology of the Great Bay Estuary, New Hampshire and Maine: An Estuarine Profile and Bibliography* (1992). Each of those books was a critical milestone in the appreciation of this region, and we hope that *Cross-Grained and Wily Waters* is a worthy successor.

Shortly before this book went to press its editor was named as the next James H. Hayes and Claire Short Hayes Chair in the Humanities at the University of New Hampshire. A decade ago the Hayes family endowed that chair to promote the study of New Hampshire's history, culture, and politics, and this book is but one of many contributions that honor their vision. We are pleased to acknowledge the inspiration of the Hayes Chair, and proud that *Cross-Grained and Wily Waters* is now part of its legacy.

"Arabesque on the Rocks," Passaconaway Inn, York, Maine. Lantern slide, circa 1915. Courtesy of Old York Historical Society.

CONTRIBUTORS

KA   Karen Alexander is a specialist in antique books and maps, and a PhD candidate in History at the University of New Hampshire. She worked as the New Hampshire map expert on the New Hampshire v. Maine boundary case argued before the U.S. Supreme Court in 2001.

RA   Robert Andersen is a freelance writer and independent scholar, currently at work on two books, a novel set in Kittery Point and a study of post-Vietnam America entitled *The Final Lesson: Vietnam and American Political Culture from the Fall of Saigon to the Flight from Washington, 1975-1995*, to be published by Basic Books.

CWA   Carol Walker Aten is project manager of the Squamscott Coalition, a community philanthropy initiative. She is the former director of the American Independence Museum in Exeter.

EWB   Emerson W. Baker is Associate Professor of History at Salem State College and co-author of *The New England Knight: Sir William Phips, 1651-1695*.

MB   Matthew Bampton is Associate Professor of Geography at the University of Southern Maine, whose research specialization is long term human modification of environmental processes.

CCB   Cathleen C. Beaudoin is the director of the Dover Public Library, in Dover, New Hampshire, and co-author of *Port of Dover: Two Centuries of Shipping on the Cochecho*.

WJB   W. Jeffrey Bolster is Associate Professor of History at the University of New Hampshire, and author of *Black Jacks: African American Seamen in the Age of Sail*.

MLB   Molly Bolster is the director of the Wentworth-Coolidge Mansion in Portsmouth, New Hampshire.

NBB   Nicholas B. Brown is a journalist and wooden boat-builder living in Eliot, Maine. His past includes naval service, coastal towing, and a lifelong love of surfing.

MEB   Maryellen Burke is a senior program officer for the Greater Piscataqua Community Foundation. She is also president of the Portsmouth Historical Society and a proprietor at the Portsmouth Athenæum. She received her PhD from the University of Florida in Victorian literature, and is co-author of *Gosport Remembered: The Last Village at the Isles of Shoals*.

RMC   Richard M. Candee is Professor of American and New England Studies at Boston University, where he directs the Preservation Studies Program. He is the author of *Building Portsmouth: The Neighborhoods & Architecture of New Hampshire's Oldest City* and other works on the architecture of the Piscataqua.

SC   Suki Casanave is a nonfiction writer whose work has appeared in national and regional publications, including *Smithsonian, Yankee, The Christian Science Monitor*, and on PBS. She is the author of *Natural Wonders of New Hampshire*.

CEC   Charles E. Clark, who was the first to hold the James H. Hayes and Claire Short Hayes Chair in the Humanities at the University of New Hampshire, is the author of many books on early American history, including *The Meetinghouse Tragedy: An Episode in the Life of a New England Town*. He is Professor of History, Emeritus, at the University of New Hampshire.

VC   Valerie Cunningham is the founder of the Portsmouth Black Heritage Trail, Inc., and the director of the African-American Resource Center in Portsmouth, New Hampshire.

SLD   Sandra L. DeChard has a master's degree from Boston University and specializes in waterfront architecture. She is assistant archeologist/architectural historian at Strawbery Banke Museum in Portsmouth, New Hampshire.

DD   Dudley Dudley served in the New Hampshire legislature for two terms and on the Governor's Council for four terms. She is a lifelong resident of the seacoast region.

JLG   James L. Garvin is the state architectural historian at the New Hampshire Division of Historical Resources, and co-author of five books, including *A Building History of Northern New England*.

RGG   Robert G. Goodby, Assistant Professor of Anthropology at Franklin Pierce College, specializes in the archeology of Native American sites in New England. He holds a PhD in Anthropology from Brown University, and recently completed a study of the 4,000-year-old Davison Brook site in Holderness, one of the largest Native American sites in New Hampshire.

MG   Michael Gowell is the former director of the Piscataqua Gundalow Project at Strawbery Banke Museum, in Portsmouth, New Hampshire. He has been rowing a dory into Piscataqua creeks, coves and guzzles since 1972.

MHA   Madeleine Hall-Arber has a PhD in Anthropology, and works at the Center for Marine Social Sciences in the Sea Grant College Program at the Massachusetts Institute of Technology. She is interested in the social aspects of regulatory change.

PFH   Paul F. Hughes has contributed to *Historical New Hampshire*, and is now writing a history of the town of Greenland.

TBJ   Thomas B. Johnson is curator at the Old York Historical Society in York, Maine, and serves as vice-chair of the Maine Historic Preservation Commission.

WBL   William B. Leavenworth earned his PhD in History at the University of New Hampshire and is currently an independent scholar researching the New England fisheries.

KM   Kelle MacKenzie is the director of the Sandy Point Discovery Center in Stratham, New Hampshire.

TCM   Thomas C. Mansfield, the architect for the New Hampshire Department of Resources and Economic Development, has overseen preservation maintenance at state owned historical sites around Portsmouth harbor since 1991, including Fort Constitution, Fort Stark, and the surviving bunkers of Fort Dearborn at Odiorne Point.

JM   John Mayer is the former curator at Strawbery Banke Museum in Portsmouth, New Hampshire. Throughout the year (when not at work or enjoying his family) he can be found in a sailboat exploring the nature and history of the Piscataqua River watershed.

SM   Sharon Meeker, a UNH Marine Extension Specialist, is director of the UNH Marine Docent program, and director of the Sea Trek Marine Education Program.

DM   Dean Merchant is an historian, clammer, and researcher of early New England history.

LSM   Lorraine Stuart Merrill is a farmer and writer specializing in agriculture, the environment, and planning. She wrote and edited *The New Hampshire Estuaries Project Conservation and Management Plan*.

PM   Peter Michaud is the Portsmouth and Exeter site manager for the Society for the Preservation of New England Antiquities.

RO   Richard Ober is executive director of the Monadnock Conservancy (a land trust serving Hillsborough and Cheshire counties), and a nonfiction writer specializing in conservation and outdoor topics.

JP   Jane Porter recently retired after many years as the keeper of the Portsmouth Athenæum.

PER   Peter E. Randall, author of *Hampton, A Century of Town and Beach, 1888-1988*, and twelve other books, is a life-long Seacoast writer, photographer, and publisher who has concentrated on the history and culture of the Piscataqua region.

RAR   Robert Alex Robertson is an Associate Professor in the Department of Resource Economics and Development at the University of New Hampshire. His current research and service activities focus on the social and cultural dimensions of the fishery management planning process in New England.

JDR   J. Dennis Robinson created and edits SeacoastNH.com, the internet portal for the Piscataqua River region. Robinson has produced over two hundred educational and promotional videos, and has written hundreds of articles and essays about Seacoast area history and culture. He writes and lives in Portsmouth.

SGR   Sarah Giffen Rooker is the executive director of the Vermont Museum and Gallery Alliance, and co-editor of *"A Noble and Dignified Stream": The Piscataqua Region in the Colonial Revival, 1860-1930*.

LHT   Louise H. Tallman, who lives in Rye, combines her interest in the natural and human history of the area through involvement in the local conservation commission and historical society.

JHT   Jeffrey H. Taylor is the director of the Office of State Planning in Concord, New Hampshire. A former deck watch officer aboard the USCG Cutter *Active* in New Castle, he now enjoys touring Piscataqua in a Bud McIntosh pulling boat.

CAV   Catherine A. Vaillancourt is the curator of collections at The Brickstore Museum in Kennebunk, Maine.

BMW   Barbara McLean Ward, director-curator of the Moffatt-Ladd House in Portsmouth, New Hampshire, is editor of *Produce & Conserve, Share & Play Square: The Grocer and the Consumer on the Home-Front Battlefield During World War II.*

DHW   David H. Watters, Professor of English at the University of New Hampshire, holds the James H. Hayes and Claire Short Hayes Chair in the Humanities, and is co-editor of *The Encyclopedia of New England Culture.*

HW   Helen Winebaum is president of the York Land Trust in York, Maine. She has served as a trustee of the Currier Gallery of Art, and is a director of the Greater Piscataqua Community Foundation.

REW   Richard E. Winslow, III, is a maritime historian and author of many books about the Seacoast region, including *Do Your Job! An Illustrated Bicentennial History of the Portsmouth Naval Shipyard, 1800-2000.*

USW   Ursula S. Wright has a master's degree in Early American History from the University of New Hampshire. She was regional administrator for the Society for the Preservation of New England Antiquities (SPNEA), managing ten house museums in Maine and New Hampshire. She is a research assistant at the Portsmouth Athenæum.

Marine Memorial, Hampton Beach, New Hampshire. Photograph by Ralph Morang, 1997. Courtesy of the photographer.

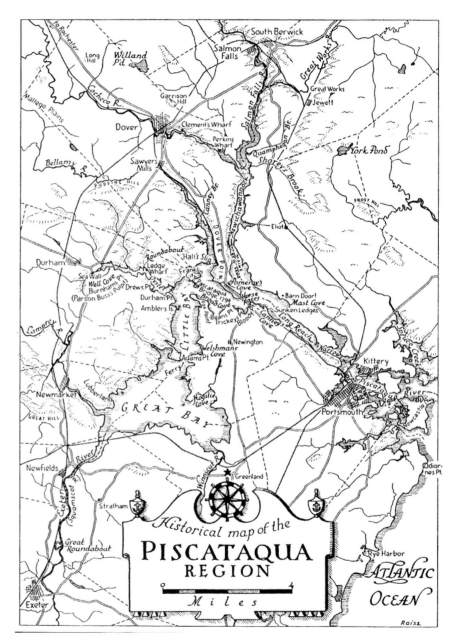

Historical map of the Piscataqua Region. *Drawn by Erwin Raisz for William G. Saltonstall's* Ports of Piscataqua, *published by Harvard University Press, 1941. Courtesy of Harvard University Press.*

FOREWORD

PIS-CAT'-A-QUA. Once you've learned where to put the accent, this is a fun word to say, the hissing in the word itself bringing to mind the fast flowing waters at Dover Point and the bubbling caldron of Boiling Rock further downstream. The term "Piscataqua," referring to both the river and the lands around it, was widely known and widely used in times past. When John Wentworth became New Hampshire's last royal governor in 1767, Portsmouth, at the center of Piscataqua, had a population of 4,500 people. Its ships and traders carried the name Piscataqua far and wide. By 1790 the Piscataqua shipping and fishing industries had made Portsmouth the fourteenth largest city in the country.

But the luster eventually wore off of the region's star, and the Piscataqua became more a locally held treasure than a national gem. First new roads, and then railroads, shifted the region's focus away from the waters. Shipbuilding remained a staple, as did some fishing, but the waterways' contribution to the Piscataqua economy was in their power, in the number of spindles they could turn in the tidewater towns of Rollinsford, Dover, Newmarket, and Exeter. But economies are cyclical, and after a while the mills closed as well.

And now growth has come to Piscataqua yet again. In York County, Maine, and Rockingham County, New Hampshire, the population increased on the order of thirteen percent between 1990 and 2000. Many here speak of the need for "balanced growth"—making sure that the new does not overwhelm the old. In order to do that effectively, one must understand and appreciate the old. Piscataqua's history is that of a waterfront community. People built homes near the shore. The rivers and coastal waters were the highways. They were the source of food, of industry, and of income.

Over time we have turned our backs on those waterways. Most of us earn our living at the end of a computer cable, not the end of a fishing line. We navigate up and down Route 95, not coasting out past Whaleback Light on a sea voyage. Even historic sites that were once approached by water now greet their visitors from the roadways. We must reconnect to that water; it is the medium that best explains the region. It is the fabric that holds the pieces together, and tells the story most fully.

In this book, Professor Jeff Bolster and his colleagues alert us to the histories and traditions of Piscataqua. They inform us of important pieces of local lore and culture. And we need to be informed. We nearly lost the Puddle Dock neighborhood in Portsmouth (later Strawbery Banke Museum) during the 1950s. In 2000 we did lose Tidewater Farm, the mansion that had graced the shores of the Cocheco River since 1815. Ongoing discussions indicate that the votes are still being counted on the future of Creek Farm in Portsmouth. And the natural areas are of concern as well. How many times must we go to the brink to save vital habitats like Portsmouth's Great Bog from becoming part of yet another subdivision? What is best for Piscataqua?

Change is the constant. The lands and waters of Piscataqua will surely change in the future as they have in the past. The question is, how, and in what manner, and with what impact? Piscataqua's is a heritage worthy of understanding, a firm foundation on which to base new actions. It is critical to the region's future that we comprehend its past.

Jeffrey H. Taylor
Director, New Hampshire Office of State Planning

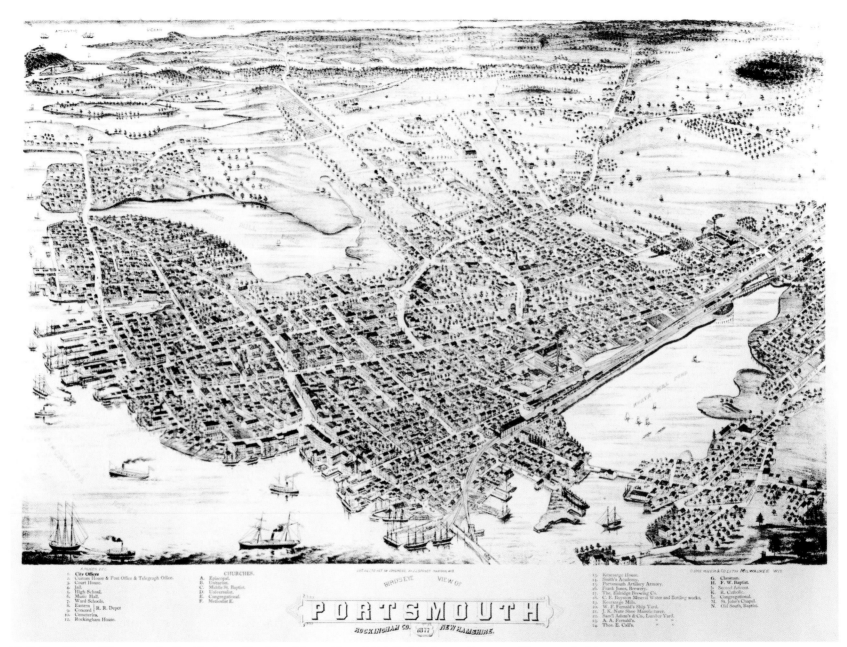

Bird's Eye View of Portsmouth, Rockingham Co., New Hampshire, *1877. By J. J. Stoner. Courtesy of Portsmouth Athenaeum.*

Introduction: The nature of This Place

One of the most enchanting and long-settled areas in America, the Piscataqua region remains somewhat undiscovered; not unpopulated, not unstudied, certainly not pristine—but undiscovered nonetheless. Here is a place almost as much water as land, a serpentine estuary steeped in maritime heritage. Inviting and approachable, the Piscataqua is nevertheless a far-flung kingdom of rivers and bays in which inspiring wildness and whiffs of the past lurk around every headland. These waters carry not only the freight of our history, but the key to our future quality of life; the stories we tell about them define who we are.

Residents no longer say they are "of Piscataqua" as did seventeenth-century settlers. References to "Portsmouth," "Kittery," "Durham," or "Seacoast New Hampshire" have replaced "Piscataqua" as a place in our minds. This change in language has been accompanied by a change in perception. Most contemporary residents and visitors do not envision the Piscataqua as a unified maritime area, a discrete historic site, or an identifiable ecosystem. They don't imagine themselves living in, or visiting, the Piscataqua. Yet the Piscataqua is a distinctive place with its own historical, environmental, and architectural footprint, a signature spot where the sea flows through an hourglass estuary to the rivers' first falls.

This region at the meeting place of Maine, New Hampshire, and the Atlantic Ocean has long beckoned people. For thousands of years, Paleo, Archaic, and Abenaki natives appreciated its shellfish and game. Then English and other Europeans were attracted by a

WENTWORTH-GARDNER HOUSE BUILT 1760, PORTSMOUTH, NEW HAMPSHIRE 2287

Postcard view of the Wentworth-Gardner House and the Mechanic Street shoreline, including the remnants of an old filled wharf. American Art Post Card Co., Boston, 1925. Courtesy of Tom Hardiman.

Gathering kelp for fertilizer, York Harbor Beach, Maine, 1889. Photograph by Fredrick B. Quimby. Courtesy of Old York Historical Society.

mind-boggling abundance of coastal codfish, along with easy water-borne access to majestic stands of white pine. Also enticing were the rapidly flowing rivers, sufficiently small that they could be harnessed for waterpower with seventeenth-century technology. One of the first sawmills in English America was built in South Berwick in 1634. By then English entrepreneurs who referred to the region as "Passcattaway," "Pascataquac," "Pascataquack," and "Pescataway," among other names, had established a rudimentary maritime economy for converting fish and timber into money.

While the spelling of its name may have been idiosyncratic, the area had well defined geographic boundaries from an early date. Those boundaries persist. Some 120 square miles, the Piscataqua region consists of the mighty Piscataqua River (one of the fastest navigable tidal currents in the United States) and its tributaries—the Winnicut, Squamscott, Lamprey, Oyster, Bellamy, Cocheco, and Salmon Falls Rivers. Connecting most of the rivers to the sea are Great Bay and Little Bay, two virtually landlocked bodies of water that are shallow, tough to navigate, and responsible for the Piscataqua's fierce ebb and flood. The bays also attract flocks of migratory waterfowl and provide panoramic vistas of an inland sea unique to this spot. From Portsmouth the region extends east to York

(once accessible by boat via Chauncey Creek and Brave Boat Harbor), and west to Seabrook. Seven miles offshore perch the Isles of Shoals, sentinels in the sea, outposts for centuries of the Piscataqua and its towns—Seabrook, Hampton, Rye, New Castle, Portsmouth, Newington, Greenland, Stratham, Exeter, Newmarket, Durham, Dover, Rollinsford, South Berwick, Eliot, Kittery, and York.

The Piscataqua is a place worth knowing, worth savoring, and worth sustaining. It is also threatened, like many other vernacular landscapes across America. The social and spiritual consequences of suburban sprawl loom large. New Hampshire's Office of State Planning reports that New Hampshire is currently the fastest growing state in the northeast, faster even than New Jersey, with a 6.8 percent rate of population increase during the 1990s. And 85 percent of New Hampshire's growth in the last decade has been in the southeast corner of the state—in the Piscataqua region. Rockingham County is predicted to grow by 66 percent between 1990 and 2020. Open space is at a premium, and going fast. The richly satisfying mosaic of field, forest, farmhouse, and marsh that long constituted the local landscape is being transformed by development. Habitat degradation is rampant. Storm water run-off tainted by automobiles and fertilizers is the number one threat to water quality in Great Bay. And more growth is inevitable.

Many of the essays in this book express concern that the Piscataqua's regional essence will be compromised as the population grows and as malls and subdivisions take root. But *Cross-Grained and Wily Waters* is not a lamentation for a lost world. In many ways it is as forward-looking as it is retrospective. Celebrating the Piscataqua, this book explains why the region looks as it does, and guides those who continue to explore by boat or car. Common threads are the estuary itself and the stories of local people interacting with an environment that has always been part land, part water. People who imagine themselves in a continuum with the past will find sustenance in these pages, as will residents for whom connectedness to place is deeply satisfying.

Earlier generations took for granted links between farm and factory, shipyard and mill, woodlot and saltmarsh, all tied together by rivers and the ubiquitous gundalow. Most people today have lost sight of those connections as they race from place to place in cars and trucks. Automobiles have made the Piscataqua more accessible and less unique. They have also drawn attention away from the rivers and bays, and the imprint of a maritime past so essential to the nature of this place.

Salt-streaked sailing ships once passed the Isles of Shoals en route to Portsmouth, the region's capitol city, and thence to towns like Exeter and Dover. Now adventurers in kayaks and outboard motor boats navigate those silted-in channels for pleasure, not profit, slipping past elegant eighteenth-century mansions, stark nineteenth-century mills, and convenient twentieth-century subdivisions. Oil tankers and early-rising lobstermen work today's tides, defining the Pis-

Henry Abbott Brickyards, Sturgeon Creek, Eliot, Maine, circa 1885. Many of the rivers in the Piscataqua region were once fringed with beds of thick blue clay, ideal for making bricks. Courtesy of Old Berwick Historical Society, South Berwick, Maine.

cataqua's contemporary maritime economy, while upstream and alongshore an ever-growing population finds new uses for old mills as condominiums and offices. Meanwhile scientists search for answers: why are eelgrass beds plagued with wasting disease? Can fish such as cod and flounder be raised in offshore aquaculture pens? To what extent has sewage treatment freed local waters and shellfish from pathogens?

As one drives west across the General Sullivan Bridge from Newington to Dover, momentarily becoming a modern skyrider on a great arc of steel and concrete, neither the bays nor the creeks and marshes appear diminished. The distant mountains form a backdrop to pines and hardwoods that have sprouted again from fields once cleared, while the tidal waters churn below, much as they did thousands of years ago. Human handiwork is evident, but not overwhelming: white church spires and factory stacks pierce the sky, while ancestral stone walls and utility lines crisscross the landscape in competing patterns of priority. This bird's-eye view of land and water puts into focus people and nature, past, present, and future. Of course, neither the landscape nor the waters themselves are timeless: the ecology of the region has changed dramatically in the last four hundred years. High on that bridge, however, there is a moment for meditation on how this region's maritime heritage and estuary has made it what it is, and how they might affect the future.

From that lofty vantage point individuals might imagine themselves as part of the natural world, intimately connected to its biological and ecological processes. Likewise, nonhuman nature might appear worthy of existence on its own terms, not simply as a servant to society. That such thoughts, nurtured by magnificent visions of the setting sun or the tidal currents' swirling eddies, can occur while driving across a technically complex bridge in the midst of bumper-to-bumper traffic is an indication that nature and human society are inextricably linked.

Consider the juxtaposition of historic man-made structures and natural environments in the Piscataqua. Eighteenth-century houses still inhabited, like the Dennett place in Kittery or many homes in the South End of Portsmouth, proclaim that this is a historic place. Meanwhile, one is never far from wildness, remnant though it may be. The harbors and coastal sea, much compromised, are still home to smelt, sculpin, and striped bass. Bald eagles routinely soar over Pease International Tradeport. Sufficient songbird habitat exists so that spring and fall migrations bring birds aplenty for watchers and predators.

This marvelous and relatively unspoiled estuary has long supported human history and pre-history. And it supports a complex and ever changing pattern of life—generally referred to as "nature." But we don't often think hard about history and nature together, or about the stories we use to link them. Stories, however, and the cultural visions behind them, tell us much about ourselves and how we imagine our place in the world.

Water sampling aboard the UNH Research Vessel Jere A. Chase. *Photograph by Jack Adams, 1979. Courtesy of Milne Special Collections and Archives Department, University of New Hampshire.*

A century ago, Colonial Revivalists with Piscataqua pedigrees told stories to perpetuate their links to heroic ancestors such as General John Sullivan of Durham, and to establish cultural proprietorship of this place. Their not-so-subtle messages about ancestry followed a script that privileged the lives and accomplishments of Anglo-Saxon pioneers over those of recent immigrants and factory workers. Stories like these condition not only how people see the past, but also how they shape the future. Individuals vote and act in part because of what they know about the world through the stories they tell and are told.

The key to regional sustainability of wild environments and vernacular landscapes in the Piscataqua may rest as much with the stories we come to tell as with environmental science. Narratives about the land and waters called Piscataqua have changed with time, and a conservationist ethos is more prominent than ever before. Nevertheless, most of our stories are still scripted in light of what we think we know about nature. For the sake of the region, it may be time to rethink them.

Just what is nature? Does nature include people or not? The answer to that question has important consequences for the future of the Piscataqua. "Nature" is a deeply paradoxical word, as historian William Cronon has pointed out. On the one hand, we use the word "nature" to describe something universal, implying that it must be common to all people, or to the universe. We say, for instance, "It's natural." On the other hand, we inscribe that word with specific values, many of them conflicting. Nature, Cronon observes, has been imagined for centuries as the Garden of Eden. In the early seventeenth century, New England was the

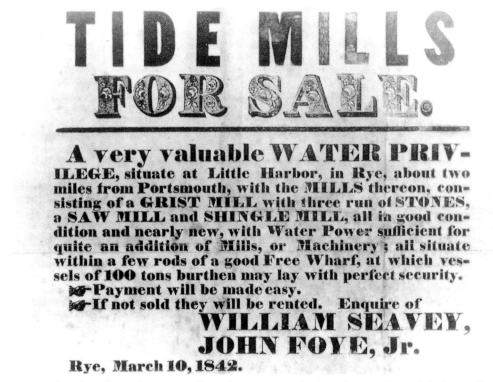

TIDE MILLS FOR SALE.

A very valuable **WATER PRIV-ILEGE**, situate at Little Harbor, in Rye, about two miles from Portsmouth, with the **MILLS** thereon, consisting of a **GRIST MILL** with three run of **STONES**, a **SAW MILL** and **SHINGLE MILL**, all in good condition and nearly new, with Water Power sufficient for quite an addition of Mills, or Machinery; all situate within a few rods of a good Free Wharf, at which vessels of **100** tons burthen may lay with perfect security.

☞ Payment will be made easy.

☞ If not sold they will be rented.   Enquire of

WILLIAM SEAVEY,
JOHN FOYE, Jr.

Rye, March 10, 1842.

Advertisement for tide mills, 1842. Most mills in the region were built at the site of waterfalls, but in flat coastal towns like Rye and New Castle, the power of ebbing and flooding tides was harnessed to saw wood and grind meal. Courtesy of Seacoast Science Center.

yet much of the popular understanding of "the environment" is predicated on the notion that if people just keep their hands off, everything will be fine. Unfortunately, the situation is not quite so simple. People have been affecting the world around them for millennia because people are *part* of the ecosystem. Yet our fundamental stories about the Piscataqua still serve to separate people from nature.

Captains Martin Pring, Samuel de Champlain, and John Smith, the first Europeans to write of New England and the Piscataqua in the early 1600s, viewed this place as a garden so rich and sublime that one stretch was evocatively named "Strawbery Banke." The conventional story about Europeans' arrival and the changing nature of this place has been one of Eden compromised. It is a woefully familiar story of forests felled, of shad and salmon gone, of waterways ultimately clogged with sawdust and tainted by chemicals.

The story was once told as the taming of wilderness and the creation of a new nation in a rich land. Predicated on Genesis, in which God said, "let them have dominion over the fish of the sea, and over the fowl of the air, and over the cattle, and over all the earth," it rationalized the extraction of resources, and suggested that technology could solve all problems. That unqualified story of progress is rarely told anymore, but we all know the script.

More prominent recently has been a tragic story of environmental decline, a tale of shrinking habitats, eroded topsoil, and slaughter. Eider and other ducks were once abundant in numbers unfathomable today. We simply have no conception of real abundance, having been affected by what fisheries scientists call "the shifting baseline syndrome," in which aggregates of creatures considered to be "normal" or

new Eden; in the nineteenth-century Yosemite was Eden; today the Amazon rain forest is considered Eden. Yet nature, he points out, also has been perceived as vengeful. Hurricanes, tornados, and shark attacks are hardly seen as edenic. Moreover, nature is still a commodity, as evidenced by New Hampshire's woodlots, Maine's lobster pounds, and real estate advertisements everywhere.

Meanwhile, nature as ecosystem is often presented as a stable community, even a "climax community," capable of enduring in a balanced equilibrium nearly forever, so long as humans do not disturb it. This is not very good science. It is not very good history, either. And

Looking southerly from Kittery Point, Maine, toward New Castle, New Hampshire, circa 1900. By then, the region's maritime commerce had long since declined, as had the wharf in the foregound. Courtesy of Strawbery Banke Museum.

The problem with these stories of progress and waste, each so true and powerful, is that they reaffirm a fallacious boundary between nature (that which is supposedly original) and the everyday world of people. The underpinnings are the same: humans are separate from nature no matter if they are using it, abusing it, or even saving it. The logical action so far for people who care about the environment is to preserve nature from human interference in as many isolated refuges as possible. The Piscataqua region has had notable successes with that strategy. Essays in this book explore the Rachael Carson National Wildlife Refuge, the Great Bay National Wildlife Refuge, and the Great Bay Resource Protection Partnership, and argue forcefully that such refuges are vital to preserve Piscataqua's estuarine ecosystem, and, by extension, its maritime heritage. So far, so good. But the problem is that governments and private agencies are not going to purchase and preserve most of the remaining open space or historically significant sites. The future of the region is largely in the hands of private citizens who will act in accordance with stories that make sense to them. This book suggests that stories told by everyday people can and do change, and that thinking people who care about the area can influence those stories that will shape the region's future.

When most people speak of "nature," historian Richard White observes, they commonly mean that it is something *not* made by

"natural" keep diminishing. Bird watchers today look for flocks of migratory waterfowl on Great Bay in the fall. Some know that market gunners once slaughtered waterfowl with small cannon in the nineteenth and early twentieth centuries. But unsustainable hunting began much earlier. About 1720 a local man named Penhallow reported Indians in canoes herding eider ducks just after they had molted and could not fly, killing 4,600 with billets of wood or paddles, and selling them to the English for a penny a dozen.

humans. But the world has been irreversibly modified by people, from the polar ice caps to the equatorial forests. One of the most ecologically diverse areas in the Piscataqua today is the Great Bay National Wildlife Refuge in Newington. More than a thousand acres of meadow, upland forest, marsh, and shoreline support numerous species and niche ecosystems near the razor wire and abandoned weapons bunkers of an obsolete Strategic Air Command base. Moreover, for centuries that land has been hunted and fished, logged and plowed, developed and abandoned. Is it still nature? It is certainly not original, nor is it untouched. And it would not be "wild" now were it not for human management. Clearly, any meaningful future conservation of mature forest, salt marsh, or biologically productive waters in the Piscataqua region can only occur in the context of human-occupied landscapes. Learning to envision nature *through time* as inextricably linked to people may be essential to the success of future preservation movements.

As we consider what was—and what is—the nature of the Piscataqua, perhaps we should begin with the insight elaborated by Simon Schama, William Cronon, Richard White, and other environmental historians, that "nature" is a human idea. Although we are accustomed to separating nature and human attitudes into two realms, they are, in fact, indivisible. The rocky intertidal zones, the beaches, the creatures, and the landscapes that we call "natural" do not stand completely apart from people. Instead, they are woven deeply with the words, images, and ideas we use to describe them. And more than ever before, the future of nonhuman nature is in human hands. Rather than assuming that modernity (the bane of the Colonial Revivalists) has increasingly separated people from nature, perhaps we should consider how modernity has increasingly squeezed humans and nonhuman nature together, forcing people to come to grips with their roles as ecological actors. Local maritime history helps make the point.

From the early 1600s to the early 1800s the natural world in the Piscataqua was envisioned at best as a source of commodities for profit. John Hatch's mural (reproduced as Color Plate IV) celebrated Durham's waterfront in that era of wooden shipbuilding and water-driven mills when loggers and farmers labored feverishly to transform "rude" or "uncultivated" landscapes into civilized and productive places. They felt

Hands-on marine biology at the Shoals Marine Lab, Appledore Island, 1979. Courtesy of Milne Special Collections and Archives Department, University of New Hampshire.

deeply that they were doing God's work, improving themselves and improving nature, which was often perceived as a threat.

By the middle of the 1800s, when textile mills dominated the landscape, the Piscataqua's maritime economy had stagnated. Maritime culture became overlain with nostalgia. From the 1860s to the 1960s recreational boaters, armchair sailors, and amateur historians alluded to that lost maritime world as an era in which hardy pioneering ancestors had created themselves, and this place, through a contest with nature. That story comprised an essential element of the Colonial Revival movement so influential in this region. Thus from first settlement until well into the twentieth century, most people here took for granted that humans were separate from nature: generally dominant, occasionally victimized, always tested.

Anxiety about the impact of a nuclear power plant at Seabrook and an oil refinery in Durham during the 1970s heightened

By the end of the twentieth century, the Moran tugs had become symbols of Portsmouth's working waterfront. Photograph by Fred Pettigrew, circa 1990. Courtesy of the photographer.

environmental consciousness. Long envisioned primarily in terms of maritime heritage, the Piscataqua was rapidly recast for the public as a marine ecosystem. Construction of marine science laboratories at Adams Point and on Appledore Island during the 1970s symbolized an important regional phenomenon, as construction of textile mills had during the 1800s, and merchants' mansions during the 1700s. Environmental scientists were the shock troops in a new battle, and their tactics paid off. Without the certainty of science, much of the Piscataqua's remnant wild areas and its distinctive wetlands landscape would have been lost. One underlying script behind the stories about the region, however, did not change.

Environmental scientists proceeded as historians before them, writing as if people operated on the environment rather than in it. Seeking scientific objectivity, some ecologists even investigated marine systems from baselines that currently existed as if they were "natural." This required ignoring the history of human interventions, a nicety jus-

tified with the rationalization that since human-induced change could not be quantified, it could not be analyzed. Recently, senior scientists writing about the Gulf of Maine (including Jeremy Jackson, Robert Steneck, and James Carlton) have elaborated problems with ahistorical ecological science, pointing out that marine ecosystems under study had already been drastically affected by overfishing, pollution, and invasive species. For example, green crabs and periwinkles, common in the Piscataqua's intertidal zone, are not native. Their invasions (made possible by humans) had serious consequences: green crabs greatly reduced soft-shell clam populations along the New England coast during the mid-twentieth century. And the intertidal zone we see today is far from "natural," if "nature" is assumed to be a web of life distinct from people. The relevant lesson is not an indictment of environmental science, but the observation that it, like maritime history, generated stories in which people were separate from nature.

At the outset of the new millennium perhaps it is not heresy to suggest that gundalows, the Portsmouth Athenæum, and saltwater farms are as much a part of the nature of this place as snowy egrets, alewives, and eelgrass. The point certainly is not to equate nonhuman nature with the flimsiest and most undistinguished elements of our consumer society, be they pre-fab buildings or strip-mall sprawl. The point is not to diminish wildness. Once a species like the Great Auk becomes extinct, replicas cannot be created, as in the case of Piscataqua wherries or historic houses. But the more we ponder the nature of this place, the more we realize that its human and nonhuman elements are inextricably entangled. Many of the people who work hardest at sustaining the Piscataqua are as passionate about its maritime heritage as its wild environments. Their informed affection for the region stands on two legs.

Ironically, despite the fact that historic users of the estuary often abused it substantially, history remains a hook for environmental preservation. Part of this irony is the somewhat naive assumption that historical development and nature are inversely related. "The more history," runs this logic, "the less nature." A glance backward at the clear-cut landscape and the sawdust-choked rivers of the eighteenth century points out the fallacies in this thinking. In certain ways, the Piscataqua is ecologically better off now than in much of the past few centuries. Invoking heritage in an unsophisticated way is often simply a nostalgic yearning for a simpler past. Informed empathy for heritage, however, reflects the recognition that connectedness to place is an essential aspect of humanity. Understanding such connections through time anchors thoughtful people to their surroundings. And genuine emotions of this sort generate results.

The contributors to this book are favorably disposed to refuges, museums, and conservation easements, each of which sustain the most worthy elements of our surroundings and make economic sense by promoting tourism and elevating property values. But the contributors recognize also that refuges and museums are not sufficient for the task at hand. Local planning and zoning boards, landowners, developers, and consumers play a major role. While such players are affected by the "bottom line," they are also affected by the scripts they have internalized and the stories they tell. Imagining the Piscataqua as a distinctive region and reconsidering humans as part of nature holds considerable promise for a future in which all things "wild" will exist in the context of human-occupied landscapes. Discovering this region anew in light of its past may be the key to a sustainable, community-based conservation that recognizes the Piscataqua's cultural and ecological heritage as vitally worth preserving.

This book can help readers construct new stories about the roles of historic people in this estuary, not separate from nature, but part of it. In the last few years, multibeam sonar images (some of which are reproduced as Color Plate V), have allowed visualization of the hidden realm below the Piscataqua River's surface. A new master narrative about the Piscataqua region, one in which history and nature are fused, may provide an alternate vision as astonishing and accurate as that of multibeam sonar. We hope *Cross-Grained and Wily Waters* is a step in that direction. –WJB

Sources: William Cronon, "Introduction" and "The Trouble with Wilderness; or, Getting Back to the Wrong Nature" in *Uncommon Ground: Rethinking the Human Place in Nature* ed. William Cronon (NY: W.W. Norton, 1996); Richard White, "Are You an Environmentalist or Do You Work for a Living?: Work and Nature," *ibid.;* William Cronon, "A Place for Stories: Nature, History and Narrative" *Journal of American History* (March, 1992); Jeremy Jackson, "What Was Natural in the Coastal Oceans?" *Proceedings of the National Academy of Sciences* v. 98 (May 8, 2001); John Brinckerhoff Jackson, *Discovering the Vernacular Landscape* (New Haven: Yale University Press, 1984); Simon Schama, *Landscape and Memory* (NY: Alfred A. Knopf, 1995); Robert Steneck and James Carlton, "Human Alterations of Marine Communities: Students Beware!" in *Marine Community Ecology* ed. Mark D. Bertness, et. al., (Sunderland, MA: Sinauer Publishers, 2001.)

Students from the Shoals Marine Lab investigating the intertidal zone in 1979. By then the Piscataqua region had been redefined in the minds of most people. No longer envisioned primarily as a maritime *region, in which waterborne commerce dominated, it was increasingly understood as a* marine *region, ecologically important in its own right. Courtesy of Milne Special Collections and Archives Department, University of New Hampshire.*

THE PISCATAQUA REGION

AN ECOLOGICAL OVERVIEW

IN A PLACE AS VARIED AS THE PISCATAQUA REGION, ecological relationships are staggeringly complex. Scientists spend lifetimes trying to understand just one piece of such an ecosystem—eelgrass or shad or razor clams or cedar trees or tidal currents or sandpipers or salinity levels or any number of other organisms and processes. It's hard enough to master one of these subjects, let alone grasp how all the parts fit together. In this sense ecology demonstrates one of the undeniable facts about the human experience: the more that is learned, the more there is to learn.

This realization should lead not to discouragement, but to a sense of wonder and a commitment to caution. As the history of the Piscataqua region shows, human beings are not just another animal species in an ecosystem; we alone have profound powers to alter the relationships not only between ourselves and other species, but also between those other species and their physical environment. Coat the bottom of the river with sawdust, the eighteenth century colonists learned, and the oysters will die. Flush untreated

Salt marsh haying. Cut and raked, Spartina patens *was carefully layered on top of staddles for curing. For centuries local residents relied directly on resources that the estuary provided. Undated photograph. Courtesy of Portsmouth Athenaeum.*

The last fish weir in the region is in the Lamprey River just downstream of the mills in Newmarket, New Hampshire. It is maintained but no longer used. A long tradition of weir fishing, which ended in the late twentieth century, linked Native Americans, English settlers, and generations of commercial fishermen. Photograph by Ann Reid, circa 1995. Courtesy of the photographer.

human and animal waste, and people will get sick. As Matthew Bampton writes in his essay on siltation, "The environmental consequences of seventeenth and eighteenth century land use practices are still playing out in the contemporary landscape, and are now complicated by nineteenth and twentieth century changes." In hindsight, this seems obvious. But is there any certainty that actions taken today won't seem equally self-destructive a century from now?

The answer is no, such certainty is not possible, especially in an ecosystem as rich and fragile as the Great Bay estuary. How complex is the estuary? The definitive book on this subject is Frederick T. Short's *The Ecology of the Great Bay Estuary, New Hampshire and Maine: An Estuarine Profile and Bibliography.* That serious volume runs to 170 pages of annotated text, charts, and graphs, and an additional forty-nine pages of bibliography. Even then, Dr. Short notes, one of his purposes in editing the book was to outline what is *not* yet known.

This much, however, is clear: the single most important ecological feature of the Piscataqua region is the fact that it *is* an estuary. Yes, there are lovely expanses of rocky coast, stretches of pavement and buildings and factories, fragments of undeveloped forests and fields, an archipelago, a moderate climate by northern New England standards, and myriad other intriguing physical and biological attributes. They all pale, however, in comparison to the estuary. That's why the place was settled so early and used so hard, that's why it is so popular today, that's why it will be vulnerable tomorrow, and that's why it is the focus of this essay. Simply put, the estuary is the Piscataqua region's greatest, and most fragile, ecological characteristic.

An estuary is a tidally dominated, partially enclosed coastal area where fresh water from rivers mixes with salt water from the ocean. Estuaries are among the richest ecosystems on the planet—the place where land and sea meet and share their gifts. Acre for acre, an estuary produces up to ten times as much organic matter as a highly cultivated cornfield in Iowa.

Estuaries are more important to the marine environment than such fishy places as the Grand Banks. Virtually all commercially viable ocean fish spend some portion of their life cycle in estuaries, or are dependent on prey that do. Globally, tens of thousands of species of fish, birds, crustaceans, and mammals live in estuaries, along with

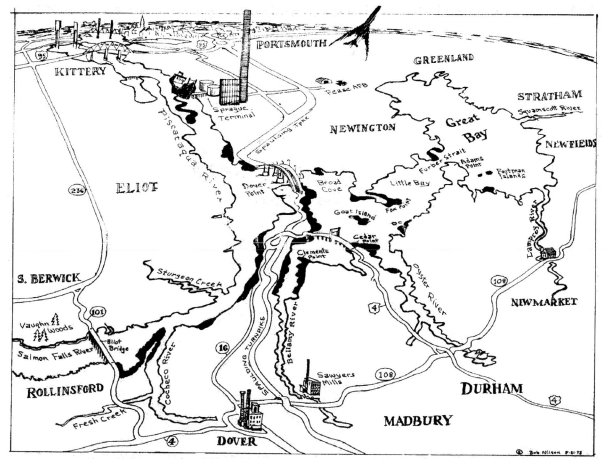

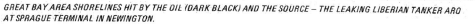

GREAT BAY AREA SHORELINES HIT BY THE OIL (DARK BLACK) AND THE SOURCE – THE LEAKING LIBERIAN TANKER ARO AT SPRAGUE TERMINAL IN NEWINGTON.

The leaking Liberian tanker Aro *at the Sprague terminal in Newington coated sections of the local shoreline with oil in 1973.* Publick Occurrences *published this map to draw attention to the potential for an ecological disaster in the Piscataqua region. Courtesy of Milne Special Collections and Archives Department, University of New Hampshire.*

striped bass, move with the tides, spawning and feeding according to salinity levels and current.

The Great Bay estuary includes Great and Little Bays and the lower Piscataqua River. It is fed by seven rivers that collectively drain a large watershed comprising forty-two towns and 930 square miles. From south to north these rivers are Winnicut, Squamscott, Lamprey, Oyster, Bellamy, Cocheco, and Salmon Falls. The constant flow of river water through the estuary and the twice-daily influx of tidal currents, which are among the strongest in the world, mix up a constantly changing organic soup of nutrients and contaminants. The flush rate is quite fast; a molecule of water entering the estuary from the Winnicut River at the top of Great Bay will take twenty-five days to exit into the ocean at the mouth of Portsmouth Harbor

Plant and animal life depends on five basic habitat types that define the estuary. In order of abundance, these are eelgrass beds, which help trap sediment, feed waterfowl, and shelter fish; mudflats, which support important prey such as worms and clams; salt marshes, through which the rivers enter the estuary and which shelter and feed waterfowl, mammals, and wading birds; the channel bottom, which is critical for navigation, larger fish species, and oysters; and the rocky intertidal zone, which supports seaweeds and algae that are the foundation of the food chain.

immense volumes of plants and microorganisms. In fact, estuaries account for much of all living matter in the world's oceans. Some species such as clams inhabit a certain niche in the estuary. Others, such as loons and eagles, are seasonal visitors. Still others, such as

Adult snowy egret. Photograph by Peter E. Randall, circa 1975. Courtesy of the photographer.

With the exception of the salt marsh and the intertidal zone at low tide, these habitats are invisible. And yet they are more basic to the region's history than the much more striking aesthetic features such as beaches, rocky shores, historic buildings, bridges, open bays, and so forth. Think of it this way: If the Portsmouth Chamber of Commerce were looking for a photograph for a promotional brochure, they would probably choose Strawbery Banke or the port over an eelgrass bed. Yet the historic district and the shipping facility might never have been founded if not for the eelgrass and other habitats that define the estuary. They are literally and figuratively built on its natural wealth.

Fish and wood were the great treasures of the New World, and the Piscataqua region had both in abundance. English settlers in the early seventeenth century found the forests thick with towering pine trees and the estuary teeming with cod, haddock, salmon, shad, bass, mackerel, bluefish, herring, alewives, and pollock, clams, mussels, oysters, lobsters, and shrimp. When they used up the wood, they could and did move inland to find more, but the estuary had more defined limits. Starting more than a century before the American Revolution, the colonists used weirs and seine nets to haul spectacular volumes of fish. Some species were showing serious decline as early as the mid-eighteenth century; by 1812 the sea bass were virtually extirpated. Overfishing had the most direct impact, but virtually all human activities eventually found their expression in the estuary.

By 1700, ninety sawmills lined the banks of the Piscataqua River, producing lumber and masts and discharging sawdust into the estuary. Other pollutants in the eighteenth and nineteenth centuries included offal from slaughterhouses and fish docks, discarded clay from making bricks, tannin from leather plants, and dyes from cotton mills. From outhouses and primitive sewer systems, untreated sewage flowed freely into the estuary. The estuary's powerful tides sucked all this refuse away in a manner that must have seemed provident to the colonists. What they didn't know was that much of the contamination was settling into the mud flats and eelgrass beds, suffocating plants and poisoning shellfish.

Industrialization and residential development in the twentieth century has taken its toll as well. Dredging for ship traffic has dramatically altered the channel bottoms; as recently as late 2000, twenty thousand cubic yards of sand and gravel were dug out of the main channel in the Piscataqua River. Treated sewage effluent flows into the estuary from six of the seven rivers; shellfishing flats are closed more often than they are open due to high coliform counts; non-point pollution runs off parking lots and roads and fertilized lawns; and incremental development is gobbling up much of the land along the shorelines. Major industrial centers in the estuary include shipping cargo facilities, an oil distribution center, two large power plants, the state fish pier, the Port Authority cargo terminal, and, of course, the sprawling Portsmouth Naval Shipyard on Seavey's Island in the Piscataqua River. These facilities all use petroleum products and spills are not infrequent. In 1999, three hundred gallons of diesel fuel spilled from a tugboat following a collision, and in February 2000 a New York barge leaked an unknown amount of heating oil. Recognizing the potential disaster of a more major oil spill, the state of New Hampshire has developed an elaborate emergency response system.

The shipyard has its own unique problems. From 1945 to 1975 the shipbuilding plant discharged into the river steady streams of liquid industrial wastes that included heavy metals, cyanide, PCBs, and petroleum. The Jamaica Island landfill, built to accept shipyard refuse, has significant deposits of sludge, ash, mercury, battery acids,

Salt marsh in Durham, New Hampshire. Photograph by Bill Finney. Courtesy of the photographer.

and other hazardous wastes. According to the *Portsmouth Herald*, an entire vault of material containing mercury has gone missing on the island. For these and other reasons the shipyard was listed in 1994 as New Hampshire's most serious Superfund site, requiring an estimated $90 million in clean-up and remediation. Heavy metals and other persistent elements are found in the sediment and throughout the food chain. Lead found in mussels at Seavey's Island exceed federal alert standards, and in 1998 PCBs were detected in lobster tamale and in migrating bluefish.

Despite these pressures and the unrelenting population growth (Rockingham County is the fastest growing region of the fastest growing state in New England, according to a 1998 study), the estuary still supports a wide variety of wildlife; bald eagles, loons, ducks, seals, and many other species peacefully coexist with humans. In all, the estuary is home to ten species of mammals, fifty-two species of fish, one hundred eleven species of birds, and more than two hundred

species and sub-species of invertebrates. Although the striped bass population has crashed twice in the past two hundred years, the resilient fish are again found throughout the estuary from spring through fall. Several clamming flats have been reopened in recent years. Some 1,300 acres of the former Pease Air Force Base are dedicated to a National Wildlife Refuge. Great Bay itself is designated a federal Estuarine Research Reserve and millions of federal dollars have been spent on science and land conservation. The University of New Hampshire's Jackson Laboratories is staffed with dedicated and talented researchers. That's all to the good.

The Piscataqua region is a remarkably rich place, with more history per acre than almost any other place in the country. It is an important industrial center, a thriving port, a center for art and culture and education, a tourism destination, a place where boats are invented and legends born, a place of mystery and peace and war. To approximately one hundred thousand people, of course, it is simply home.

But from an ecological perspective the region is only what it is: a fine example of one of the richest ecosystems on the planet—an estuary, the place where the land environment and the sea environment meet, mingle, and do their fertile dance. That alone, even without all the other wonderful aspects, makes the region worth attention and care. As Dr. Short writes, "As open space, as a buffer for point and nonpoint source pollution, as wildlife habitat, as a recreational location, the Estuary has value beyond measure. Although some parts of the Estuary are quite undeveloped and even protected from future development, other parts are already heavily developed and showing signs of degradation. What will its future be?"

The more people who ask that question, the better the answers will ultimately be. –RO

Sources: Frederick. T. Short, ed., *The Ecology of the Great Bay Estuary, New Hampshire and Maine: An Estuarine Profile and Bibliography* (NOAA-Coastal Ocean Program, 1992); NOAA publications and web site (www.noaa.gov); Great Bay Estuarine Research Reserve web site (www.greatbay.org); *Portsmouth Herald* archives.

TIDAL WRITERS

THE EBB AND FLOW OF PISCATAQUA LITERATURE

IF THE PISCATAQUA EXISTS AT ALL in the minds of Americans, it may be due to the region's extraordinary production of literature. National recognition has come to Thomas Bailey Aldrich, Celia Thaxter, Sarah Orne Jewett, Ted Weesner, James Patrick Kelly, Joe Coomer, and Anita Shreve, all of whom relied on a sense of place. In each era, from the early national to the present, Piscataqua writers present the distinctive social and natural environment of the region, always concerned about the tension of preserving the past amid currents of social and economic change.

Many of Portsmouth's writers write as insiders, creating a sense of place from "local knowledge," an interweaving of community, place, and history. This sense of place in turn attracts outsiders from larger urban and suburban places who yearn for a rooted life, at least while on vacation. To make a bad pun, Portsmouth has always been a port with a mouth, an opening that swallows what the world offers, but also a mouth that gives voice to a diversity of writers. Ports were and are the sorts of places that produce literary culture, for trade requires literacy and a press, and successful trade creates the wealth that sustains education and a taste for fine arts.

By the 1790s, Portsmouth's elites saw themselves as part of an Atlantic culture, and they communicated among themselves through letters, poetry and essays, occasionally printed in the local newspaper, *The New Hampshire Gazette*. Such literary expression contributed to the creation of a regional, public identity. The Portsmouth slave Nero Brewster made a claim for inclusion in this identity during the American Revolution through a petition asking that "the name of slave may not more be heard in a land gloriously contending for the

Celia Thaxter in her garden. Undated photograph from the collection of Peter E. Randall.

sweets of freedom." His voice was the product of a maritime world, in which free and enslaved blacks mixed with whites on shipboard and in port. Another literary center was Exeter, where the Odiorne press reprinted English poets and fostered a community that included Tabitha (Gilman) Tenney, whose *Female Quixotism* (1801) is one of the first novels published by an American woman. Like the tributary-fed river itself, regional literature's many currents are expressed by many voices.

Thomas Bailey Aldrich put the Piscataqua region on the national literary map. He created the image of "an old town by the sea" in the book by that name, as well as in his best-selling *The Story of a Bad Boy* (1869). There is something very old in his work—the nostalgic evocation of a colonial identity for Portsmouth culture in the face of industrialization and immigration. But there is also something very new in his presentation of local knowledge as part of a symbolic system by which modern people construct culture and themselves in opposition to the cultural centers of Boston and New York. A provincial self-consciousness, salted with irony, characterizes literary Portsmouth from Aldrich's day to our own. If Portsmouth as an economic and literary society was at ebb tide in Aldrich's youth, a flood of memoirs, histories, and local-color writing by Charles W. Brewster, Aldrich, Jewett, and Thaxter made the region a focus of cultural preservation efforts by the end of the century.

Aldrich created an image of an old town by the sea to oppose the commercial spirit, immigration, and industrialization of his era, especially as these forces threatened an imagined community of secure social relations and hierarchies. In *The Story of A Bad Boy*, Aldrich looked back nostalgically on a city of neighborhoods, where the classes, based in various employments—from seamen and servants to bankers, merchants, and teachers—mixed in social rituals centered in city squares, parks, and cemeteries. His nostalgic memoir, *An Old Town By The Sea* (1893), revealed a beautifully landscaped city and an appreciation for historic sites: "From this elevation [the roof of the Portsmouth Athenæum] the navy yard, the river with its bridges and islands, the clustered gables of Kittery and Newcastle, and the illimitable ocean beyond make a picture worth climbing four or five flights of stairs to gaze upon. Glancing down on the town nestled in the foliage, it seems like a town dropped by chance in the midst of a forest."

Nature, culture, and historic neighborhoods made Portsmouth appealing to writers like Aldrich, who hoped an aesthetic appreciation of the community would provide a model for a modernizing New England. Yet his writing, based on local knowledge, prefigured elitist Anglo-Saxon fears expressed in the Colonial Revival. His poem, "Unguarded Gates" (1895), warns against the so-called racially impure immigrants from southern Europe and Jews filling the Puddle Dock neighborhood behind his ancestral home. "Wide open and unguarded stand our gates, /And through them presses a wild motley throng— /…In street and alley what strange tongues are loud, /Accents of menace alien to our air." He asks, "O Liberty, white Goddess! is it well /To leave the gates unguarded?" Preservation, then, has had more than one meaning for Piscataqua writers.

Celia Thaxter created a different conservation ethic in her historical writing, nature essays, and poetry. Thaxter's point of view emerged not from the predominantly male institutions of the city, but from her parlor, garden, and conservatory on Appledore Island. Like Henry David Thoreau, she was dedicated to "love and careful scrutiny" of nature, but she linked traditional imagery from women's local color writing about seascape and garden to a critique of modern consumerism. When a gray freezing fog effaces Portsmouth, she recalls "delight as I have known a single rose to give, unfolding in the bleak bitterness of a day in February, when this side of the planet seems to have arrived at its culmination of hopelessness, with the Isles of Shoals the most hopeless speck upon its surface." One can hear in Thaxter the start of a conversation that will stretch across the water decades later to the York, Maine, home of May Sarton. The harsh beauty of land and sea and the recognition of an existential despair and aloneness at the core of being combine in a chronicle of a solitude that offers a sacrament of simple gifts in the heart of a single rose. For Thaxter, the preservation of historical memory and place are acts of faith.

Sarah Orne Jewett's work deepened Thaxter's tints of local color. Her first novel, *Deephaven*, explores the quaint, old homes and their residents, but later stories present a darker view of the psychological costs of clinging to a past gone by. In "The Landscape Chamber," the overmantel painting of a fine colonial mansion stands in stark contrast to the decayed current state of the home, in which a young woman is trapped by her moody father. Jewett, like her contemporaries Edith Wharton and Edwin Arlington Robinson, feared an allegiance to the past was potentially incestuous, a turning back from the energies of the dawning twentieth century.

Contemporary Portsmouth writers also have explored the consequences of economic decline and transformation in the region. A grittier Portsmouth, populated by fishermen, workers scrambling to make car payments, sometime-students, and the elderly, finds voice in Ted Weesner's *The True Detective* (1987) and *Harbor Lights* (2000), and in Joe Coomer's *Beachcombing for a Shipwrecked God* (1995). In Weesner's novels, the Piscataqua region of the late twentieth century is fragmented. Highways and bridges create a network of places in transition, where there are many margins and marginal lives. The preserved buildings and cultural spots, such as Prescott Park, Strawbery Banke, or Ceres Street Bakery, which present islands of stability for middle-class Portsmouth, don't really fit together for Weesner's characters. If Portsmouth was seen for three centuries from the sea and river, now it is observed from a speeding car on the interstate, a change in perspective that speaks volumes about the invisibility of locals in the eyes of tourists and newcomers. One character observes, "the bridge arcs through the sky like something more modern than the city, and in reverse focus he imagines the view of Portsmouth below, its buildings and houses, the wide river, its lobster boats, and at last—would he be visible? —himself standing here. No, he thinks."

In recent years, it has been just such a sense of life at the margins, the Piscataqua as a place apart from Boston or New York, that has sustained writers. Joe Coomer chronicles the lives of Portsmouth's displaced—young and old—who try to attach themselves to the region by reading history, participating in a dig at Strawbery Banke, or living on a houseboat beneath Memorial Bridge. Portsmouth's recent poet laureates Esther Buffler and Robert Dunn, published with others in *Under the Legislature of Stars: 62 New Hampshire Poets* (1999), accept their public office with good humor and irony. Robert Dunn takes the position of the ironic insider, as if he is himself a ghostly reminder of the local in the struggle over the region's identity:

> Some people say,
> "This is the land of our fathers."
> Others say,
> "This is the land of our children."
> And a lot of people call it real estate
> because it's more businesslike
> if you never love
> anywhere.

The uncertainties of the Piscataqua region's position in a global economic and literary marketplace resonate in the science fiction of James Patrick Kelly's "Pogrom," set in a Durham gone bad from global warming, and "Faith," in which a singles ad leads to a surreal Portsmouth romance. Similarly, Brendan DuBois's *Dead Sand* (1994), *Black Tide* (1995) and *Shattered Shell* (1999) are mysteries probing the darker social ecologies of the region. The sense of mystery has long helped "sell" the region in the popular imagination. Foremost is the story of the March 5, 1873, murders by Louis Wagner of two women on Smuttynose Island. This gruesome tale confirmed Celia Thaxter's fame when her account, "A Memorable Murder," spurred sales of her book, *Among the Isles of Shoals* (1873). As a tourist, Anita Shreve came upon this story two decades ago, and the story lingered in her mind until she wrote *The Weight of Water* (1997), a controversial, brilliantly written, retelling of the story. The appearance of a major motion picture version of the novel will surely emblazon the image of the Piscataqua region on screens across the country. For Thaxter, the murders were a violation of the social and natural environment, "that beautiful broad river, the Piscataqua, upon whose southern bank the quaint old city of Portsmouth dreams

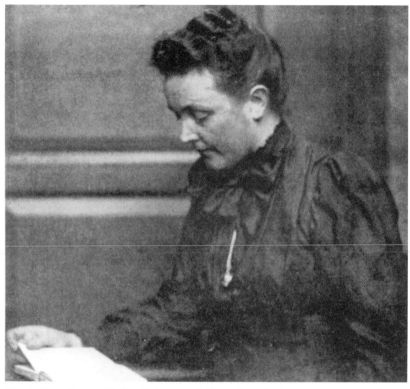

Sarah Orne Jewett. Undated photograph from the collection of Peter E. Randall.

When I look now at the pictures of Smuttynose, I ask myself if I have captured the soul of the island. For I believe that Smuttynose has a soul, distinct from that of Appledore or Londoner's, or any other place on earth. That soul is, of course, composed of the stories we have attached to a particular piece of geography, as well as of all the cumulative moments of those who have lived on and visited the small island. And I believe the soul of Smuttynose is also to be found in its rock and tufted vetch, its beggar's-ticks and pilewort, its cinquefoil brought from Norway. It lives as well in the petrels that float on the air and the skate that beach themselves—white and slimy and bloated—on the island's dark beach.

The fragility of stories and the coastal environment means that "no one can know a story's precise reality." So the very changeability of Portsmouth and the inhospitable landscape of the Shoals both challenge the human imagination to construct and preserve a sense of place. In Piscataqua region literature, the sense of place shifts with the tides of memory and migration, but for four centuries, it has been a home for those who came to write. –DHW

Sources: Charles W. Brewster, *Rambles About Portsmouth* (Somersworth, NH: New Hampshire Pub. Co., 1971-72); Robert C. Gilmore, *New Hampshire Literature: A Sampler* (Hanover, NH: University Press of New England, 1981); Rick Agran, Hildred Crill, Mark DeCateret, *Under the Legislature of Stars: 62 New Hampshire Poets* (Durham, NH: Oyster River Press, 1999); Thomas Bailey Aldrich, *The Story of a Bad Boy* (Boston: Fields, Osgood, 1870); David H. Watters, "'Build Soil': Language, Literature, and Landscape in New Hampshire," in *At What Cost? Shaping the Land We Call New Hampshire*, ed. Richard Ober, (Concord, NH: NHHS and SPNHF, 1992); Julia Older, ed., *Celia Thaxter: Selected Writings* (Hancock, NH: Appledore Books, 1997).

its quiet days away…Before another sunset it seemed to me that beauty had fled out of the world, and that goodness, innocence, mercy, gentleness, were a mere mockery of empty words." But such nightmares are the dream of the tourist industry.

In Anita Shreve's version, the loss of innocence involves the shock of learning that one cannot ultimately know a place or oneself. If Maren, Karen, and Anethe were adrift, so Jean is off-soundings in her life, when she becomes obsessed with the story of the murders and with suspicions about her husband's fidelity. Jean explores how a place can elude an immigrant or a tourist.

A SAMPLER OF PISCATAQUA WRITERS

THOMAS BAILEY ALDRICH, *The Story of a Bad Boy* (1869)

As we drove through the quiet old town, I thought Rivermouth the prettiest place in the world; and I think so still. The streets are long and wide, shaded by gigantic American elms, whose drooping branches, interlacing here and there, span the avenues with arches graceful enough to be the handiwork of fairies. Many of the houses have small flower-gardens in front, gay in the season with china-asters, and are substantially built, with massive chimney-stacks and protruding eaves. A beautiful river goes rippling by the town, and, after turning and twisting among a lot of tiny islands, empties itself into the sea.

The harbor is so fine that the largest ships can sail directly up to the wharves and drop anchor. Only they don't. Years ago it was a famous seaport. Princely fortunes were made in the West India trade; and in 1812, when we were at war with Great Britain, any number of privateers were fitted out at Rivermouth to prey upon the merchant vessels of the enemy. Certain people grew suddenly and mysteriously rich. A great many of "the first families" of to-day do not care to trace their pedigree back to the time when their grandsires owned shares in the Matilda Jane, twenty-four guns.

Few ships come to Rivermouth now. Commerce drifted into other ports. The phantom fleet sailed off one day, and never came back again. The crazy old warehouses are empty; and barnacles and eel-grass cling to the piles of the crumbling wharves, where the sunshine lies lovingly, bringing out the faint spicy odor that haunts the place—the ghost of the old dead West India trade! (26-27)

SARAH ORNE JEWETT, "River Driftwood" (1881)

Where the river is wide, at low tide one can only see the mud flats and broad stretches of green marsh grass. But when the tide is in, it is a noble and dignified stream. There are no rapids and only a slow current, where the river from among the inland mountains flows along, finding its way to the sea, which has come part way to welcome the company of springs and brooks that have answered to its call.

ESTHER BUFFLER, "May June" (1988)

> lilacs in Portsmouth, N.H.
> mauve—white—and indigo
>
> the wind shifts
>
> to the ear-killing drone of
> Air Base FB-111 bombers
> announcing readiness to death
> with carbon ribbons
> streaking the sky . . .
>
> the wind shifts
>
> as to the homestead I fly,

stumble on the crumbly stone-
wall, plunge to the fullness
of an old white lilac bush
bent like a cane
leaning next the kitchen door

the wind shifts

and a fragrance drop by drop
touches the wind with the chiming
of tiny blossom bells
glorioso lilaceous
mauve—white—and indigo.

Joe Coomer, *Beachcombing for a Shipwrecked God* (1995)

I read in the mornings: Mays's *Early Portsmouth History* (1926), Brewster's *Rambles About Portsmouth* (1859), and from a fine leather-bound 1825 edition of Nathaniel Adams's *Annals of Portsmouth*. The area's written history began as early as 1603 when Martin Pring, an Englishman, visited the coast and rowed up the Piscataqua ten or twelve miles. I wanted to familiarize myself with the old city so that on my afternoon walks I'd have some historical sense of the things I saw. Portsmouth seemed to be full of opportunities for an historical archeologist, almost four hundred years of recorded occupation. Many eighteenth-century residences and commercial buildings were still standing. Portions of the city had been burned and rebuilt on three separate occasions, in 1802, 1806, and 1813, which should have left substantial debris over which new structures were built, predom-inantly of brick. Puddle Dock, a tidal creek extending into Strawbery Banke, had been completely filled and built over at the beginning of this century. In my mind it formed an almost perfect time capsule, every artifact pickled in mud beneath a protective layer of dirt and debris. I supposed that one could dig on any square meter of the city and find some evidence of culture….As I walked through Portsmouth, stepping to one side of the sidewalk for the living, I walked arm in arm with the dead, among the tangible evidence they'd lived lives: their homes and shops, the names of their streets, our stony and silent inheritance that requires a true diligence to decipher. I knew I was only walking on the surface of the past. (43-44)

Theodore Weesner, *Harbor Lights* (2000)

Seas were placid and it was unseasonably warm for October. The pastures of harbor water were as thinly green as old mirrors, with fissures of air escaping fault lines here and there as if hissed from whales. Fishing boats passed soundlessly in the distance, and all around was the solitude that came with the livelihood of one man hauling traps within sight of land. Larger boats carrying radar and crews went far out and stayed weeks at a time, but were neither as solitary nor as philosophical as the one-man entities.

Lobstering and independence went hand in hand. Within a hundred yards of shore were depths over forty fathoms, and within the volume of black water along reefs and seaweed-draped valleys lay promises of treasure in forms of fish and crustacea, together with daily threats of death and discouragement. Questions were ever present for lobstermen: Can you stand the loneliness? What of the cold water on your hands, the smell of bait in your lungs and rowing out before dawn in snow squalls, pouring rain, uncompromising walls of wind? What of your oilskins getting tangled and finding yourself pulled over the side? What of the times when lobster aren't feeding, or when a glut is on the market? And your family—will they provide the support on land a lobsterman needs to succeed at sea? Why not trade some of that mean independence for a seat at the wheel of a backhoe, for wages, regular hours, the camaraderie of a factory with dry wooden floors, heated air, a candy machine? For coffee and talk with friends…at least until a foreman came cracking the whip? (3-4)

ISLES OF SHOALS

THE ISLES OF SHOALS

ON SMUTTYNOSE, ONE AWAKENS TO GULLS bickering on the roof of the Haley cottage, their voices growing louder with the rising sun. It is easy to awaken before dawn on the Isles of Shoals; indeed it is difficult not to. All nine islands harbor an abundance of birds, including herons, ibises, and egrets, and more than 125 species of pelagic and inland birds that use the islands as migratory resting spots. The islands' bird population has not always been so strong; gulls and other sea birds were endangered at the turn of the nineteenth century, hunted for the feathers prized for use in women's hats. Black backs, herring gulls, cormorants, eiders, and terns were all hunted aggressively from 1850 to 1900, despite the protests of early island conservationists such as Celia Thaxter.

Now a constant focus of conservation efforts, the Shoals have changed dramatically over four hundred years of human habitation. This obscure group of tiny islands, four in New Hampshire and five in Maine, played a central role in the settlement of the New World. Fishermen from Europe in search of better fishing grounds may have exploited the marine habitat north of this area as early as the 1550s. But not until 1614 were the islands formally put on the map; John Smith (of Jamestown fame) charted them in his *Description of New England*, published in 1616. A fine mapmaker and promoter, Smith named the islands after himself. Although his name for the islands did not stick, another of his terms, "New England," did.

In the seventeenth century fishermen's fortunes were made from *dunfish*, high quality dried cod, a commodity that fed Catholic

Tourism has been important to the region since the middle of the nineteenth century. Summer guests arriving at the wharf on Appledore Island, Isles of Shoals, New Hampshire. Undated photograph. Courtesy of Laing Collection.

Europe. Smith boasted, "he is a very bad fisher, that cannot kill in one day with his hook and line one, two, or three hundred cods." The windswept islands made an ideal place for drying cod on racks called "flakes." By the 1640s, fishermen had built permanent dwellings and

Smuttynose Harbor, circa 1880. Courtesy of Laing Collection.

the name Isles of Shoals had come into use. Situated in the midst of a thriving fishing ground, the Shoals became a frontier boom camp, attractive to the lucky or calculating few who became prosperous, such as William Pepperrell, father of baronet Sir William Pepperrell. Others barely eked out a living, constantly in debt to the merchants who staked them to a season's equipment.

Eventually taverns, a meetinghouse, and even a school rose on the islands, which governed themselves independently of the Puritans in Massachusetts for at least a while. The resident population fluctuated year-by-year and island-by-island. Through the archeological work of Faith Harrington and others, we know that from 1650-1680, more than 250 people lived on the islands. By 1715 the New Hampshire Provincial Assembly had named the Star Island township Gosport to designate the New Hampshire territory of the Shoals.

From 1732 until his death in 1773, Reverend John Tucke ministered to the Shoals community. A physician as well as a clergyman, he

was also an excellent record keeper. Tucke's parishioners loved him, and regularly added quintals of fish to his salary. His papers reveal, among other things, that at least two slaves lived in Gosport. Tucke's society, though stable during his tenure, was only as deep as the island topsoil. Instead of following the course of many New England towns whose early settlements often grew steadily, the islands' population was sustained by a fragile relationship with fish production, a dependence on trade, and the politics of the young republic. At the outbreak of the American Revolution, residents were ordered to remove from the island. Those who could afford to, floated their homes across to New Hampshire or Maine. Some, like Samuel Haley, may have defied the order and stayed on island.

By the turn of the nineteenth century, some inhabitants had returned. The fishing boom was long past, and Shoalers were destitute. The Society for Propagating the Gospel Among the Indians and Others in North America sent missionaries, teachers, and material goods to the year-round residents—always less than one hundred in number. Tourism, however, had more impact than the SPG missionaries. In 1848 Thomas Laighton opened the Appledore House on Appledore Island. His daughter, Celia Thaxter, achieved fame through her poetry and her summer salon during the 1870s and 1880s. Boston's finest poets, painters, writers, and musicians summered at Appledore, where Childe Hassam created many of his famous American Impressionist paintings.

Tourism spread to Star by the 1870s. A man named Poor bought property from all but two of the last year-round residents of the island (George Beebe and John Downs), and built a grand hotel called the Oceanic. Although it burned a few seasons later, the stage was set for Star Island to become, like Appledore, a summer haven for tourists. After the fire, Mr. Poor was able to combine and expand existing buildings on Star to erect what we see today, the new Oceanic. In 1897 Thomas Eliot and his wife, Lilla, convinced their fellow churchgoers

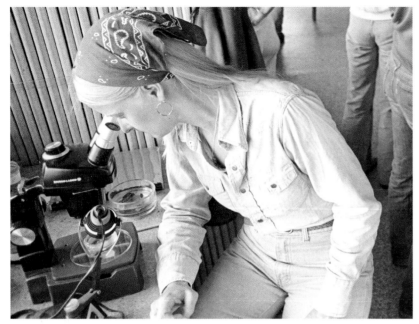

Microscopic marine biology at the Shoals Marine Lab, Appledore Island, 1979. Courtesy of Milne Special Collections and Archives Department. University of New Hampshire.

that the Oceanic was an ideal place for the summer conference of the Unitarian Universalist church. For the next hundred years, the Star Island Corporation, which bought the island in the 1920s, continued to operate summer religious conferences for families and adults. Currently, Star Island is home to nearly four hundred conference-goers and staff at the height of the summer. Appledore Hotel met the fate of most seaside resorts; it burned in 1914 after falling into decline following Celia Thaxter's death in the 1890s.

Star Island Corporation also owns most of Appledore Island, which they lease to the Shoals Marine Laboratory, operated since 1973 by the University of New Hampshire and Cornell University to study bird and marine life. The marine lab is the largest undergraduate facility of its kind in North America. According to director James Morin, Appledore Island is wilder than at any point since the first European set-tlers arrived nearly four hundred years ago. Black-backed and herring gulls numbered around eight thousand at last count, and are now the most populous inhabitants, outnumbering people at the height of the summer twenty to one. They dominate Smuttynose Island in particular, where only a handful of people ever spend the night. Volunteers known as the "Smuttynose Stewards" act as caretakers during the summer and fall, staying at the Haley cottage, the restored home of Samuel Haley, a fisherman who lived on Smuttynose in the late eighteenth century. Today, "Haley Island," as it had been known, is no longer the site of a productive fishing industry. The old fish houses are gone, as are the vast shoals of cod that once defined the islands. There is no sign of Haley's orchard, gristmill, or ropewalk. The Mid Ocean House inn and the store once run by Thomas Laighton, before he moved to Appledore, are now difficult to locate precisely. A small sign and stones are all that indicate the foundation of the Hontvet house, site of the infamous Smuttynose murders in 1873. But the archaeological remains and the oral history legends have become a sidebar to the forward-looking concerns of the Stewards today. With the cooperation of island owners, they plan to designate Smuttynose Island as a conservation area, limiting use, preventing development, and protecting the natural environment.

Those who are fortunate enough to attend a conference on Star Island or classes at the Marine Lab become acutely aware of the islands' limited natural resources. Conferees, for instance, must attend a thirty-minute orientation to the three types of water and the ways they are used and reused. Today, the Shoals' richest resource is its oft-recycled history. Dozens of stories about pirates, shipwrecks, lost loves, and murder have been repeated and republished since the nineteenth century. Though the accounts vary in accuracy and entertainment, all preserve the essence of the Shoals, the stern and lovely scene that is these nine rocky islands. –MEB

Sources: Celia Thaxter, *Among the Isles of Shoals* (Portsmouth, NH: Peter E. Randall, 1997); *A Stern and Lovely Scene* (Durham NH: University Art Galleries, University of New Hampshire, 1982); Peter E. Randall and Maryellen Burke, eds., *Gosport Remembered: The Last Village at the Isles of Shoals* (Portsmouth, NH: The Portsmouth Marine Society, 1997).

LOCAL SMALL CRAFT: THE HAMPTON BOAT, THE ISLES OF SHOALS BOAT, AND THE PISCATAQUA WHERRY

AFTER A GOOD LOOK AT THE PISCATAQUA RIVER, particularly where the rush and roil of the tidal current rips through the bridges, very few people are likely to think that it looks great for rowing. But during the centuries before boat engines and bridges, the need to travel up, down, or across the river made rowing a routine part of life.

Local watercraft made this possible. After generations of evolution, distinct styles of boats emerged from the Piscataqua region uniquely suited to its waters. The resulting craft reflected their environment and the work they did, and were representative of local craftsmanship and available materials. Marine historians call such vessels "indigenous small craft." Sometimes they stand out because they fit a place so well, and sometimes they are hard to see for the same reason.

The best-known and farthest-reaching local type was the New Hampshire Hampton boat. It was a double-ended, two-masted sailboat of 17 to 25 feet used in the nearshore fishery of Hampton and Seabrook. Enoch Chase is credited with the Hampton boat's invention in 1805. By the 1830s, New Hampshire boats, as they were often called, were carried aboard cod fishing schooners from Maine and New Hampshire to the waters off Newfoundland. Once the fishermen filled their holds, they often sold their small boats in New Brunswick, Newfoundland, or Labrador before heading home. The striking resemblance of the "Newfoundland boat" and the "Labrador boat" to New Hampshire Hampton boats may be rooted in those sales.

Rowing a dory on the Piscataqua River near the Sheafe Warehouse, in its original location, just downstream of the Puddle Dock inlet, circa 1900. Courtesy of Strawbery Banke Museum.

Some historians believe New Hampshire's Hampton boats were predecessors of the square-sterned Maine Hampton boats of Casco Bay in the late 1800s. Marine historian Howard I. Chapelle is doubtful, but discusses the idea carefully in his highly regarded book,

American Small Sailing Craft. Suffice it to say, the New Hampshire Hampton boat was a very successful local type. It spread seed-like upon northeastern waters, fetched up on distant shores, and took root there either in its original form or as a type from which later boats evolved.

A direct descendant of the New Hampshire Hampton boat, the Isles of Shoals boat originated in the same coastal fishing communities, but was used nearer the islands for which it was named. Initially fishing vessels, Isles of Shoals boats became popular excursion craft for summer guests at the grand hotels built after the Civil War on the Isles themselves. Like the Hampton boats, they were double-ended and rigged with two masts, but the Isles of Shoals versions were distinctively larger, in both length and beam.

The Piscataqua wherry evolved in protected waters inside the rivermouth. It was common transportation on the lower Piscataqua River, and became the preferred water-taxi to and from the busy Portsmouth Navy Yard for over a hundred years. The boats were lapstrake built, meaning their side planks overlapped each other. They were narrow at the waterline but full (plenty wide) at the rails. Judging from the few that have survived from the nineteenth century, seventeen feet was a common length.

The wherry is a member of the dory family, a general type of workboat that has been associated with northeastern waters since the late 1700s. Dozens of local varieties exist between Boston and Halifax but they all share a few distinguishing traits. All dories are lapstrake and flat-bottomed. Those bottom-planks run fore and aft instead of athwartships. Dory construction has its roots with the Vikings and by 1800 had been reduced to essentials; there are no unnecessary parts. The most well known variety is the Banks dory, a beamy workhorse synonymous with the stormy offshore fishing grounds for which it is named. The Piscataqua wherry is related, but because its purpose demanded speed on swiftly moving but relatively sheltered waters, it had less wetted surface, or underbody, and a more complex and elegant shape than its fishing cousins on the Grand Banks. As the old-timers said, "She's a working girl, but she's a lady."

Oscar Laighton, brother of poet Celia L. Thaxter, in a Piscataqua wherry, circa 1935. Courtesy of Strawbery Banke Museum.

Only four known Piscataqua wherries remain from what may have been thousands during the great age of oar in the 1800s. One is displayed at Strawbery Banke Museum in Portsmouth; another at the Kittery Historical and Naval Museum in Kittery, Maine; Mystic Seaport in Connecticut has one; and the last known in private hands belongs to Howard Huntress of Eliot, Maine, where all four surviving boats were built.

Howard grew up along the Eliot shore of the Piscataqua and remembers salvaging timbers and collecting driftwood off the beaches with his father in their wherry during the Depression years. "Oh, jeez, we'd load her right down," he said, "until there was only one plank showing." The Huntress family had relatives across the river on the New Hampshire side. "We didn't own a car in those days and neither did they, but we had that wherry." The New Hampshire family used a loud horn to hail their relatives across the water. "They usually wanted something from town [Portsmouth or Kittery] and

A lapstrake cat-ketch, typical of local inshore fishing boats in the mid-to-late nineteenth century. Very few photographs exist of Isles of Shoals boats or Hampton boats. This may be an apple-cheeked Isles of Shoals boat, to which that twig of a bowsprit has been added as an after-thought. Photographed off New Castle, 1925. Courtesy of the Society for the Preservation of New England Antiquities.

my father would row over there, hear them out, and then row off to collect whatever it was." The round trip is several miles. "We didn't think anything of it," Howard said, "always felt safe in that wherry."

People still row on the Piscataqua, usually because they want to. The notorious current is a blessing when it is with you, but only a fool tries rowing against it mid-channel. Every cove conceals a counter-current that can carry the knowing boater against the main flow for a time, without taking a stroke. Of course, there is no substitute for ability and local knowledge, and Piscataqua wherries have both built-in. –NBB

Sources: Howard I. Chapelle, *American Small Sailing Craft: Their Design Development, and Construction* (New York: W.W. Norton & Co., 1951); Maynard Bray, *Mystic Seaport Museum Watercraft* (Mystic, CT: The Museum, 1979); John Gardner, *The Dory Book* (Camden, ME: International Marine Publishing, 1978); Eric McKee, *Working Boats of Britain: Their Shape and Purpose* (London: Conway Maritime Press, 1983).

SEABROOK

SEABROOK AND SEABROOK STATION

OF ALL THE TOWNS ALONG THE NEW HAMPSHIRE SEACOAST, perhaps none has had such a strong maritime tradition as Seabrook. Once a part of Hampton and then Hampton Falls, Seabrook was established as a separate town in 1768.

The Hampton River estuary sustained many early Seabrook residents. Boat building, trapping, hunting, fishing, and marsh haying were often necessary occupations for the independent-minded residents of Seabrook, but the pursuit of the soft-shell clam is most strongly identified with the town.

Generations of Seabrook families were supported by the clam industry during the late nineteenth and early twentieth centuries. From the productive clam-flats of Hampton River, hard working diggers extracted bushels of clams during low tide. The clams were washed, shucked, and the meat packed into containers for retail or wholesale. In the twentieth century, commercial clam houses hired local people, mostly women, to shuck clams dug from Hampton River as well as those imported from Plum Island and Ipswich, Massachusetts, and from Maine. Most shucked clams were sold throughout New England for frying and chowder.

Fishing boats at Seabrook Harbor, circa 1975. Photograph by Peter E. Randall. Courtesy of the photographer.

By 1940 the Seabrook clam industry was worth $200,000, but the following year hardly a clam could be found in the Hampton River. Over digging, periodic natural fluctuations in the clam population, and green crabs (an introduced predator) impacted the industry. Although each town had regulated its own clam-flats in an effort to maintain the harvest and control the diggers, little scientific research had been conducted to support the local rules. A 1950 survey indicated that the clam population would recover with proper management. As a result, in 1951 the legislature gave the state control of the flats. Digging was prohibited in many areas for two years, and then only one peck of clams could be dug per day, for personal use only. Commercial digging came to an end. Residents of New Hampshire may still dig clams but only for personal use. The season is restricted and the flats are often closed due to red tide or suspected water pollution. A few clam houses remain in Seabrook, maintaining a tradition that seems certain to continue as long as residents and tourists have a taste for fried clams.

Before roads crossed the marsh and bridges crossed the creeks, Seabrook residents went to clam-flats on tidal creeks that flowed from the river to the uplands. At the end of Farm Lane, at the edge of the marsh, the remains of a narrow canal dug to provide access to the river is visible. Except for the beach cottages across the marsh from this spot, the landscape appears to have changed little from the days when Native Americans camped here. Ironically, less than a mile north of Farm Lane at the foot of Rocks Road stands the greatest modern intrusion into the Seacoast area: Seabrook Station.

Rocks Road was once a primary point of entry to Browns River, which clammers and fishermen navigated to reach the Hampton River. That changed in 1972 when Public Service Company of New Hampshire announced plans to build a nuclear-powered electric generating station on the site. The complexity of construction, corporate financial woes, myriad federal regulations, and fierce opposition from local, regional, and national organizations delayed completion of the project until 1990. The controversial station was designed and planned in an era when nuclear power was thought to be answer for all of America's electricity needs. By the time Seabrook was completed, however, one of its two units and all other planned stations across the country had been cancelled, leaving Seabrook as the last nuclear plant to be built in the United States.

Clearly visible across the marsh from many locations, Seabrook Station has a visitor's center open to the public. The Science and Nature Center of Seabrook Station has exhibits related to energy and

Seabrook Station, the controversial nuclear power plant. Photograph by Peter E. Randall, 1988. Courtesy of the photographer.

nuclear power, sea life tables, and a one-mile nature trail through woods to the marsh.

Seabrook Station pays most of the town's property taxes, and frugal residents have used this windfall to build a new town hall, a recreation center, a library, police and fire stations, and a sewer system. At Seabrook Harbor, the local fisherman's cooperative uses a large wharf originally built as part of the Seabrook Station construction project. –PER

Sources: Joseph Dow, *History of Hampton, New Hampshire*, Volume I (Portsmouth, NH: Peter E. Randall, 1988[1894]); Peter E. Randall, *Hampton, A Century of Town and Beach, 1888-1988* (The Town of Hampton, NH, 1989).

THE CLAMSHELL ALLIANCE

THE 1970s SAW A MODEST REGIONAL renaissance in some of New England's small towns. Many idealistic young people left increasingly crowded and violent cities or banal suburbs, going, as they saw it, "back to the land." They adapted to the somewhat rural, small-town lifestyle, and many long-time residents learned to overcome their initial suspicions and to appreciate fresh blood on the local conservation committees and volunteer fire departments. These two populations—newcomers and natives, working together to protect the region they loved—fought the major environmental battles in the Seacoast during the 1970s. Those battles have preserved much of the Piscataqua region from industrial blight and continue to inspire conservation efforts decades later.

The longest and hardest fight was against the giant nuclear powered electric generating station proposed for Seabrook. On February 2, 1972, the front-page headline of the *Portsmouth Herald* announced that Public Service Company of New Hampshire (PSNH) would be building a nuclear power plant in Seabrook at the edge of the state's largest salt marsh. The twin 1.1 million kilowatt reactors with their associated buildings, roads, and infrastructure, would be the

A New Hampshire State Trooper drags off one of nineteen anti-nuclear demonstrators outside the front gate of the Seabrook Station. The nineteen were charged with disturbing the peace after being warned by police. August 25, 1978. AP laserphoto.

largest construction project the state had ever seen.

Local citizens, fisherman, and members of the scientific and academic communities voiced strong opposition. Four years of citizen forums, studies, and publications followed. Even the town of Seabrook itself, a famously blue-collar community that initially had supported the project because of promised jobs, voted in their 1976 town meeting against the nuclear plant.

There were also lawsuits; the Society for the Protection of New Hampshire Forests and the Audubon Society, joined by a relative newcomer, the Seacoast Anti-Pollution League, were concerned about heated water discharged into an eight-square-mile salt marsh, the destruction of a rare stand of Atlantic white cedar, and the impact of high-voltage transmission lines. They lost case after case, frequently on narrow technical grounds. Gradually their critique escalated to the dangers of nuclear power itself, but courts and federal boards consistently ruled against them.

On July 7, 1976, the Nuclear Regulatory Commission voted two to one to issue a construction permit to PSNH. Within a few days the Clamshell Alliance emerged.

The impetus for a more militant opposition to the nuclear plant had been growing for several years as the inadequacy of legal opposition became clear. Environmental activists who formed the Clamshell Alliance took their name from the best-known users of the Hampton-Seabrook estuary, the clammers. Every year several thousand clammers would come from as far away as the White Mountains to dig their peck of soft-shell (or "steamer") clams. The Clamshell Alliance saw themselves as protectors of this environment and its traditional culture.

The Clams (as they called themselves) had a new tactic. They were going to "occupy" the construction site, blocking construction with their own bodies. Quaker advisers from the American Friends Service Committee had considerable influence on the Clamshell Alliance. They introduced the ideas of decision-making by consensus or unanimity rather than majority rule, and a non-hierarchical structure. The Quakers also suggested organization into "affinity groups" of a half-dozen or so protesters who trained together in non-violence tactics and came to trust one another.

On August 1, 1976, the Clamshell Alliance held a rally at the Hampton Falls common. From there, five hundred people marched to the edge of the Hampton-Seabrook marsh. After speeches and musical performances, eighteen pre-selected and non-violence trained New Hampshire residents marched onto the nuclear plant site. Ignoring a PSNH spokesperson who warned them to leave, the protesters tried to engage in a token reforestation of the bulldozed site by planting corn and maple saplings. The Seabrook police arrested the Clams and took them to Hampton Beach jail, where they offered the option of release on personal recognizance rather than a cash bail. For reasons of conscience, the Clams chose jail. The next day they were taken to a hastily organized Sunday court session where they pleaded not guilty to charges of disorderly conduct, resisting arrest, and criminal trespass. They were released pending trial.

"Nuke Protest Fizzles" blared the headline of the *Manchester Union Leader*, the state's archly conservative newspaper, but the Clams knew otherwise; the rally turnout had been excellent, the symbolic occupation had proven the value of non-violence training, and the refusal to bail themselves out of jail had caused considerable trouble for the legal system. With larger numbers the Clam could expect real impact.

Three weeks later, on August 22, 1976, 179 people walked onto the site while another individual rowed a dory up Brown's River. This time the arresting officers were New Hampshire State Police; the resources of the local police department were unequal to the task. The Clams were careful to be respectful of the police, feeling that respect was a necessary component of nonviolence. They were arrested and taken to the Portsmouth National Guard armory. Once again they refused to bail themselves out. Faced with the need to feed these prisoners, the police turned to a nearby McDonalds, but when informed that many of the prisoners were vegetarians, the police made half the orders "Big Mac, hold the mac." Respect worked both ways. Within twenty-four hours everyone was arraigned in district court and released.

The Alliance announced that the next occupation would occur on October 23, 1976. Some long-time activists, however, felt that too much energy was being spent organizing the occupations and that more work needed to be done to educate the general public about the dangers of nuclear power. So the October event was changed to an Alternative Energy Fair at Hampton State Beach, with demonstrations of wind and solar power, energy conservation, and speeches against nuclear power. This drew approximately three thousand attendants, but the absence of political confrontation disappointed many Clams.

The next action was set for April 20, 1977. The goal was to mobilize one to two thousand occupiers. A tremendous amount of organizing, such as recruitment, training, camping, and parking arrangements, was necessary. The first serious disagreements among Clams began to emerge over the issue of destruction of property. Those committed to nonviolence felt that any violence—even cutting a hole in a fence—was a violation of principle as well as counterproductive public relations. Others felt that while nonviolence was a useful tactic, no occupation could be successful until the site was totally accessible. At the last moment the nonviolent view prevailed, but the conflict foreshadowed things to come.

On Saturday April 30, 1977, hundreds of Clams approached the site from each of four directions; they met on the employee parking lot and organized a tent community called Freebrook. Facing them were local police, New Hampshire State Police, and squads of state police from most of the other New England states. The Clams were too numerous for a mass arrest and an impasse ensued.

There was a triumphant feeling among the Clams that they had organized a successful mass nonviolent community. But early Sunday afternoon New Hampshire governor Meldrim Thompson arrived and demanded that the Clams leave. They booed. He ordered everyone arrested.

The governor appeared at the Portsmouth National Guard armory, which was being used to process arrested Clams, and ordered that all out-of-state Clams must post cash bail; only New Hampshire residents could be released on personal recognizance. The Clams quickly passed the word for "bail solidarity" and no one bailed out. Meanwhile busses from Seabrook were arriving with more and more Clams. Hurriedly armories were opened all across the state. Guardsmen were called in from their homes and jobs to act as jailers. The final arrests were not made until after sunrise Monday morning. New Hampshire had 1,414 Clams in their armories.

This was serious stuff. The story was of national interest, and the state saw an influx of press that rivaled the presidential primary season. The 1,414 people were sorely missed by their families, friends, and employers, who began to complain.

The Clams held out for two weeks before reaching an agreement with the state to guarantee the return of out-of-state Clams for their trials. The entire event had been an organizational triumph and groups sprang up across the country applying Clamshell Alliance tactics to their own local situations.

But in New Hampshire the local Clams, especially the organizers and local support folks, were tired and emotionally drained. More people began questioning the tactic of occupation, particularly since PSNH had continued construction and invested hundreds of millions of dollars in site work. The logical next step was unclear.

On Wednesday March 28, 1978 an accident at the Three Mile Island nuclear power plant in Pennsylvania resulted in a near-melt-down. Tension simmered nationwide for a week before the plant stabilized. Tremendous public reaction to the accident ensued, and opposition to nuclear power became much more popular.

Two months later an executive decision of the Clamshell Coordinating Committee transformed an occupation planned for June of 1978 into a three-day legal rally. This attracted about twelve thousand members of the public and six thousand trained Clams. The event was successful in its public impact, but many Clams were disappointed by the decision to "go legal," and felt that the principle of decision-by-consensus had been violated.

Within the Clam, militants who advocated fence-cutting split off into the Coalition for Direct Action at Seabrook. On October 6, 1979, more than sixteen hundred Coalition protesters stormed the fences at Seabrook. They were beaten back by state police who made few attempts at arrests; clubs, tear gas, and fire hoses were used instead. Coalition members eventually gave up. They tried again on May 24, 1980, with even less success.

The Clamshell Alliance as an organization had seen its glory days. The people who organized it dispersed to engage in other organizations, other activities. And ultimately, despite a ruling by the Atomic Safety and Licensing Appeals Board that the regional evacuation plan was unworkable, the Nuclear Regulatory Commission granted Seabrook Station an operating license. Tests began in 1989, and the plant began generating electricity shortly thereafter. Recently, when asked to sum up the Clamshell Alliance and Seabrook, one original Clam said, "PSNH got to build only one of their two planned reactors. They went bankrupt in the process. Seabrook was the last nuclear power plant built in the U.S. in the twentieth century. We lost the battle but won the war." –MG

Sources: Etahn M. Cohen, *Ideology, Interest Group Formation, and the New Left: The Case of the Clamshell Alliance* (New York: Garland Publishing, Inc., 1988); Clamshell Alliance Papers, Special Collections, Dimond Library, University of New Hampshire.

HAMPTON & NORTH HAMPTON

HAMPTON: TOWN AND BEACH

WHEN HAMPTON'S FIRST SETTLERS ARRIVED BY BOAT in 1638, they found a heavily forested landscape. Hampton River with its surrounding tidal marshes provided settlers with food and hay for their livestock while they cleared fields and built houses. The marsh was so valuable that the original grantees received a portion of marsh along with their upland. A large area, the so-called "Great Ox Common" adjacent to Great Boars Head, was reserved "to the world's end" as common land for use by all Hampton residents.

The Hampton marshes account for approximately 1,800 acres of the 3,000-acre Hampton River estuary. For more than 250 years after settlement, the marshes were considered as valuable as any land in the Seacoast. The marsh grass, called *Spartina patens*, was harvested by farmers as hay for bedding and feed for livestock. Farmers in many surrounding towns owned sections of the marsh, and at an annual gathering scores of men and boys from fifty or sixty area farms cut the hay by hand and stacked haycocks on circles of posts called staddles, which kept the drying hay above the tidal waters. More than 1,000 loads of hay were produced and usually

Mace fish houses and dory, Hampton. Photograph by Ralph Morang, 1998. Courtesy of the photographer.

23

removed in the winter; some men lost their lives in the cold water while carrying out this hazardous task. Staddles can be seen today along Route 1 where it crosses the marsh between Hampton and Hampton Falls.

When farming declined in the early years of the twentieth century and marsh hay was no longer needed, the perception of the marshes began to change. As Hampton Beach grew, developers leveled the barrier beach's sand dunes and began to fill the marsh to create lots for cottages and tourist businesses. Long considered by many residents as nothing more than a breeding ground for mosquitoes, the marshes seemed poised for destruction. About this time biologists began to understand the value of marshes as a nursery for commercially valuable fish and as an important buffer for floodwater during storms. Although filling continued on a reduced basis into the 1980s, state laws finally protected the marshes and, in the 1990s, efforts were made to rehabilitate marsh areas that were damaged by filling and road construction.

The Rev. Stephen Bachilor and his followers who settled Hampton in 1638 were anxious to create homesteads and farms and had little interest in the seashore. They followed the Hampton River inland to the first high ground and laid out a large common now known as Meetinghouse Green about a quarter mile from the marsh. Their first meetinghouse was erected here and settlers' lots surrounded the green. The area is bounded today by Lafayette Road (Route 1), Park Avenue, and Winnacunnet Road. Many of the town's oldest houses are located here, as is the Pine Grove Cemetery, established in 1654 and now the oldest public burial ground in New Hampshire.

Meetinghouse Green is one of the oldest common spaces in New Hampshire that retains its original location and its purpose as a public space. Here is Founders Park with its ring of stones bearing the names of Hampton's founding families, and the Tuck Museum. Owned by the Hampton Historical Society, the museum is open to the public from mid-June to Labor Day. Its varied collections of books, paintings, photographs, genealogical material and artifacts, and its changing exhibits cover all aspects of Hampton history. Adjacent is the fire department museum and Tuck Memorial Athletic Field.

Hampton continued as a farming community until the turn of the twentieth century, but the coastal location also provided an opportunity for fishing. Before the development of gasoline-powered engines, the fishing business was located at the foot of High Street, where Hampton's two remaining fish houses, once used to store gear and bait, are still located. According to tradition, fishmongers from as far as Vermont and Canada came to Hampton Beach each winter with huge sleds to purchase and haul dried, salted, and frozen fish to inland markets. About 1800, Moses Leavitt operated "a house of entertainment" for these fishmongers. In 1806 Daniel Lamprey built a house at the base of Great Boar's Head and began to take in a few summer guests, mostly seafowl hunters. Soon there was a hotel at Boar's Head and others were built along Hampton Beach. A rough road led from the town to the seashore, and once there visitors had few attractions other than natural surroundings. Most of the beachfront was undeveloped and lined with sand dunes.

All this changed in 1897 when the town agreed to lease (for ninety-nine years at $500 per year) what is today most of the main beach to a corporation of local developers. These developers in turn subleased a small area for the same $500 a year to the Exeter, Hampton, and Amesbury Street Railway Company. To attract riders to the beach, the railway company built a large entertainment center and bathhouse, today the Hampton Beach Casino. Before long, Hampton Beach was transformed into a major New England tourist resort.

With the leveling of sand dunes for building sites, the barrier beach no longer provided protection from storms. Hurricanes and northeasters smashed into the beach, eroding the shore and destroying buildings. Unable to cope with the cost of repairs, the town reluctantly voted in 1933 to turn the beachfront over to the state in exchange for a promise to build a seawall and other improvements. Hampton Beach State Park now stretches from Hampton River north to High Street. –PER

Sources: Peter E. Randall, *Hampton: A Century of Town and Beach, 1888-1988* (The Town of Hampton, NH, 1989).

Hampton's most prominent landmark, Great Boar's Head, and the congested main beach. The Underwood Bridge is at the top left and Seabrook Station, the nuclear power plant, at top right. Photograph by Peter E. Randall, circa 1986. Courtesy of the photographer.

CLAMMING

On a brisk November Friday, about an hour before low tide at Hampton Harbor, it is easy to find a great troop of New Hampshire residents dressed in rubber boats and comfortable clothing, armed with buckets and clam hoes, staring at the tide flats. Although the double domes of the nuclear power plant loom as a backdrop to the marsh, the scene is reminiscent of the California gold rush. Braced against the wind, the throng is pursuing the famous Hampton and Seabrook soft-shell clams, also known as "steamers."

Even as those in line wait to be shuttled by boat to the clam beds, fellow clammers already have been zipped across the water to the Middle Ground. They depart from either the Hampton or Seabrook pier to the fast-emerging land mass of the tidal flats. Backs bent to task, these early arrivals pluck bivalves from the sand, while boats shuttling four or five clammers at a time crisscross each other's wakes, engines humming, hulls slapping the whitecapped waters. Perched above them all, behind the Fishermen's Coop, green-clad state Fish and Game officers with green pickup trucks keep a watchful eye on the activities.

It is opening day of New Hampshire's recreational clamming season. Clammers who have been chafing at the bit to harvest *Mya arenaria*, the soft-shell clam, flock to the

Aerial view of the Blackwater River and Seabrook marshes and beach, December 12, 1998. Courtesy of the New Hampshire Coastal Program.

productive beds of the harbor. Digging is extremely restricted compared to years ago, and is now limited to Friday and Saturday only. Traditional digging grounds in the adjoining rivers and creeks remain closed to clamming. Nevertheless, by sunset on Saturday approximately one thousand diggers, each having taken their ten-quart daily limit, may have reduced the stock of a given bed by twenty percent.

New Hampshire's human-clam relationship dates back thousands of years. Approximately 7,000 years ago the "Red Paint People" consumed clams in the Hampton region. By 4500 B.C. other maritime peoples plied Hampton's coastal waters, gathering clams from the intertidal areas where fresh and salt waters met, and setting out to sea in pursuit of swordfish. Many generations of Native Americans followed their ancestors to the clam-flats of Winnicumet. They abandoned winter camps in time for spring fish runs, planted pumpkins and corn when the oak leaf was as big as a mouse's ear, and lived on the coast until the fall hunt. Summer brought clambakes, combined with digging, drying, and stringing clams for later consumption or for trade with inland people.

The arrival of European settlers in the 1620s began a new ecological chapter in Hampton's clam history. The settlers were quick to adapt to the use of clams both as a reliable food source and as bait. Fish houses soon lined the shore. Hampton enjoyed a mackerel fishery as well as its cod fishery, and with the advent of the mackerel jig in the 1820s, clams were chopped into chum to attract fish. Clams were

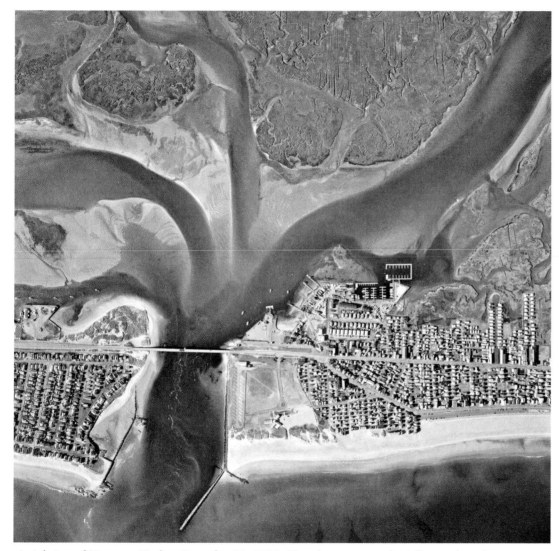

Aerial view of Hampton Harbor, December 12, 1998. Note the currents and swirling sands as the Blackwater (left) Brown (center) and Taylor Rivers (right) converge at the mouth of the Hampton-Seabrook Estuary, enroute to the open ocean of the Gulf of Maine. The large, exposed flat to the left of center is the Middle Ground, home to some of the most sought-after clams in the New Hampshire coastal region. Courtesy of the New Hampshire Coastal Program.

also salted by the barrel to be used as bait in the offshore Labrador fishery, in which Seabrook men participated. By the middle of the nineteenth century, the increasing leisure food and hotel trade at the Hampton beaches fueled a demand for fresh Hampton River clams. The new canning industry also began to put up clams in cans. Soon the whole East Coast saw dwindling clam stocks.

During the ensuing decades clamming became integral to existence for many of Hampton's coastal families. Indeed, during the Depression, the soft-shell clam regained its role as a lifeline, as it once was for the colonists and natives before them. Clamming provided immediate food as well as supplemental seasonal employment. It provided a kitchen enterprise for some of Hampton's and Seabrook's residents and for a few led to thriving businesses such as clam factories and clam stands. A handful of such factories still exist on South Main Street in Seabrook. But today's clams are trucked in from out of state.

Clamming as a commercial enterprise came to an abrupt end in New Hampshire. During the 1950s an army of green crabs marched up the coast, totally devastating soft-clam populations. When the state took over management of the flats in 1951 it faced empty clam beds left behind by the green crabs, an introduced species. Commercial digging has been off limits ever since, although infamous tales persist of bootlegged clams snatched from under the glow of miners' lamps.

Clamming for recreational diggers has been varied for the past half century as introduced species and human pressure affected the estuary. License sales reached about 12,000 during banner years and dwindled to just a few thousand during others. The 1980s saw pollution closures, an awareness of clam neoplasias, and an increase in HABs—harmful algae blooms. HABs such as "red tide" do not generally affect Hampton harvests, since blooms typically occur during warm summer months when the flats are closed. Of major concern today however, is the threat of a major clam pandemic.

General environmental awareness, however, makes the future look brighter for clams and clammers as citizens learn to protect this precious resource. –DM

Sources: Interviews with Bruce Smith, New Hampshire Fish and Game; Carl Randall of Rye, Bruce Brown of Seabrook, Richard Schanda of Newmarket, Beverly Hollingworth of Hampton.

Hampton Marsh, looking toward Route 1 and Interstate 95. Photograph by Peter E. Randall, circa 1987. Courtesy of the photographer.

LITTLE BOAR'S HEAD, NORTH HAMPTON

LITTLE BOAR'S HEAD IS LOCATED AT THE FOOT of Atlantic Avenue in North Hampton. Early settlers farmed there, and at the base of the Head, fishermen—as early as 1804—built fish houses and rowed their dories out to sea in search of cod, haddock, and other finfish. Twelve old fish houses remain today, now converted to summer cottages. Adjacent is North Hampton State Beach.

By the middle of the nineteenth century, summer boarding houses began to attract visitors to Little Boar's Head. Batchelder's Hotel opened in 1868, and soon the rich and famous arrived to build three-story summer "cottages." Constructed by bankers, captains of industry, and state and national politicians, these Victorian houses, now mainly year-round homes, line Route 1A and adjacent Atlantic and Willow avenues. The family of former Massachusetts Governor Alvan T. Fuller owned several large houses. He also built the beautiful Fuller Gardens off Willow Avenue, now open to the public in season. Nearby is the 1877 Union Chapel, which is open for summer services.

To view these houses and the surf crashing against the cliffs of Little Boar's Head, park at North Hampton State Beach and walk north past the old fish houses and a beautiful public garden, then along the shore. The two-mile sidewalk ends at the Rye Beach Club. One can often watch a variety of seabirds and occasional harbor seals, as well as surfers who ride the waves year round. On the horizon are the nine Isles of Shoals. –PER

View toward Great Boar's Head from Little Boar's Head with historical fish houses. Photograph by Peter E. Randall, 1975. Courtesy of the photographer.

Sources: Joseph Dow, *History of Hampton, New Hampshire*, Volume I. (Portsmouth, NH: Peter E. Randall, 1988[1894]); Stillman Moulton Hobbs and Helen Davis Hobbs, *The Way it Was in North Hampton* (North Hampton Historical Society, 1994[1978]); Peter E. Randall, *Hampton, A Century of Town and Beach, 1888-1988* (The Town of Hampton, NH, 1989).

Rye

Odiorne Point: Four Centuries of Land Use

THE SEACOAST SCIENCE CENTER AT ODIORNE POINT in Rye sits at the birthplace of New Hampshire. For nearly four hundred years (the era of its documented history), this site at the confluence of tidal river, ocean, and marsh has been used and understood in many ways. As a fishing station, farm, mill site, resort hotel, gentleman's estate, fort, and park, it has been exploited, romanticized, and preserved. To understand the story of Odiorne Point is to understand the story of much of the Piscataqua region.

Captain John Smith's voyage to North America in 1614 produced a remarkable map of this region and rekindled in Plymouth, England, interest in a settlement north of Virginia. English nationalists and entrepreneurs hoped to create profitable colonies like those in Spanish America. And with the success of the enclosure movement that drove commoners off their traditional lands, England appeared to have a surplus population suitable for overseas plantations. In 1620 the newly created Council for New England received royal authority to grant land in North America, and within two years Sir Ferdinando Gorges and Captain John Mason obtained titles to land extending sixty miles inland between the Merrimack River and the Kennebec River.

One of Gorges's well-connected employees was David Thomson, an experienced fish merchant and overseas trader. After apprenticing to a seagoing apothecary in 1607, Thomson voyaged to New England. Backed by three Plymouth merchants with whom he would share profits, Thomson arranged for a grant of six thousand acres of the Mason/Gorges land. He arrived in March of 1623 at Little Harbor (also known as Pannaway), an area he had singled out on earlier voyages. Thomson built a house at the place now called Odiorne Point. This frontier foray, however, was unsuccessful; after a brief stay Thomson moved his family to an island in Massachusetts Bay where he died about 1629. That island still bears his name.

John Mason and Ferdinando Gorges, still in England, then backed a venture called the Laconia Company. Other settlers arrived at Little Harbor, led by Captain Walter Neale, an ambitious military man who named the area Rendezvous, a designation that stuck until the American Revolution. Neale delegated tasks such as fishing, fish processing, and salt production to his stewards and explored interior New Hampshire in hopes of finding valuable minerals. When a disappointed Neale returned to England in 1633, the Laconia Company dissolved, and most activity in the area shifted to Strawbery Banke, a truly protected deep-water harbor.

After that first decade of English settlement, it is not clear who remained at Pannaway. It is likely, however, that a few fishermen and their families continued to use the area, perhaps seasonally, until John Odiorne purchased it in 1660. Odiorne had previously owned a fishing interest on Smuttynose, one of the Isles of Shoals, and he continued to fish commercially and farm after his move. Generations of his descendants referred to a ridge on the family farm as "Flake Hill," a reference to the open-air drying racks for curing cod.

Daily activities on John Odiorne's farm were typical of coastal farming during the seventeenth and eighteenth centuries. Householders had to be as self-sufficient as possible, cultivating livestock, gardens, and fruit trees, even as they produced fish or agricultural surplus for sale. Most activity on the Odiorne farm centered on the original buildings, closer to the inland marsh than to the ocean.

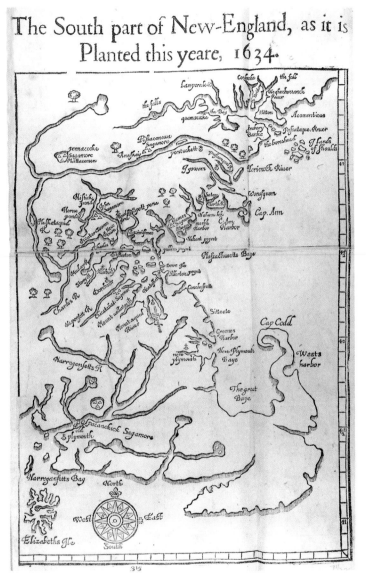

The South part of New England, as it is Planted this yeare, 1634.
Woodcut from William Wood's New Englands Prospect. *Boston Public Library, Rare Books Department, Courtesy of The Trustees of the Boston Public Library.*

John Odiorne died in 1707, and his direct descendants continued to farm the land. In 1800 Ebenezer Odiorne built the farmhouse that stands today. The farm included a blacksmith shop, located in a corner of the cemetery where the Settler's Monument, erected in 1899 during the Colonial Revival, now stands. The Odiornes also operated a tidal sawmill and gristmill at the narrow part of Seavey Creek, just north of the present wooden-decked highway bridge. The mills burned in September 1862 and were never rebuilt.

For two centuries the Odiorne family lived on a parcel of uplands, surrounded by ocean and estuary. Like other moderately prosperous coastal families, they provided much of their own sustenance, while always producing commodities for the market. As fishermen, farmers, and millers, they capitalized on local resources and secured financial stability.

By the Civil War, however, agriculture had generally declined as a viable means of support in Rye. Inshore fishing and milling had also become marginal means of survival. But East Coast urbanization and industrialization created a new demand for summer resort communities. By the 1870s, the era of the grand hotel had begun. Sagamore House, one of the most sumptuous new hotels in Rye, was located on Frost Point at Little Harbor. It began as a modest boarding house in the 1850s, but expanded dramatically under the ownership of George and James Pierce during the 1860s. They cultivated an elite clientele, until the Sagamore House burned to the ground in 1871.

Coastal summer estates became more popular during the late-nineteenth and early-twentieth centuries, a phenomenon accentuated by the development of the automobile. The history of the Foye farm abutting the Odiornes is a case in point. The Foyes began to farm the property in 1799. They prospered, eventually building a twenty-four-room house with a large attached barn and outbuildings. In 1920, however, Foye descendants sold to the Whitcombs, who refashioned the farm into a gracious summer retreat. As a vacation home in the 1920s the property was no longer commercially viable, and it was perceived in ways that would have been foreign to generations of Odiornes and Foyes. The Whitcombs completely remodeled the house and barns. The most noticeable changes as seen from Route 1A were the many added

The Sugden House, originally built of beach stones in 1920, became incorporated into the Seacoast Science Center. This photograph was taken in 1992. Courtesy of Seacoast Science Center.

dormers. But the Whitcombs's peaceful enjoyment of the property was brief, as the United States government obtained this estate and eleven others during World War II. Kathleen Whitcomb's garden is the only remaining fragment of that era. Roses still bloom here, thanks to volunteers who now call it the Heritage Garden.

With the advance of the German forces in Europe in 1939 and 1940, the U.S. Army had quietly chosen positions on both the Atlantic and Pacific coasts to protect military assets should the U.S. become involved in the war. An elaborate defense plan for the Portsmouth Naval Shipyard was prepared, but not made public. Odiorne Point was a key site in that plan.

After the attack on Pearl Harbor in 1941, the federal government initiated action to obtain the land in the Odiorne Point area. In the ensuing months, some land owners sold property to the government at deflated appraisal prices, while others balked and were compelled to surrender their holdings by court proceedings. Former owners were assured that they would be given priority to repurchase the land if and when it was declared surplus. This area became Fort Dearborn, named in honor of a Revolutionary War hero, General Henry Dearborn. The guns at the fort were never fired in anger, but the government's temporary acquisition of the property significantly affected its destiny.

After the war, in 1949, the Odiorne farm land to the west of Route 1A was declared surplus and offered for sale to the former owner. Mr. Odiorne declined, and Mr. Ralph Brown purchased the land. Later that year, Congress passed the Federal Property and Administrative Act, which contained no language giving previous owners priority in securing land acquired by the federal government. On the short coast of New Hampshire, this provoked considerable resentment.

In 1959 the federal government declared the Odiorne Point land to the east of Route 1A as surplus. The State of New Hampshire, next in line under the 1949 act, made application for the properties, and by the fall of 1959 had passed a bill to fund the purchase "if the owners…of 75% of the property… shall not have succeeded in obtaining federal legislation enabling them to repurchase the property." Attorney Edward Gage, a son of Odiorne Point landowners, led a spirited fight to return the land to its former owners. His efforts led to legislation passed by the U.S. Senate for the return of the properties. But for reasons never made public, that legislation was not introduced in the House and the initiative died. The state acquired the land in 1960 for $91,000. Those who had loved this quiet summer retreat felt betrayed, and many children of the former owners inherited their parents' bitterness. But their unwilling sacrifice ultimately became a worthy

The Whitcombs modified the Foye house and barn extensively during the 1920s, converting it into an elegant retreat on the coast. This photograph, circa 1930, was taken from Route 1A. Nothing remains of the estate today except part of its garden. Courtesy of Seacoast Science Center.

bequest to the public, and to the region's environmental health, as Odiorne Point is now a public park.

For almost ten years the newly acquired state land was not managed in any consistent fashion, although the deed stipulated that it be used for "recreational purposes." Not until Mrs. Annette B. Cottrell gathered a group of scientists and specialists to produce a book about the property entitled *Natural Science and Historical Studies* did the state agree that the park should be preserved as a natural area and used for environmental education. In 1971 it opened as a state park. Two years later, the Audubon Society of New Hampshire converted an abandoned Air Force firehouse on the site into a nature center that operated during July and August.

By the 1970s an environmental movement had gained momentum nationwide, fueled in part by highly publicized oil spills that demonstrated the fragility of coastal environments. Local people rallied behind environmental protection in the fall of 1973 when Aristotle Onassis announced plans to build the world's largest oil refinery in Durham. That same year Public Service Corporation of New Hampshire (PSNH) applied to the Atomic Energy Commission for a permit to construct a nuclear power plant at Seabrook, and protesters soon marshaled considerable opposition. The preservation of coastal and estuarine environments took on increased urgency during those years, affecting the way that politicians and citizens in New Hampshire perceived Odiorne Point.

In the summer of 1977, the University of New Hampshire Cooperative Extension Program conducted a Marine Awareness Program at Odiorne Point, and in January of 1978, the UNH Marine Advisory Program joined the New Hampshire Division of Parks and Recreation and the Audubon Society as a partner there. Educators were offered continued use of the firehouse or of Sugden House, the summer home built on the shore at Odiorne Point by Robert Sugden in 1920. They chose Sugden House, and a team of UNH students and faculty established a marine educational exhibit there. Sugden House became the park's interpretive center.

A management plan developed for the park in 1986 recommended an improved visitor center that would meet the demand for environmental programs and increased visitation. In an unusual move, the State of New Hampshire agreed to fund $400,000 for the construction of the center, provided that a like sum could be raised from private sources. The required sum was raised, testimony to public passion for the site. The improved center, now called The Seacoast Science Center, opened in 1992.

The park expanded in 1989 when The Trust for New Hampshire Lands and the Land Conservation Investment Program bought sixty-five acres on the west side of Route 1A from Mr. Ralph Brown. Two and one-half acres surrounding the 1800 Odiorne farmhouse and barn were purchased by the state in 1993. In 1995 a non-profit volunteer group, The Friends of Odiorne Point, became the fourth partner in the park's educational consortium. The park exists today not only because of a public shift towards environmentalism, but because several agencies and private groups pooled their resources and expertise for a worthy common goal.

Of course the park is by no means in a "natural state." Generations of cutting, plowing, and farming have biologically redefined Odiorne Point. Since 1941 upland habitats have changed dramatically, with previously open fields succumbing to woody plants like buckthorn and sumac. The U.S. Army planted oriental bittersweet as camouflage, and the invasive vines now climb and strangle old apple trees, breaking their tops. Honeysuckle shrubs crowd roads and trails, and poison ivy appears virtually everywhere. Groundskeepers discourage the worst invasive plants, while trying to nurture indigenous species and old garden plants. It is a real challenge, for this historic site is ecologically still quite dynamic.

A master plan developed for the park in 1999 stipulated that all efforts at Odiorne Point should be devoted to conservation and education. This new philosophy is a departure from four centuries in which this land was occupied by Europeans and their descendants and used in distinctly different ways. The Odiorne family understood the land and marsh as a productive resource, a source of food and profit. The Whitcombs envisioned it as a serene retreat from the stress of modern life and an emblem of their success, while military planners in World War II defined it as a strategic asset. Most people in the Piscataqua region believe that a park is the best use for this historic spot and, as such, Odiorne Point will remain dedicated to public access and environmental conservation for the foreseeable future. –LHT

Sources: Langdon B. Parsons, *History of the Town of Rye, New Hampshire: From its Discovery and Settlement to December 31, 1903* (Concord, NH: Rumford Print. Co., 1905; reprinted by Heritage Books, Bowie, MD, 1992); Howard S. Crosby, Wendy W. Lull, and Richard T. MacIntyre, *Footprints in Time: A Walk Where New Hampshire Began* (Bath, Great Britain: Alan Sutton, Ltd., 1994).

Fort Dearborn

ODIORNE STATE PARK, ON THE SOUTHERN JAW of the mouth of Portsmouth Harbor, is a legacy of World War II. Before the war, eleven private estates and summer residences occupied this prime seacoast real estate. But in the ominous days of 1940 when it seemed that England might be overwhelmed and Germany would control the North Atlantic shipping lanes, the War Department decided that Odiorne Point was needed for coastal defense—particularly for the protection of the Portsmouth Naval Shipyard. As soon as war was declared in December of 1941, plans were implemented for the construction of Fort Dearborn on this strategic, scenic, and formerly residential point of land.

Odiorne Point residents received official notice of eminent domain on March 12, 1942, and were given one month to vacate their property. Eight months later soldiers occupied the land and construction of Fort Dearborn began. Harbor Defense Board planners believed they needed Odiorne Point as a location for modernized

Fort Dearborn, June 21, 1944. After one day of test-firing the huge guns were never fired again. Courtesy of Seacoast Science Center.

batteries to protect Portsmouth Naval Shipyard. The batteries were to consist of two 16-inch guns capable of firing shells weighing 2,240 pounds twenty-six miles, and two 6-inch guns capable of firing 138-pound shells fifteen miles. The 16-inch guns were of staggering proportions. Each was sixty-eight feet long from muzzle to breach and weighed 142 tons. They were housed in Battery Seaman, a reinforced concrete structure with a 500-foot long gallery between the two gun ports. The entire structure was buried under an earth mound that rose fifty-five feet above the surrounding grade. The more modest 6-inch guns were mounted in Battery 204 adjacent to the present Seacoast Science Center building. This was a concrete "casemate" or bunker buried in an earth mound that covered a 200-foot long gallery between the two guns. The guns were pedestal mounted and protected by a cast steel shield that was four to six inches thick.

Radar was in the early developmental stages, so the 16-inch guns depended on a network of remote observation towers to locate and aim at targets that were often out of sight of Battery Seaman itself. Sixteen of these gray concrete towers or "base end stations" were built to control the guns defending Portsmouth Harbor. They were connected via telephone lines with the plotting room in a casemate near Battery Seaman. Target coordinates called in from various stations allowed plotters to calculate enemy vessels' position and direction of motion by triangulation. The guns could then be accurately aimed at targets up to twenty-five miles away.

Battery Seaman was completed in June of 1944 and Battery 204 was completed one month later. On June 21, 1944, the big 16-inch guns were test fired with three shells each. They were never fired again. The tide of the war had turned decisively, and by October 1944 the army was reorganizing coastal defenses, redirecting troops to Europe and the Pacific, and downgrading the importance of Atlantic coastal artillery. On July 25, 1945, all batteries on the Atlantic coast were put on caretaker status.

In the rapid advance of military strategy and technology during World War II, coastal artillery emplacements like Fort Dearborn had receded in importance. Aircraft had displaced ships as primary attack weapons, and the refinement of amphibious assault meant that coastal artillery could be bypassed or outflanked. By the end of World War II, the coastal artillery around which Fort Dearborn had been built was obsolete. Nevertheless, the Air Defense Command retained a station on the site from 1949 to 1959.

Initially, unhappy landowners had been promised the opportunity to reacquire their properties when the government no longer needed them. But after the war, new laws allowed the state of New Hampshire to take over the property; it did so in 1961. Public access to the shore at Odiorne Point State Park thus came at the expense of a cruel loss to private landowners, many of whom wondered if the coastal defense construction had ever been necessary. Since then, however, the park has served to connect visitors to the maritime heritage of the Piscataqua. –TCM

Sources: Howard S. Crosby, Wendy W. Lull, and Richard T. MacIntyre, *Footprints In Time* (Bath, Great Britain: Alan Sutton Ltd., 1994); The Thoresen Group, *State Coastal Properties Project* (Concord: New Hampshire Office of State Planning, June 1983); Jack P. Wysong, *The World, Portsmouth, and the 22nd Coast Artillery* (Missoula, Mont.: Pictorial Histories Publishing Co. Inc., 1997).

LIFESAVING IN THE PISCATAQUA REGION

United States Lifesaving Service boat and station at Jenness Beach, circa 1900. Photograph by Clarence Trefry. Courtesy of Seacoast Science Center.

PROVIDING ASSISTANCE TO MARINERS IN distress has been a critical service in coastal communities for hundreds of years. The Piscataqua region is no exception. The current U.S. Coast Guard claims Hopley Yeaton of Portsmouth as its first commissioned officer. A veteran of the *Raleigh*, which was built in Portsmouth during the Revolutionary War, he became captain of the Revenue Cutter *Scammel* in 1790. For nineteen years Yeaton patrolled the waters of Maine and New Hampshire looking for smugglers and vessels in distress.

The development of shore-based assistance to endangered shipping came surprisingly late. Even through the 1840s, this assistance generally consisted of unmanned caches of food, blankets, and other emergency supplies that a survivor might encounter in shelters along the shore. All too frequently, though, when a sailor did reach one of these, he found that either rodents or the neighbors had gotten there first.

The winter of 1870-71 saw a tremendous loss of life in marine accidents along the Atlantic coast. Congress soon undertook an aggressive program to protect mariners' lives, establishing a series of lifesaving stations with permanent superintendents and adequate equipment along the eastern seaboard. This became formalized as the U.S. Lifesaving Service in 1872.

Rye Station, located near the north end of Jenness Beach, became one of the first stations of the new service. Its full-time keeper directed a crew of six experienced surfmen from September to April. Although replaced by a more modern station in 1889, this original facility (with most of its Victorian gingerbread details intact) still stands on Jenness Beach, now as a private cottage. Other stations were established at Jerry's Point on Wild Rose Lane in New Castle and on Wallis Sands in Rye between 1887 and 1890. By 1903 there were four stations in New Hampshire, with Hampton Station having been added north of Boar's Head.

The pattern of activity and service for these stations was typical of the Lifesaving Service. Crews were charged with keeping a constant vigil on the ocean from the station during daylight hours, and with walking the beaches in patrols that linked one station with its neighbor during hours of dark and storm. Two tools were available for rescues: the double-ended surf boat, which could proceed to a vessel in distress and remove passengers and crew directly, and the Lyle line throwing gun, which would shoot a line to the vessel requiring assistance, and remove people via a breeches buoy that moved along the line.

Effective use of either rescue system required considerable practice, particularly as rescues were typically needed only in very severe weather. Reports brim with fearsome stories of boats capsized at launching, then righted and taken on long rows to distressed vessels in blowing snow and temperatures well below zero. In 1893 the Jerry's Point Station reported forty-four rescues in its five years of operation. Each member of the crew was awarded a gold medal worth $125 for the rescue of the schooner *Oliver Dyer* off of New Castle on November 26, 1888, in a storm that many think exceeded the ferocity of the "Portland Gale" ten years later.

In 1908 the Jerry's Point Station was decommissioned and replaced by Portsmouth Harbor Station, which was then located on Wood Island, a part of Kittery. The Jerry's Point Station was demolished to make way for the expanding Fort Stark. The Wood Island facility was itself decommissioned in 1948, and its crew transferred back to New Castle to the Fort Constitution site. Today the decaying hulk of the Wood Island facility remains an attractive picnic site for rowers and kayakers passing over the shallow ledges of the Maine shore.

Piscataqua lifesavers continue to provide aid to coastal and offshore vessels in distress through the Coast Guard's Portsmouth Harbor Station in New Castle and the cutter *Reliance*, based at the Portsmouth Naval Shipyard. The days of the double-ended surfboat are gone, but traditions of marine service and protection continue. –JHT

Sources: Chester B. Curtis *Bi-Centennial Souvenir of New Castle, NH, 1693-1893* (privately published, 1893; copy available NH State Library, Concord, NH); Langdon B. Parsons, *History of the Town of Rye, New Hampshire: From its Discovery and Settlement to December 31, 1903* (Concord, NH: Rumford Print. Co., 1905; reprinted by Heritage Books, Bowie, MD, 1992); Joseph W. Smith, *Gleanings from the Sea* (privately published, Andover, MA, 1887; reprinted by Harding Publishing Company, Wells, Maine, 1987).

U.S. Coast Guard Cutters Active *and* Decisive *at the new base in New Castle, 1970. Courtesy of Jeffrey H. Taylor.*

NEW CASTLE

GREAT ISLAND

A BOLD ROCK WITHIN THE SEA, New Castle's Great Island is one of the oldest, smallest, and fishiest places in the Piscataqua region. Its current population is just under 850, and only 449 people called it home on the eve of the American Revolution. But New Castle has always had its aficionados, and in the hands of storytellers like John Albee, author of *New Castle: Historic and Picturesque* (1884), and Helen St. John, author of *Inalong, outalong, downalong: Reminiscences of New Castle, New Hampshire* (1985) and *From Mrs. Tredick's Inn: More Reminiscences of New Castle, New Hampshire* (1987), the essence of the town's past endures.

Now primarily a bedroom community, New Castle was born in an age when fishermen rowing heavy shallops wished to live as close as possible to the fishing grounds, and when military control of the "Passcattaway River" demanded a garrison's presence. Seventeenth century documents testify that between 1623 and 1635 "planters" (their word for settlers) built "many houses upon the great island which lyeth at the entrance" of the river. New Castle has been populated ever since, and while its residents have changed the island's landscape considerably, there is no place in the region that feels so historic. Neither the new condominiums and marina at Wentworth-by-the-Sea, nor the increasingly frequent decisions of newcomers to raze houses and build anew in their stead, has overcome the essential antiquity of New Castle's crooked lanes and cheek-by-jowl clapboard houses.

New Castle also makes an exquisite subject for aerial photographs. The image of the northern part of the island, from which Fort Constitution and the Coast Guard pier protrude like a lobster's claw, contains the heart of the old village. Just to the left of the long Coast Guard pier is the town wharf, and just north of it is striking evidence of the cross-grained and wily waters with which locals have always contended. The moored boats are arranged in a circle, as if in a vortex, even though the vessels moored upstream of them are arranged linearly with the ebbing tide, as one would expect. Cod Rock is to blame. Lurking just under water beyond the town wharf, it is a prominent little seamount. (Cod Rock is easily visible in the multibeam sonar images of the Piscataqua printed as Color Plate V.) It twists the current off Middle Cove into an eddy long familiar to those who fished near it or who approached the wharf—especially under sail. The juxtaposition of this aerial shot and that sonar image, never before published together, explains one of the Piscataqua's distinctive quirks.

West (or left) of Cod Rock in this aerial shot is Salamander Point, and west of it is the prominent Portsmouth Yacht Club facility. Just to the west of that is Upper Cove, the largest cove on this shore of Great Island. During the nineteenth and early twentieth centuries New Castle's coal pier was in Upper Cove, and great heaps of coal were piled along shore and on the wharf. To the left, or west, of Upper Cove is the "Fish Pasture," where cod were split and sun-cured when New Castle men still fished for a living. Today the "Fish Pasture" is the place from which the causeway (just out of this aerial picture) departs for Portsmouth.

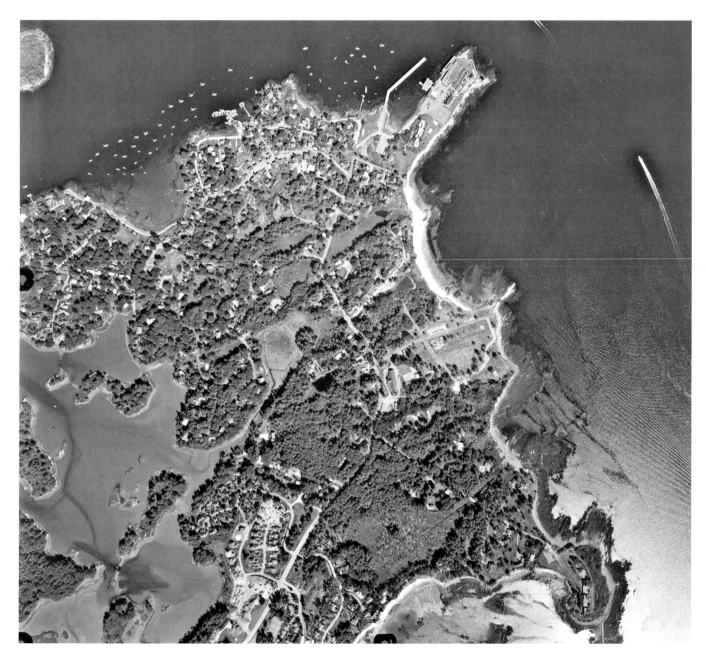

Eastern side of Great Island, New Castle, New Hampshire. Photograph by J. W. Sewall, Inc., September 29, 1998. Courtesy of the New Hampshire Coastal Program.

The aerial photograph of Great Island's southern shore is even more dramatic, including as it does the Wentworth-by-the-Sea Hotel, the marina, the bridge over Little Harbor to Rye, and extraordinarily productive mud flats and salt marsh that surround Odiorne Point. Two granite breakwaters now make Little Harbor a much more protected anchorage than it was when the Odiorne family fished here. The breakwaters also make Little Harbor difficult to approach in darkness and thick fog, especially in vessels without radar, for the current runs hard, and that granite is unforgiving. One breakwater juts south from Fort Stark; the longer one extends north from Frost Point.

As fishing village, military garrison, artists' colony, yachters' haven, and wharf-studded seaport, New Castle's Great Island has long been at the heart of the Piscataqua maritime region. Moreover it is the only town in the area that can be circumnavigated. Every year boaters in motor vessels small enough to clear the bridges, and row boats and kayaks of all descriptions, make their way around Great Island, savoring the nature of the place and the continuum they share with those who navigated these waters in years past. –WJB

Little Harbor at southern end of Great Island, New Castle, New Hampshire. Photograph by J. W. Sewall, Inc., September 29, 1998. Courtesy of the New Hampshire Coastal Program.

New Castle, New Hampshire, circa 1978. Photograph by Peter E. Randall. Courtesy of the photographer.

FORT CONSTITUTION (FORT WILLIAM & MARY)

FORT CONSTITUTION, situated on Fort Point of New Castle Island, marks the southern portal of the main channel into Portsmouth Harbor. This pivotal location at the entrance to the harbor has been fortified for almost as long as Portsmouth has been a haven for sailing vessels. As early as 1633 the British maintained four guns in an earthwork on the site to guard the harbor entrance. Since then, Fort Point has been fortified in every war through World War II.

Viewed from land, most of the visible brickwork at Fort Constitution remains from the fortifications built for the War of 1812, including the brick ramparts, the gateway with portcullis, the powder magazine, the ramps for moving guns, and the terraplain platform for firing the battery. But from the harbor side of the fort, the most notable feature is the massive cut granite wall pierced with dark openings for cannon. The center section of the wall is incomplete, giving the impression that the fort might have been breached under the cannonade of some unknown battle. The wall was actually a victim of premature obsolescence. Great granite forts were the state of the art in harbor defense prior to the Civil War. With the onset of that war, many new fortifications of this type were built, including Fort Constitution and Fort McClary in Portsmouth Harbor. Subsequent development of naval artillery, however, and rapid improvements in firepower and accuracy became more than a match for granite forts. A wall whose destruction formerly would have required extended close range bombardment could now be shattered with a single exploding shell. Under these circumstances, the granite walls became more dangerous to the fort's defenders than to the enemy, as the shattered stone would be additional shrapnel. Construction of granite fortifications was abandoned as soon as this became apparent, and Fort Constitution's wall was never completed.

The most dramatic episode in the fort's history occurred in the tense months leading to the outbreak of the Revolutionary War when Sons of Liberty from surrounding towns overpowered the half-dozen British soldiers stationed there. The patriots carried off sixteen cannons and five tons of gunpowder in one of the American revolutionaries' first violent acts against the King.

In more recent wars Fort Constitution defended the harbor, particularly the Portsmouth Naval Shipyard. During the Spanish-American War, mine laying equipment was installed so that electronically controlled mines could be strung across the harbor channel. Two eight-inch guns were mounted in a concrete battery known as Battery Farnsworth located south of the older fortifications. A second battery of two three-inch guns, Battery Hackleman, was in place before World War II at the site of the current Coast Guard building. At the peak of operations during World War II, eighteen buildings were in use at the fort. Those wooden buildings are gone now, but the remains of the masonry fort exist and are open to the public as the Fort Constitution State Historical Site. The opening in the incomplete granite wall frames the boat traffic moving in and out of Portsmouth Harbor, as it has for over 140 years. –TCM

Sources: Bruce Sloane, *New Hampshire's Parklands* (Portsmouth, NH: Peter E. Randall, 1985); The Thoresen Group, *State Coastal Properties Project* (Concord: New Hampshire Office of State Planning, June 1983); Jack P. Wysong, *The World, Portsmouth, and the 22nd Coast Artillery* (Missoula, MT: Pictorial Histories Publishing Co. Inc., 1997).

Fort Constitution. Photograph by Davis Brothers, circa 1900. Courtesy of Portsmouth Athenaeum.

A Short Row from Portsmouth to Revolution

That warm June night should have been an absolute pleasure, especially in a New Hampshire garden. Flowers and trees were just coming into their own for the summer season. But as he raced with his young family from his back door to the shore of South Mill Pond, the scent of fresh buds and blossoms must have been the last thing on the mind of Royal Governor John Wentworth.

It was June 13, 1775, a Tuesday. Circumstances in New Hampshire had deteriorated to a point unimaginable to Governor Wentworth and his supporters as recently as six months ago. Despite New Hampshire's participation in the First Continental Congress in Philadelphia in September 1774, the colony's voice was then still relatively mild in its call for independence. Wentworth, ever a moderate, hoped for wise heads to prevail on both sides of the Atlantic and for some accommodation to be reached that would be acceptable to all.

In December 1774 there had been a critical turn of events in Portsmouth. On Tuesday the 13th, Paul Revere had arrived from Boston with word that King George III had forbidden any further export of cannon, gunpowder, or other munitions to the colonies. With only limited production capacity of its own, this would put the patriotic military at a disadvantage should fighting occur. Revere further warned that British troops had boarded vessels in Boston on Sunday. It was rumored they were headed for Fort William and Mary in New Castle, to enhance the modest troops there, and to join them in protecting the colony's supply of arms and gunpowder.

Revere's message alarmed local patriot leaders. The next day, Wednesday, December 14, John Langdon led a troop of some two hun-

Governor John Wentworth (1737-1820), *1769. Pastel on paper mounted on canvas, John Singleton Copley. Courtesy Hood Museum of Art, Dartmouth College, Hanover, New Hampshire.*

dred Portsmouth men downriver by boat to the fort, where the Piscataqua makes one final turn before it heads to the open ocean. En route they were joined by men from Kittery, Rye, and New Castle, who doubled the force. At the fort they challenged the commander and his five soldiers to release the arms stored there. The commander asked for orders authorizing this action, and, when none were forthcoming, ordered his men to fire into the crowd. Miraculously, no one was injured. The enraged crowd soon stormed the poorly maintained fort, overcame the small garrison, and lowered the royal colors. Over the course of the afternoon Langdon's men loaded one hundred barrels of gunpowder onto two gundalows and returned to Portsmouth. Langdon sent word inland to militia major John Sullivan at Durham, and left to him decisions about the distribution and storage of the gunpowder, as well as the question of whether to return to the fort to remove the remaining cannon and small arms.

Sullivan led a group that retook the fort at 10 p.m. on Thursday, December 15, again with only token opposition. By eight o'clock the next morning they had loaded sixteen light cannon, ten cannon carriages, and forty-two muskets onto waiting gundalows, leaving behind some seventy heavier cannon, according to the governor. As they sailed up the river to Portsmouth, they stalled against a strong ebb current near the town. Here they waited for the evening's flood tide to carry them further upstream and through the churning currents of the Horse Races at Dover Point. By Friday evening, December 16, the gundalows were coming up the Oyster River. Thick ice in the river had to be broken by hand, slowing progress considerably. Over the weekend, however, the supplies were offloaded at the Durham town landing and hidden.

British vessels soon arrived to restore order. The sloop *Canceaux* dropped anchor in the cove above the fort on Saturday, December 17, and the man-of-war *Scarborough*, under command of Captain Andrew Barkley, arrived on Wednesday, December 21. Governor Wentworth again was caught squarely in the middle. Over the next eight months he would find himself locked in negotiations between town officials, whose constituents were regularly shooting at the *Scarborough's* boats as they patrolled the river, and Captain Barkley, who, with equal regularity, offered to bring the *Scarborough* upstream to level the town of Portsmouth with his ship's guns.

Governor John Wentworth House. Courtesy of Mark H. Wentworth Home.

Governor Wentworth was overwhelmed by circumstances beyond his control. Throughout the spring of 1775 he had been at odds with the Provincial Assembly as well. Unlike his uncle, Governor Benning Wentworth, whom he relieved as royal governor in 1767, John Wentworth worked hard for the best interests of the entire colony. He expanded the county system so that inland farmers would not have to travel to Portsmouth to attend court. He undertook a major road building program to connect the interior lands with the coast. He established Dartmouth College as a fixture in the Connecticut Valley. Unfortunately for him, such improvement and conciliation were simply too little too late.

Governor Wentworth had called and dissolved the Provincial Assembly repeatedly since the attacks on the fort, each time hoping that cooler heads might prevail when the members returned, or that new elections might bring members less inclined to the rhetoric supporting revolution. He had tried to stem the tide of revolution by extending the ballot to towns where his supporters lived, in hopes that they would elect delegates who would reduce the tensions by diluting his opposition. His efforts were to no avail.

Among the beneficiaries of Governor Wentworth's decision to extend the vote to new communities was John Fenton of Plymouth, a supporter of the governor. Throughout its opening session on June 13, the assembly refused to seat Fenton or delegates from Orford or Lyme, arguing that the governor had no right to extend the ballot to these communities without legislative approval. Tempers ran high. Fenton did little to improve the situation, making strong statements in favor of Governor Wentworth and the administration of George III. The day's session at the state house in Market Square adjourned with Fenton and the other challenged delegates still not seated. Fenton left to have dinner with the governor and his wife at their home on Pleasant Street, a short walk away. After dinner, with the governor and Fenton downstairs and Mrs. Wentworth upstairs with their five-month-old son, word reached the house that a mob was approaching.

Governor Wentworth opened the door to face a large crowd milling in the street, all demanding that Fenton be released to them. The governor refused and returned inside. The crowd approached the house and began beating on it with sticks and clubs. The governor opened the door again, only to be faced with a cannon aimed at him, and a call from the crowd for Fenton or the death of everyone in the house. At that point, Fenton released himself to the crowd and was carried off by the mob to face the Colonial Congress, then sitting in Exeter.

Governor Wentworth had earlier called for a boat from the *Scarborough*. High tide allowed the boat to be rowed over the dam at the entrance to South Mill Pond and directly to the foot of the gardens behind the governor's home. He, his wife and baby, and a few servants ran through the gardens to the boat and the safety of the

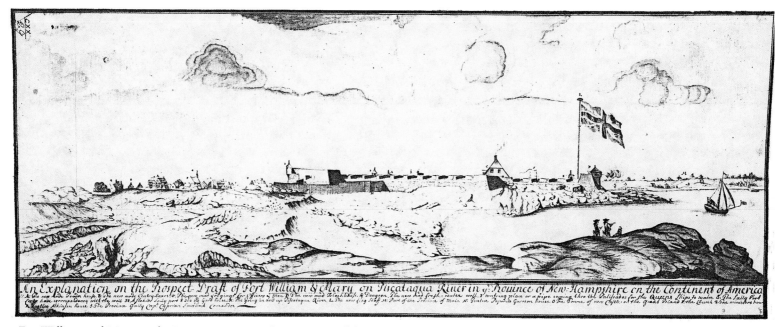

Fort William and Mary on the Piscataqua River, 1699. Courtesy of the Portsmouth Athenaeum.

Scarborough and the fort. As fears escalated that Fenton might not be enough to satisfy the mob's anger, and that it might return for the governor and his family, the men pulled on their oars and moved the boat toward the mill dam near today's Marcy Street.

Directly in front of the fleeing governor would have been Little Island, a point of reference in Portsmouth's back channel to this day. If the tide were still sufficiently full, Wentworth's boat would have slid over the bar that connects the lower end of Peirce Island with Shapleigh's Island, part of the current road to New Castle. If it were not full, the vessel likely turned to port after leaving the millpond, cruising the gut between the mainland and Peirce Island before entering the main channel of the Piscataqua near Four Tree Island.

Ironically, while passing through the gut, Wentworth would have traveled directly in front of the home we now know as the Wentworth-Gardner House, which his mother had built in 1760 as a wedding gift for his late younger brother Thomas. As he passed the foot of what is now Prescott Park, he would have crossed the mouth of the water that flowed from Puddle Dock, adjacent to which was a home that had belonged to his namesake and grandfather, Lieutenant Governor John Wentworth, who had served regularly as New Hampshire's acting royal governor until his death in 1730.

By either route, whether passing inside or outside of Peirce Island, at its foot Wentworth could have looked to starboard to see The Pool, the site where so many mast ships had been loaded with the white pines that were the mainstay of the colony's export economy and his family's fortune. Beyond The Pool, beyond Pest and Leach Islands, would be the candlelit windows of his Uncle Benning's home, now occupied by Benning's young widow and her new husband, yet another Wentworth.

Beyond that Wentworth home lay Sagamore Creek. Here the patriot leader John Langdon had grown up in a house that is now part of the Urban Forestry Center. On that creek Langdon learned the small boat skills that would later lead him to be a master mariner, a man fully capable of leading a group of skiffs and barges on a winter trip down the Piscataqua to attack the fort. And finally, further down the main channel of the river, the New Castle shore itself would appear to starboard, bringing Governor Wentworth and his retinue to the fort. Here they took up residence in a two-room building, much open to the wind and weather, under the watchful eyes and protective guns of the *Canceaux* and *Scarborough*.

Governor Wentworth stayed in these difficult quarters for ten weeks. He was there on June 17, when General John Stark and his New Hampshire men made such good use of the stolen powder and arms at the Battle of Bunker Hill. He was there on June 22, when militia major John Sullivan of Durham was made a brigadier general in the Continental Army. He was there on August 9, his thirty-eighth birthday. On August 24, when the *Scarborough* had to leave to be re-supplied in Boston, Wentworth realized that he must sail with her in order to assure his own safety and that of his family. And yet, as he sailed down the channel past Wood Island, taking with him all royal authority, the governor apparently still could not fully grasp what had happened to him and what was about to happen to the English colonies.

After reaching the safety of Boston, Governor Wentworth made one last futile gesture. On September 21 he secured a vessel and sailed to Gosport Harbor on the Isles of Shoals. From there he sent a message ashore to Portsmouth, adjourning a session of the Provincial Assembly that he had previously ordered to convene later that month. The next day, September 22, 1775, Royal Governor John Wentworth, native son of Portsmouth and third generation in his family to rule the province, sailed back to Boston, never to return to New Hampshire. The Revolution had begun. –JHT

Sources: Lawrence Shaw Mayo, *John Langdon of New Hampshire* (Concord, NH: The Rumford Press, 1937); Paul W. Wilderson, *Governor John Wentworth and the American Revolution: The English Connection* (Hanover, NH: University Press of New England, 1994); David Hackett Fischer, *Paul Revere's Ride* (New York: Oxford University Press, 1994); Charles C. Parsons, *The Capture of Fort William and Mary* (Paper delivered at the New Hampshire Historical Society 77th Annual Meeting; reprinted by The William and Mary Committee of the New Hampshire American Revolution Bicentennial Commission, Concord, NH, 1976).

FORT STARK

LOOMING UP FROM THE SLENDER PENINSULA at the southern tip of New Castle Island is an unusual concrete building that resembles the superstructure of an ocean liner; a calculated piece of deception intended to confuse enemy ships. This building is the most prominent structure among the remains of Fort Stark. During World War II it served as the Harbor Entrance Control Post for Portsmouth Harbor. It was built between 1901 and 1905 during a frenzy of coastal defense construction inspired by the Spanish-American and Russo-Japanese wars. The peninsula has long been of strategic importance, dividing as it does Portsmouth Harbor's main channel from the back channel through Little Harbor. Forts and batteries have been positioned here for hundreds of years.

The spot was first fortified in 1746 in preparation for an English military expedition against Louisburg, Nova Scotia, when nine 32-pound guns were mounted there. During the Revolutionary War, New Hampshire's government built a more permanent fort of sods, earth, and stone walls. In fact, Fort Stark was named for a Revolutionary hero, Major General John Stark of the First New Hampshire Regiment and Continental Infantry. After the Revolution the site was improved when war with England again seemed imminent. And in 1874 military planners began, but then aborted, construction of an 8-gun battery.

During the first decade of the twentieth century, when coastal forts still had a clear advantage over naval artillery, a comprehensive system of American coastal fortifications was constructed. Fort Stark's armaments at the time consisted of Battery David Hunter (two 12-inch guns on disappearing carriages); Battery Edward Kirk (two 6-inch rapid-firing guns on disappearing carriages); Battery Alexander Hays (two 3-inch rapid firing guns on pedestal mounts); and Battery William Lytle (two 3-inch rapid fire guns on pedestal mounts.)

During the world wars, advances in naval artillery rapidly outstripped coastal defenses. In 1917 the two 6-inch guns in Battery Kirk were decommissioned, and by World War II the 12-inch guns in Battery Hunter were considered obsolete because of vulnerability to "plunging fire" from above. The two 3-inch batteries were maintained during World War II for close-in harbor protection, and an antisubmarine net was run between Wood Island and Fort Stark.

Fort Stark's primary role in harbor defense during World War II was as the Harbor Entrance Control Post. All harbor defense units, both army and navy, were coordinated from the ship-like building. Today the ruins of the four batteries and the camouflaged Harbor Entrance Control Post are all open to the public as New Hampshire's Fort Stark Historic Site. –TCM

Sources: Bruce Sloane, *New Hampshire's Parklands* (Portsmouth, NH: Peter E. Randall, 1985); The Thoresen Group, *State Coastal Properties Project* (Concord: New Hampshire Office of State Planning, June 1983); Jack P. Wysong, *The World, Portsmouth, and the 22nd Coast Artillery* (Missoula, MT: Pictorial Histories Publishing Co. Inc., 1997).

Fort Stark, October 1999. Photograph by Thomas C. Mansfield. Courtesy of the photographer.

Lighthouses of the Piscataqua

As one views the Piscataqua region from the sea during daylight, the sweeping arc of the Interstate 95 Bridge, the sky-piercing cranes of the Portsmouth Naval Shipyard, and Mount Agamenticus dominate the rather bland coastal topography. At night, however, lighthouses prevail. Although the coast is aglow with building and street lights, it is the reassuring fixed green of the New Castle Light and the powerful double white flash of Whaleback Light that dominate the night. Offshore, at the Isles of Shoals, White Island Light flashes once every fifteen seconds. It has been flashing, in darkness and in fog, since 1820. For the last 230 years, except during wartime, at least one lighthouse has marked the Piscataqua.

Those lighthouses have been photographed, sketched, and painted innumerably, and they are clearly among the most enduring symbols of the region's maritime heritage. But for fishermen, yachtsmen, and commercial mariners, they are infinitely more meaningful, even in this age of precise electronic navigational devices.

Electronics can fail or produce false positions. But all competent mariners know that they can fix the position of their vessel by taking compass bearings on lighthouses and plotting those bearings on a chart. For nineteenth-century skippers, taking such bearings was no exercise in nostalgia, nor a measuring of the accuracy of the human hand against the hum of electronics. It was a routine matter of critical importance, and sometimes one of life or death. Well into the twentieth century, captains had no accurate way to position their vessels at night, save for lighthouses. Those stately beacons, now icons of the region, were essential to the development of American shipping and essential to the safety of generations of Piscataqua mariners.

Few lighthouses existed in America during the colonial era. Boston Light, built on Little Brewster Island in 1716, was the first. Mariners simply knew that at night they had to take their chances, and their chances were not always promising. In December of 1768 a Portsmouth schooner returning from Guadeloupe in the French West Indies piled up on White Island. The crew was rescued, but the schooner and its cargo of molasses were a complete loss. The public outcry energized New Hampshire's Royal Governor John Wentworth to champion lighthouses. With funds approved by the Provincial Assembly in 1771, Wentworth authorized the first lighthouse in the province. Situated at New Castle, it was only the tenth lighthouse in British North America, and the first north of Boston.

The first New Castle Light was a wood frame structure, 78 feet tall. Located adjacent to Fort William and Mary, it perched on a ledge against the upstream side of the fort. Fish oil fueled that first light, which was tended by the fort's modest garrison—the same garrison that attempted to protect the king's gunpowder and cannon during the patriots' raid in 1774. By 1803 the New Castle Light was in need of substantial repair. Congress directed that a new light be built, more visible to coastal shipping. New Hampshire's first lighthouse had always been partially blocked to mariners approaching from the eastward by Gerrish Island on the Maine shore of the Piscataqua. Builders situated the second New Castle Light downstream of the fort on the site of the current light. It became operational in 1804, during the presidency of Thomas Jefferson.

Shipping flourished in the early nineteenth century, and the new federal government invested considerable resources in lighthouses. Contemporaries saw them as markers of progress, demonstrating Americans' determination to overcome nature's threats. In 1811 a lighthouse was constructed at Boon Island Ledges, off the coast of York. An engineering marvel that seemed to rise straight out of the sea, it was nonetheless twelve miles northeast of the Isles of Shoals, and of limited utility for mariners bound for the Piscataqua. A few years later a Spanish vessel named *Conception* was wrecked on Smuttynose, one of the Isles of Shoals, with the loss of fourteen sailors. Local men knew that they could be next, and endorsed the construction of a lighthouse on White Island in 1820. Finally, after

Whalesback Light. *Pen and ink drawing by Abbott F. Graves from John Albee's* New Castle: Historic and Picturesque, *1884. Courtesy of the Milne Special Collections and Archives Department, University of New Hampshire.*

more than two hundred years of shipping in the region, the Isles of Shoals were visible at night.

Offshore marine construction was a new and developing art in the 1820s. The mortar used in the first White Island Light began to crumble almost immediately. By 1824 the lighthouse was sheathed in wood and shingles to keep it from further deterioration. This was the structure that welcomed Thomas Laighton, father of poet Celia Laighton Thaxter, when he and his family arrived to assume their duties as lighthouse keepers in the fall of 1839. Visitors to White Island today will note that the covered walkway linking the keeper's house to the light does not enter that structure directly, but rather winds through a series of adjacent foundations. These are the base of the original light.

In a final attempt to get a coastal light out from behind the shadow of Gerrish Island, Congress in 1829 authorized a new light to be built on the shallow ledges running southerly from Gerrish and Wood Islands at the mouth of the Piscataqua River. The ledges were known locally as Whale's Back, and Whaleback Light it became. Once illuminated, it completed the triumvirate of Piscataqua lights that exist today.

Lighthouses appear as firm, fixed sentinels. But fully exposed to both the wrath of gales and the constantly corrosive marine environment, many early lighthouses did not last long. By 1851 the impact of the elements had taken its toll on the second New Castle Light, severely damaging the upper levels of the wood frame structure. The rotting upper portion was simply lopped off, reducing the light to only sixty feet above mean high water, and giving the once graceful tower a squat and inelegant appearance.

White Island Light continued to deteriorate, and in 1859 a new light was constructed immediately adjacent to the first. This is the 58-foot brick structure (painted white) that stands today. Engineering techniques had improved substantially by the mid-nineteenth century. The first light lasted only thirty-nine years, whereas the second White Island Light is over 141 years old, and still going strong. Whaleback Light also had to be replaced after forty years, and a second light was built immediately adjacent to the first. The base of the original light may still be seen, but the reassuring double pulse of Whaleback that

The third, and current lighthouse at New Castle, New Hampshire, August, 1903. Courtesy of the Society for the Preservation of New England Antiquities.

appears every night—and in every fog—flashes from the newer tower built in 1872. Old photos reveal that after part of the original Whaleback Light was removed, its base supported a steam-powered foghorn and a vegetable garden for the keeper's summer fare.

Even the truncated New Castle Light could not last forever, built as it was of wood. By the 1870s, cast iron was being used widely to produce buildings and other architectural features, including lighthouses. The current New Castle Light, with its Victorian arched windows, is made of cast iron plates. Eight feet shorter than the light it replaced, and smaller in diameter as well, it was assembled inside the older tower.

Timbers were removed from the older structure, and the light apparatus itself was lowered into place on the new cast iron tower. Later the old wooden structure was peeled away. The New Castle Light has been painted white since the early twentieth century, but it was originally a rusty brown color. Writing in 1885, New Castle historian John Albee called it a "corpulent length of stovepipe," revealing himself as a traditionalist rankled by the modern metal lighthouse. The Nubble Light in York was fabricated from the same molds as the New Castle Light.

The lighthouses remain, but the keepers are gone. Whaleback was automated in 1963, and White Island followed suit in 1986. No longer

The second White Island Light from Star Island. Courtesy of the Laing Collection.

do crews of keepers or their families labor in the confinement and isolation of a light tower, living on a ledge like Whaleback, awash at every high tide. Of course, stories persist of lighthouse keepers and their families maintaining a vigil for others despite their isolation, and struggling through storms to keep their beacons burning. But today the relationship of Piscataqua people to the sea is significantly different. Fewer people earn their livelihood there, and fewer still imagine themselves pitted against the sea. Instead we understand that human commercial and technological progress—the very forces that once made lighthouses imperative to preserve mariners from the sea—must now be harnessed to preserve the sea itself. – JHT

Sources: John Albee, *New Castle, Historic and Picturesque* (Boston: Cupples, Upham and Company, 1885); Clancy, Adams, and Roy, Consultants, Inc., *Portsmouth Harbor Light, Supplemental Filings, Application for National Register of Historic Places*, and *Isles of Shoals (White Island) Light Station, Supplemental Filings, Application for National Register of Historic Places* (Unpublished documents on file with the New Hampshire Division of Historic Resources, Concord, NH, 1989); Kirk F. Mohney, *Whaleback Light Station, National Register of Historic Places Registration Form* (Unpublished documents on file with the Maine Historic Preservation Commission, Augusta, Maine, 1987).

WENTWORTH-BY-THE-SEA

NEW CASTLE ABOUT 1890. This view from Odiorne Point across Little Harbor shows a wonderful range of pleasure craft and the Wentworth-by-the-Sea Hotel during its glory years. On the far right is an Isles of Shoals boat, strictly indigenous to this area and a type of which no existing model remains today. They were used first for fishing between the mainland and the Shoals and were later used as excursion boats for hotel guests. Where the fine yawl and fan-tailed steam yacht in the background are anchored, there is now a sprawling marina with docks for a hundred vessels, some of which carry their own aircraft. While much has changed here since 1890, Little Harbor is still the realm of aquatic excursions great and small, and public access to the shore from which this photograph was taken has endured. –NBB

Courtesy of Strawbery Banke Museum

PORTSMOUTH

CHARTING THE PISCATAQUA

THE PISCATAQUA RIVER figured prominently on seventeenth-century maps of New England thanks to the excellence of its harbor and the quality of its nearby fishing grounds. John Smith was particularly impressed by the area; on his *Map of New England* (1616), the Isles of Shoals appeared as "Smith's Isles," but the name never caught on. The mountain named Agamenticus became the English "Snadoun Hill," and "Boston" was provisionally applied to a settlement site near the Piscataqua. That name caught on further south. Smith depicted the Piscataqua region's coastline, navigable rivers, and good natural harbors—the infrastructure of transportation and communication—with great care. In fact, Smith's *Map* was the most accurate printed chart of those waters for almost a hundred years.

The colorful manuscript *Masathusett, Mason's Patent and the Province of Mayne,* probably drawn about 1650, shares important characteristics with Smith's *Map* (see Color Plate I). Mount Agamenticus served as an important landmark for mariners voyaging to the Piscataqua, and a profile of "Agamenticus Hill" graced the southwestern

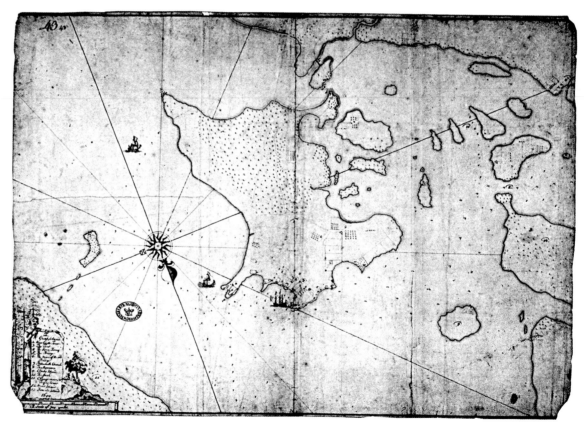

New Castle, 1699. Attributed to Col. William Wolfgang Romer. Romer's map was the first to include soundings for mariners, and its meticulous detail remained unsurpassed for seventy years. Note that north is at the bottom, and the open ocean is to the left. Courtesy of the Portsmouth Athenaeum.

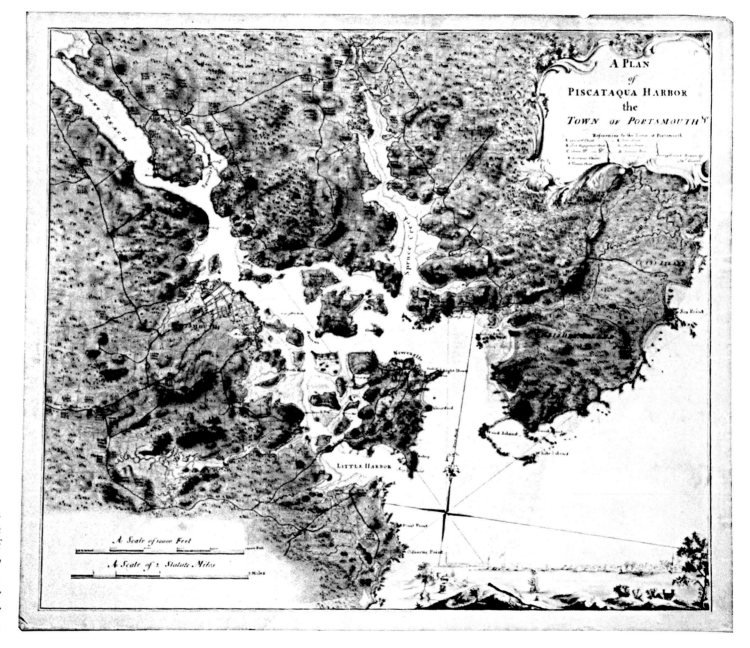

Plan of Piscataqua Harbor and the Town of Portsmouth, *by James Grant, 1774. Courtesy of the New Hampshire Historical Society.*

Mayne shore. The sea was not divided into a regular Cartesian grid of latitude and longitude on seventeenth-century English portolan charts, for mariners could not calculate longitude. Dead reckoning allowed a skilled navigator to figure his position by knowing the direction in which he sailed, the time elapsed from his last fixed position, and the speed of the vessel. A sea chart featured a scale for distance traveled and rhumb lines radiating out from intersecting points like spider webs. At a few of these intersections, elaborate compass roses resolved the converging lines into directions, with North indicated by a *fleur de lis*. West often lay at the top of New England charts, a useful orientation for the voyage from Europe.

Piscataway River in New England by I. S. was probably drawn in the 1670s after the First Dutch War had made Piscataqua-area mast pines a vital strategic commodity. (See Color Plate II.) It was the first map to focus on the local shoreline, which was depicted as one scattered community of towns tied together

An Accurate Map of His Majesty's Province of New Hampshire in New England, Taken from Actual Surveys of All That Is Inhabited . . . Together with Adjacent Countries Which Exhibit the Theatre of This War in That Part of the World, by Col. Blanchard and the Rev. Mr. Langdon. *[London]: Thomas Jefferys, 1761. Courtesy of the New Hampshire Historical Society.*

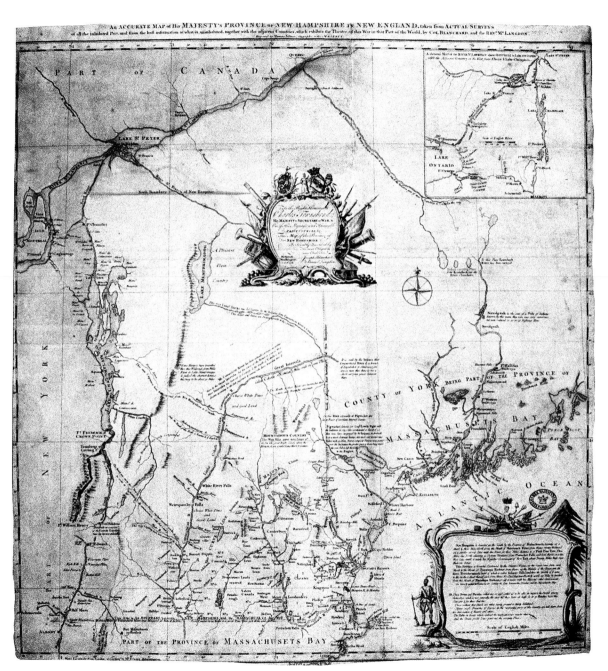

On May 29, 2001, the United States Supreme Court dismissed New Hampshire's suit against the state of Maine for jurisdiction over the whole of the Piscataqua River and Portsmouth Harbor. New Hampshire claimed historical control of commerce, navigation and defense on the waterway while Maine relied on the language of King George II's 1740 Boundary Decision. However, the Court looked no further back than the 1977 Lobster War for the basis of its opinion. In 1977 Maine and New Hampshire agreed to the boundary shown here to end the dispute over lobster grounds between the mainland and the Isles of Shoals. The Supreme Court stated twenty-four years later that New Hampshire, having once approved a middle of the river boundary, cannot now go back on its word even if the stretch in question is further up the river. This map, presented by New Hampshire in Oral Arguments, was reproduced with minor changes in the Supreme Court's decision.

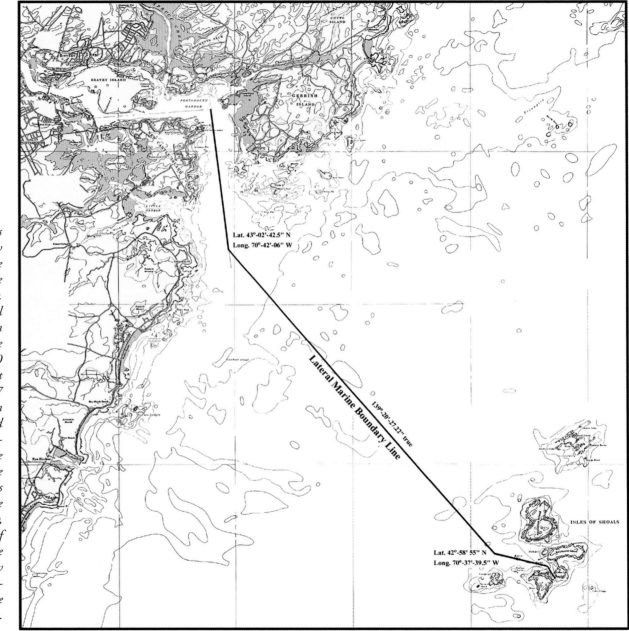

by ribbons of water. Landmarks and hazards like "Boiling Rock" at the entrance to "Long Reach" already bore familiar colloquial names. A very fine dotted line between Brave Boat Harbor and Pepperrell Cove may indicate a navigable saltwater channel along Chauncey Creek. William Pepperrell dredged here around 1700, possibly to combat siltation from farming. Silt had already begun to choke shallow waterways and to foul millponds in heavily settled areas.

"I. S." was probably John Sellers, "Hydrographer to the King," who began to print crude English sea charts in the 1670s from old Dutch copper plates. On the New England chart, the Piscataqua looked like a tiny grasping hand, its fingers forming the tributaries to Great Bay. Nevertheless his *English Pilot* (1671), which combined charts with sailing directions, was the standard printed sea atlas for English seamen for a hundred years. Captain Cyprian Southack's necessary corrections to the New England chart, published in Boston in 1720 as the *New England Coasting Pilot*, were eventually incorporated into later editions of the *English Pilot, Forth Book*.

When Wilhelm Wolfgang Römer arrived in New Castle in 1699 he commenced to survey the Piscataqua for Governor Jonathan Dudley with an eye toward defending it from the French. His map of *Great Island*, besides depicting such minute details as wharves, roads, ferries, plowed fields, orchards, and house lots, is the first to offer soundings. His fortification strategy was revealed in a series of meticulous manuscript maps and profiles unsurpassed in accuracy for seventy years.

During the eighteenth century, parallels and meridians replaced rhumb lines on sea charts as improved instruments made possible mathematical accuracy in surveying and navigation. As John Harrison labored to perfect his chronometer, a group of British officers recognized the need for accurate charts of the North American shoreline before the next French war. Samuel Holland, who labored hard to implement their project, became surveyor general for the North District of North America in 1763. For a time in the early 1770s, his team of hydrographers and land surveyors headquartered at Portsmouth triangulated the coastline and its rivers.

Holland sent William Hogg, master of the Royal Navy ship *Canceaux*, to triangulate the Piscataqua coast. On his sketch, preserved in the Hydrographic Office, Taunton, U.K, Chauncey Creek no longer runs into Brave Boat Harbor. Its eastern end is a marsh, with Gerrish and Cutts Islands appearing connected to the mainland. Little Harbor is partially choked by sandbars. James Grant, who published the well-known *Plan of Piscataqua Harbor and the Town of Portsmouth*, also worked for Holland as a deputy land surveyor. Their results went into Joseph F. W. des Barres's *Atlantic Neptune* (1777), one of the greatest examples of scientific art ever published.

Holland, des Barres, and their colleague in the South, De Brahm, were correct about the war. Their maps and charts were important to both sides during the American Revolution, although the British had most of the copies. Rochambeau's French forces made at least two sketches of the Piscataqua during the last year of the war. It bristled with shoreline redoubts and island forts.

After the Revolution, Newburyport publisher Edmund Blunt, Sr., Americanized nautical publishing with a successful edition of sailing directions for American harbors. The fact that whole passages were copied from Southack and the *English Pilot, Forth Book* bothered no one. Charts were added in 1804 to the fourth revised edition of Blunt's *American Coast Pilot*, and his "Harbour of Portsmouth" was the first chart to employ that name instead of "Piscataqua Harbor."

During the nineteenth century the construction of lighthouses and deployment of buoys and channel markers improved coastal navigation. Precision instruments and methodical procedures moved surveying from an art to an institutionalized science. Blunt's charts were supplanted by better government surveys, including the huge (1 inch = 1/10 mile scale), six-part engraving, *Survey of the Harbor of Portsmouth NH With a view to its Defense,…1842, 43, & 44*. This exhaustive effort incorporated "298 points of triangulation fixed on land; 41 points fixed on water to locate the lines sounded; 13,111 soundings; 813 tides registered at high water; 820 tides registered at low water; 298 miles coursed and chained to delineate the shores of the harbor and the sea coast; the ponds, marshes roads and the topography of the interior; 19,730 points the heights of which were ascertained by the level."

Under the direction of Alexander Dallas Bache, great-grandson of Benjamin Franklin, the civilian Coast Survey finally assumed responsibility for accurately surveying the coast by mid-century. Their charts were sometimes printed on heavy paper, or thin paper was laid on stiffened fabric to make the charts roll neatly like British bluebacks for storage in a tight cabin.

Bache and his Coast Survey vessels periodically operated off the Piscataqua, and the *Preliminary Chart of Portsmouth Harbor, New Hampshire* was issued in 1854. Four years later the Gosport town clerk recorded that "a U.S. Surveying Steamer enlivened our harbor by her prolonged presence and her soundings were evidently made with care and completeness."

The Coast Survey and its successors, the Coast and Geodetic Survey and NOAA, recognized that people were changing the geography of the coastline. Bridges for railroads and highways spanned the Piscataqua and its tributaries. Siltation on the Squamscott, Cocheco, and Oyster Rivers obstructed what had been deepwater ports in Exeter, Dover, and Durham several generations earlier. The Army Corps of Engineers recommended several modifications to improve navigation on the Piscataqua, including removing Boiling Rock and dredging Pepperrell Cove. Henderson's Point, locally known as "Pull and Be Damned Point" because it was so difficult to round, was dynamited out of existence in 1905 to widen the main channel and temper its fierce current. For safety, new navigational aids as well as physical changes had to be accounted for. Beacons positioned on Peirce Island and just east of Fort McClary marked the main ship channel with a lights-on-range approach and required new printings of C&GS Chart 329 in 1942 and 1957.

Today's NOAA charts of the New Hampshire/Maine coast descend directly from A. D. Bache's *Preliminary Chart of Portsmouth Harbor*. Although the theory remains the same, methods of surveying and navigation have advanced far beyond the techniques of his day. Gyroscopes have replaced magnetic compasses. Aerial photography had replaced sea level surveys by the 1980s. Long Range Navigation, or LORAN, uses signals from two related transmitters to fix positions with a radio receiver. Currently printed NOAA charts show LORAN contours, fixed aids to navigation, tide tables, and soundings, as well as coastwise geography and possible hazards such as sub-surface rocks or underwater cables. Navigational satellites, part of the Global Positioning System, give precise latitude and longitude to anyone with a GPS device. This does not eliminate the need for charts that tell sailors of immediate dangers and where to find safe harbor; accordingly, weekly updated nautical charts are now available from NOAA online. –KA

Sources: William Patterson Cumming, *British Maps Of Colonial America* (Chicago: University of Chicago Press, 1974); NOAA web site (www.noaa.gov); Tuck Library Special Collections, New Hampshire Historical Society, Concord, NH.

THE WENTWORTH-COOLIDGE MANSION

"THE SITUATION OF THE WENTWORTH MANSION is very retired, being a mile from any highway and reached by a road of its own" observed John Albee, author of *New Castle: Historic and Picturesque*, in 1884. "Little Harbor washes its walls, however, and this, in old times, was the more common way of going to it, as well as to all other dwellings around the adjacent shores. It is still the most pleasant manner of approach. You see at once that [all of the old homes in the area], and especially the Wentworth Mansion, were planted and constructed with reference to the water ways, and not the land."

If Royal Governor Benning Wentworth's Piscataqua was a kingdom of rivers, his house was in a class of its own. Wentworth's mansion, perched on the edge of Little Harbor, has been described in detail by generations of poets, historians, journalists, and artists. Those who have written about the house since the 1750s consistently comment on its

As Katharine M. Abott wrote in 1908, "The Old Wentworth Mansion lies across the river [from the "new" Wentworth Hotel]; it is a most delicious experience to float with the tide down Sagamore Creek to this oddly built house of many wings, assorted in such a variety of shapes and sizes to appear a succession of after thoughts; its history is more romantic than any other of the splendid houses standing in fine old maritime Portsmouth." Old Paths and Legends of New England (NY: G.P. Putnam's Sons, 1908), p. 259. Photograph courtesy of Wentworth-Coolidge Mansion.

"odd" and "freakish" silhouette, its unique architectural style, its incomprehensible floor plan, the ancient lilacs hugging its walls, and its dramatic proximity to the harbor's shore. Countless artists have tried to capture its architectural nuances on paper, and it remains a popular gathering place for artists in the summer. But despite the mansion's

closeness to the shore, most visitors now approach by car or bicycle from Little Harbor Road.

The royal governor, however, appears to have arrived often by boat. Wentworth likely made his rounds between Portsmouth, Little Harbor, and other places aboard his "barge," as boats of state, or gentleman's boats, were called. Apparently sixteen to twenty-four feet long, with a six-foot beam and a soft chine, Wentworth's barge was propelled by six oars. It is likely that on occasions of state the oarsmen wore livery. Dr. Alexander Hamilton visited Portsmouth in the summer of 1744, and wrote in his diary: "After breakfast we waited upon Governour Wentworth, who received me very civilly and invited me to take a soldier's dinner with him, as he called it, at the fort. At ten o'clock we went by water in the Governour's barge to Newcastle...where the fort stands upon a little island. The tide in these narrows runs with great rapidity and violence, and we having it in our favour and six oars on the barge, we were down at the fort in about ten minutes."

Much is known about Royal Governor Benning Wentworth's political career, including his role as Surveyor General of the King's Woods, his involvement in the mast trade, and his numerous land grants extending far beyond the current boundaries of New Hampshire. He made a fortune in timber and land speculation, and left his mark on the provincial landscape. However, because relatively little is known about Wentworth's domestic lifestyle, interpretations of his personality have taken on the same enigmatic character as his house. Myths abound, but facts are few and far between.

We do know, however, that when the General Assembly refused his requests to purchase the elegant Macphaedris-Warner House in Portsmouth for him, Wentworth moved his family to Little Harbor in 1753. His parents owned a 100-acre farm there with an assortment of outbuildings, but no proper dwelling house. During the following eight to ten years, Wentworth had carpenters add to the original warehouse or shop until it was described, with some exaggeration, as having fifty-two rooms with a stable large enough for thirty horses. This included the council chamber, whose elaborate mantelpiece was said to be an imitation of that of Prime Minister Walpole's.

Benning Wentworth governed New Hampshire from 1741 to 1767—the longest-serving royal governor in British America. His house, at once awkward and elegant, was the political and social heart of late provincial New Hampshire. After he died in 1770, his second wife, Martha Hilton Wentworth, inherited the property, much to the dismay of Benning's siblings. Martha lived in the mansion with her new husband for thirty-five years before auctioning its furniture and selling the estate to Charles Cushing in 1816. During the seventy years that Cushing and his descendents owned the property, the mansion was re-envisioned and promoted as a historic shrine, and it became one of the first such sites in America to be opened to the public.

J. Templeman Coolidge, a Harvard graduate, amateur artist, and sailor, bought the mansion in 1886 at the height of the Colonial Revival movement. Coolidge avidly promoted arts education in Boston. A trustee of the Museum of Fine Arts, Boston, and the Boston Athenæum, he was also a member of the Council of the School of Drawing and Painting of the Museum of Fine Arts, the Committee on Fine Arts at Harvard, the Society of Arts and Crafts of Boston, the Exhibition Committee of the Copley Society, and the Boston Art Commission. His network of friendships with artists led to the development of an elite and creative summer colony at Little Harbor, centered on the rambling colonial house. Templeman Coolidge died in 1945, and his widow generously donated the entire property to the state of New Hampshire in 1954.

Since the mid 1960s, the mansion has been operated as a historic house museum, with emphasis on the colonial era, the Colonial Revival, and—more recently—the turn-of-the-century artists' colony. In 1982 the Wentworth-Coolidge Commission, a private, non-profit organization, was established to work with New Hampshire Parks and Recreation at the site. This public-private partnership is dedicated to keeping the property central to the artistic and cultural life of the Seacoast. With its waterfront location, including two outlying islands, and its three-hundred-year pedigree, the Wentworth-Coolidge Mansion is emblematic of the Piscataqua's distinctive cultural landscape—a mix of the estuarine and the historic. –MLB

Sources: James L. Garvin, "Historical and Architectural Report and Furnishing Plan for the Wentworth-Coolidge Mansion Owned by the State of New Hampshire." (1978); John Albee, New Castle: Historic and Picturesque (Boston: Rand Avery, 1884); Woodard Openo, "The Summer Colony at Little Harbor in Portsmouth, New Hampshire, and its Relation to the Colonial Revival Movement." (PhD dissertation, University of Michigan, 1990).

URBAN FORESTRY CENTER

BEQUESTS WORK IN DIFFERENT WAYS. When the King's Council for New England granted land in what is now Portsmouth to Captain John Mason in 1629, the goal was privatization and economic productivity. It worked. Within about twenty-five years Tobias Langdon owned some of that land, and successive generations of Langdons accumulated more. The Langdons developed the land and prospered. More than a century later John Langdon helped lead the colony to independence, and became the first elected governor of New Hampshire. When John Elwyn Stone, a direct descendent of Governor Langdon, bequeathed part of the family tract to the people of New Hampshire in 1976, his goal was preservation of, and public access to, that historic saltwater farm. His vision also paid off. Nestled between Sagamore Creek, Lafayette Road (U.S. Route 1), and Elwyn Road are 180 acres of fields, woods, and marshes known today as the Urban Forestry Center. Its hiking trails, tree farm, and sanctuary for birds and wildlife provide an antidote to Portsmouth's rapidly urbanizing environment. Public programs there focus on forest management, wildlife habitat, urban landscaping, conservation, and gardening. Moreover, the center integrates an appreciation of history with its emphasis on environmental stewardship. The site is protected from future development, but its brochures and explanatory signs make abundant references to the historic nature of the property and its changing use through time. Visitors can see evidence of prior land use plainly before them.

While these staddles are located in Seabrook, similar ones are also visible at the Urban Forestry Center. Photograph by Peter E. Randall. Courtesy of the photographer.

Along the Urban Forestry Center's northern edge abutting Sagamore Creek is approximately sixty acres of a salt marsh border. Salt marshes have always provided the Piscataqua region with a natural area for flood control. Although it is a complex ecosystem consisting of birds, fish, mammals, plants, and insects, the salt marsh was historically viewed as a source of commodities rather than a system beneficial in its own right. Residents used salt marshes as pasture, harvested marsh grasses for hay, and reclaimed tidal areas for development. These actions left their mark; at the Urban Forestry Center, evidence remains in the form of wooden staddles that were once used to dry marsh grass, stone walls that contained livestock, and straight ditches designed to control the mosquito population.

The history of the Piscataqua region is not just the story of great men like John Langdon, but also of a coastal landscape used in ways both benign and exploitative. At the Urban Forestry Center, those tales are woven together—food for thought for the inquisitive visitor. –WJB

STRAWBERY BANKE

THE EARLY RECONNAISSANCE OF THE PISCATAQUA by Englishmen revealed, among other things, a high bank close to the river on which grew luscious strawberries in abundance. Now crowned by Saint John's Episcopal Church, that bank gave the settlement its first name. The more prosaic sounding "Portsmouth" was not adopted for decades.

Today Strawbery Banke is an outdoor history museum located along the western shore of the Piscataqua River, near the center of Portsmouth. The museum operates a ten-acre site with forty-three historic buildings that range in date from the 1690s to the 1950s. Some were taverns and inns, some were garages or storage buildings, but most were homes. The Sherburne House, built in two periods from 1695 to 1705, is the oldest house on the site. Like its neighboring houses, it once had a wharf and was flanked by outbuildings, shops, and warehouses that told of an era of seaborne commerce.

Visitors today see a cluster of restored buildings lining small streets and alleys, and a number of other features—fence lines, foundations, gardens, and pathways—that speak to different periods in the history of the site. But much of the nautical character of Strawbery Banke has disappeared, and it takes imagination to envision this old urban enclave as a thriving maritime community.

From the first English settlement in the early 1600s through the last period of private use in the 1950s, the site kept changing, remaking itself in response to commercial pressures even as it sustained links to the past, however inadvertently. Part of the museum's charm is that it accepts this cheek-by-jowl assemblage of buildings from a three-hundred-year span, interpreting snapshots of neighborhood life from dramatically different eras.

Originally, a tidal inlet known as "the cove" dominated the settlement. By about 1800 it was called Puddle Dock. Lined by wharves and warehouses, it supported merchants, ship captains, tradesmen, and shopkeepers into the nineteenth century. For two centuries this neighborhood lived by the sea, but as the local economy shifted to industry and larger-scale operations, the tidal inlet and the small-scale wharves and shops lost their importance. Furthermore, nearby residents complained that the inlet was a nuisance, a foul smelling and polluted cesspool. Beginning in the 1890s, city officials decided to fill the inlet and build a roadway on top of it. In its glory days, Puddle Dock had probed inland from the mighty river all the way to South Millpond, and a person in a skiff could pass from one to the other on a moon tide. Today it is solid land. Small areas of macadam from the roadway are still visible in the grassy field where Puddle Dock's tides once ebbed and flooded.

Walsh House, circa 1796, and the recreated Goodwin Garden. Photograph by Frank Clarkson, 1987. Courtesy of Strawbery Banke Museum.

By the late nineteenth century, new types of residents were living in the neighborhood. Houses built in the seventeenth, eighteenth, and nineteenth centuries continued to serve as homes, but often were converted into multi-unit tenements. Portsmouth Naval Shipyard employees, factory workers, and immigrant families found inexpensive housing here. Around 1900, after the tidal inlet was filled, several scrap-yards lined the new roadway, and most residents looked inland away from the river.

During the twentieth century, private citizens and public officials dramatically altered the waterfront area that includes Strawbery Banke

Lowd House, circa 1810, and Sherburne House, built in 1695 and 1705. Photograph taken in 1987. Courtesy of Strawbery Banke Museum.

and Prescott Park. Beginning in the late 1930s and with financial support from a trust created by the Prescott sisters, Mary and Josie, property along Marcy Street and the river was purchased, and dilapidated buildings demolished. The goal was to create a public park in place of the brothels and bars long associated with the tawdry waterfront.

While not directly connected to the park, the creation of Strawbery Banke was an extension of this gentrification. In 1958 concerned citizens began working with federal, state and city officials to use urban renewal funds for a historic site. The Marcy-Washington Street Urban Renewal originally called for replacing all buildings on the Strawbery Banke site with a public housing project. Local negotiators shifted the focus to preserve selected historic buildings and create a "colonial village," thereby developing a tourist attraction. A fundamental element of the urban renewal philosophy was elimination of blight. Forty-four non-historic buildings were thus demolished, and the families who inhabited them were relocated.

As a consequence of this demolition, only a fraction of the buildings that had stood in the 1920s, when neighborhood density was greatest, still stand today. Many building forms have either entirely disappeared or are barely represented. The stores, saloons, and boarding houses that lined Marcy Street have disappeared. The wharves and warehouses that lined Puddle Dock and the Piscataqua are likewise gone. All aboveground evidence of eighteenth-century tanneries, nineteenth-century tenements, and early twentieth-century junkyards has been lost.

In 1965, after several years of work, the first restored houses at Strawbery Banke opened to the public—the Chase and Goodwin houses. Since that time, Strawbery Banke has opened other restored buildings. Because buildings on the grounds were built in different periods and were occupied nearly continuously until the late 1950s, museum staff can interpret the changing nature of life in the neighborhood. At the Shapley house, visitors see the furnished interior of a late eighteenth-century wharf-front shop adjacent to a 1950 apartment. They see the interior of an upper-class home from the early 1800s at the Chase house, and the home of Russian immigrants circa 1910 at Shapiro house.

The Strawbery Banke outdoor history museum today interprets a neighborhood's epic tale with many twists—environmental degradation, seafaring entrepreneurship, ethnic immigration, and selective historic preservation. It all began in a fetching spot where wild strawberries grew within a stone's throw of the cross-grained and wily waters. –JM

Sources: Mark J. Sammons, ed., *Strawbery Banke: A Historic Waterfront Neighborhood in Portsmouth, New Hampshire-Official Guidebook* (Portsmouth, NH: Strawbery Banke, 1997); Paige W. Roberts, "The Politics of Preservation: Historical Consciousness and Community Identity in Portsmouth, New Hampshire." (PhD Dissertation, George Washington University, 2000); Records of the Portsmouth Housing Authority, Marcy-Washington Streets Urban Renewal Project, and Thayer Cumings Library at Strawbery Banke Museum.

PUDDLE DOCK

Puddle Dock, circa 1870, looking west from Liberty Bridge. Courtesy of Strawbery Banke Museum.

HUMAN MANIPULATION OF THE ESTUARINE environment is dramatically revealed by the story of Puddle Dock. Today this site is a lawn at Strawbery Banke Museum. When the first English settlers arrived it was a pristine tidal pond, and they built Portsmouth's first neighborhood on its shores. By the time this photograph was made, buildings flanked Puddle Dock, but it was well past its heyday as both a tidal ecosystem and a commercial center. Note that the warehouse in the left foreground has a doorway on the first floor facing the water. Vessels (most likely medium-sized gundalows) loaded or discharged cargo there. The warehouse sat atop a cob wharf made of logs and filled with stone rubble. The mud bank just west of that warehouse, one of the few underdeveloped bits of shoreline remaining, stands proud of the water level and sports a vestigial patch of salt marsh. The building at center right is clearly a warehouse, given its single chimney and few windows. Despite pollution and sedimentation, Puddle Dock may have still attracted common species of fish like white perch and mummichogs even in this diminished state.

Puddle Dock, circa 1890, looking west from Liberty Bridge. Courtesy of Strawbery Banke Museum.

The edge of the river has always been in flux from both natural and human forces. Note the changes to the warehouse in the left foreground: owners moved it about thirty feet farther west to rest upon pilings. It has new shingles and new windows but the first floor doorway and second floor porch are gone. At the time of the photograph, this building was doing business via the road, not the river. Meanwhile, as the waterway silted in, the mud bank beyond had become almost level with the bottom of the channel, becoming less hospitable to intertidal flora and fauna. And the large building at center right now displays more chimneys and windows, having been adapted from a warehouse into a tenement. Sadly none of these waterfront buildings survive today.

Puddle Dock, circa 1895, looking east. Courtesy of Strawbery Banke Museum.

Note the tin cans and debris in the left foreground encroaching on the waterway. The days of a ballastmaster enforcing laws against mariners casually disposing ballast into waters close to piers and wharves—and thus reducing the navigable depth—were long past. By the time this photograph was made, complaints of evil smells from Puddle Dock at low tide had been common for years. The yacht club just beyond Liberty Bridge even claimed that sewage and effluents yellowed the white paint of their boats. So the city determined to fill Puddle Dock. Beginning around 1897, 25,000 cubic yards of material—much of it coal waste that needed disposal—was dumped into the historic waterway. Originally an estuarine cove, and then a commercial dock, Puddle Dock was dry land by 1904.

Newton Avenue looking east, circa 1930. Courtesy of Strawbery Banke Museum.

Portsmouth constructed an east-west gravel road from Washington Street to Liberty Bridge atop the old Puddle Dock channel and named it Wallace Avenue, honoring Portsmouth Alderman and State Representative George Wallace, who had shepherded the act enabling the filling project through the legislature. Ironically Wallace Ave. was renamed Newton Ave. within a year. It seems the surveyors strayed in laying out the street and crossed onto the property of Elwin and Sherman T. Newton. The new land created by filling in docks and slips adjacent to the old wharves was granted to the old abutters. For the most part, they sold it to speculators and entrepreneurs, and the area quickly developed into a hodge-podge of auto repair shops, junkyards, and tenements.

Puddle Dock, Strawbery Banke Museum, circa 1968, looking east. Courtesy of Strawbery Banke Museum.

In 1958 Strawbery Banke Museum was founded to prevent the wholesale bulldozing of the neighborhood by the Portsmouth Housing Authority, which intended to erect "modern low income housing." Many of the most ramshackle buildings were destroyed at the insistence of the PHA and it took a while for the new museum to develop its vision and make plans. One early experiment is seen above. Taking advantage of archaeologist Roland W. Rollins's large-scale excavations on Puddle Dock, the museum left part of the original wharves exposed. Unfortunately, the level of the water was uncontrollable. It rose and fell with the tide, exaggerated by droughts and rainstorms. Judged a hazard, this last remnant of Puddle Dock was filled for the second and perhaps final time after a few years of exposure. Today this site is just in

Puddle Dock, 1998. This is how Puddle Dock looked at the end of the twentieth century. Photograph by Bill Fish. Courtesy of Strawbery Banke Museum.

front of the Strawbery Banke boat shop. But Puddle Dock lives on in memory, and throughout Portsmouth one can encounter people who lived in the neighborhood a half-century or more ago and still identify themselves as "Puddle Dockers". –MG

Sources: Patch Collection, Strawbery Banke Museum archives; Ray Brighton scrapbook (unpublished), Portsmouth Athenæum.

From Piers to a Park

PRESCOTT PARK'S MANICURED AND idyllic public access to the waterfront is a far cry from the bustling commercial wharves of previous eras. Gone are the stout ships, coal heaps, and prostitutes that made Water Street (now Marcy Street) a gritty "sailortown." During the Great Depression, Josie and Mary Prescott, two spinster sisters with Progressive principles and philanthropic inclinations, changed the face of this old town by the sea.

Prescott Park began as tidal mud flats, part of the Piscataqua's productive estuary. Beginning in the 1690s the area just inland from what is now the park was sectioned into narrow parcels and sold. Only after this subdivision did numerous wharves begin to appear, reaching into the river and foreshadowing what would later become dry land. Over the next century Portsmouth became a prominent seaport, boasting some of the most substantial wharves and warehouses in New England. The longest of the Portsmouth Pier Company's wharves, for instance, located just

These piers were located where the Memorial Bridge now crosses the river just north of what is today Prescott Park. Photograph by Staples, January 5, 1921. Courtesy of Portsmouth Athenaeum.

Postcard view of the five-masted schooner Paul Palmer *at the Walker coal wharf on Market Street, Portsmouth, 1908. Published by Detroit Publishing Co. Courtesy of Tom Hardiman.*

ing, is a remnant of the type of warehouse constructed during Portsmouth's most prosperous time in the late eighteenth century. It sat on a wharf once extending into the river, where today there is grass and asphalt. Two hundred years ago, boisterous stevedores labored on the docks, discharging heavy cargoes from bluff-bowed brigs and schooners along this wharf. Later, piles of coal and lumber stood on the wharf waiting for distribution. Now Shaw's Warehouse holds offices and storage space for the Prescott Park Arts Festival and Prescott Park Maintenance.

Sheafe's Warehouse was moved to its present waterfront location in the mid-twentieth century from the site where the bridge to Peirce Island now stands. It is the oldest warehouse in Portsmouth and the sole survivor of a type of building once found throughout the Piscataqua River basin.

south of the present-day Memorial Bridge ramp, stretched 320 feet, and boasted a three-story warehouse sectioned into fourteen stores that contained trade goods from the West Indies, South America, Europe, and Russia. By 1813, ten wharves jutted into the Piscataqua River between the present-day Liberty Pole and the north side of the Memorial Bridge ramp. Larger warehouses sat closer to shore, with smaller one-story buildings and storage sheds farther out.

Two historic warehouses survive in Prescott Park, tying it to the town's maritime past. Shaw's Warehouse, the three-story frame build-

Several brick structures were built on the east side of Marcy Street in the early nineteenth century, when fear of fire discouraged wooden construction. The only one still standing is the Player's Ring Theater. It was the head house for the Portsmouth Marine Railway (the rails for which were located to the north of Sheafe's Warehouse's present location) and later a factory for cement drainpipes. This building went from servicing commerce to industry to the arts.

By the late nineteenth century this section of the waterfront had begun to decay. By the 1920s it was an impoverished district, where

local grocers kept shop next to notorious, raunchy saloons and brothels that served fishermen, naval sailors, and errant husbands. Flamboyant prostitution and more than a few murders earned Water Street an unsavory reputation. So when Josie and Mary Prescott inherited their fortune in 1933, they decided to bequeath a waterfront park to the city and name it after their father. Visionary, philanthropic, and determined, the Prescott sisters purchased properties in the Water Street neighborhood where they had grown up, and removed what were considered unsightly buildings. Granite bulkheads, now visible along the water's edge, were constructed and the docks filled and wharves covered. Formal sunken gardens with three fountains replaced two commercial gas tanks. C. E. Walker's Coal piers, once located in the north end of the park, became a tree-lined parking lot. Gardens in the south end sprouted over what once was the inlet to Puddle Dock. Most traces of commerce and industry were obliterated, along with the tawdry side of town.

The trees that the Prescott sisters planted have grown magnificently, and the respectable citizens that they hoped to attract have arrived. Today the park is still managed by the trust established by Josie Prescott, and summer plays and other events hosted by the Prescott Park Arts Festival are staples of community life. How many actors and spectators know, however, that the region's maritime past lies just below the surface of the lawn? –SLD

Sources: Ray Brighton, *The Prescott Story* (Portsmouth, NH: Portsmouth Marine Society, 1982); Richard M. Candee, *Building Portsmouth: The Neighborhoods and Architecture of New Hampshire's Oldest City* (Portsmouth, NH: The Portsmouth Advocates, Inc., 1992); Sandra L. DeChard, "The Importance of Ordinary Buildings: A Case Study of the Portsmouth, New Hampshire Waterfront." (Master's thesis, Boston University, 2000).

Prescott Park flower gardens, 2000. Photograph by Grace Peirce. Courtesy of the photographer.

Contemporary Ship Operations on the Piscataqua

Portsmouth remains a working port and is proud of it. The coexistence of gritty port activities and coifed downtown retail businesses is increasingly rare in waterfront cities today, and Portsmouth owes much of its character to that contrast. A towering Peruvian salt ship along with a perfect fandango of swaying cranes and swinging buckets unloading thirty-five thousand tons of salt exists in close proximity to the boutiques, clothiers, and cafés that all too frequently displace working ports. The freshly painted Moran tugboats at a berth surrounded by shops and restaurants are emblematic of the city itself—a clean, working waterfront whose soul is largely intact.

The new millennium found the New Hampshire State Port Authority stuck between the Iron Age and the intermodal era. Its recent past as a scrap-metal storage and export facility has left its directors looking for cleaner cargoes, but the facility's piers have been quiet during a slow transition. As a state-run entity, the Port Authority's responsibilities include administration of a loan fund to aid the commercial fishing industry, orchestration of all dredging on state waterways, and management of fourteen hundred moorings on the New Hampshire side of the Piscataqua. The Port Authority plays a broad role in an otherwise healthy and steadily growing port.

"I've been working on this river for forty years and the tonnage has increased every year," said Portsmouth Pilot, Capt. Richard Holt, Sr. About five million tons of cargo crosses Piscataqua piers annually. Port facilities stretch from the drydocks of the Portsmouth Naval Shipyard to the petroleum and dry-bulk terminals three miles upriver in Newington. Salt ships, gypsum carriers, passenger vessels, commercial fishing boats, and nuclear submarines typically call at the

A bulk carrier unloading at the Granite State Minerals pier. Photograph by Fred Pettigrew, circa 1997. Courtesy of the photographer.

Portsmouth, Newington, and Kittery piers. Most of the coal and petroleum products—gas, kerosene, diesel, and asphalt—as well as propane, cement, and more salt are discharged at terminals lining the Newington shore.

Most of the Piscataqua's cargoes are imports. Salt, spread by New England highway crews on winter roads, comes from Peru, the Bahamas, and Ireland. Gypsum comes from Halifax, Nova Scotia, and

Getting this liquefied petroleum gas (LPG) ship through the Route 1 bypass vertical lift bridge is a tight squeeze, but all in a day's work for Portsmouth pilots and tug captains. Note the Coast Guard escort because the ship has a dangerous cargo. Photograph by Fred Pettigrew, circa 1997. Courtesy of the photographer.

is pressed into sheetrock locally. Fuels for everything from jets to residential furnaces arrive here for distribution, quenching the region's petroleum thirst.

The Piscataqua's two principal export cargoes represent the height of contrast: fiber optic cable and tallow. Fiber-optic cable is no bigger around than a garden hose and can handle 240,000 telephone calls a second. Tallow is inedible grease made from boiled animal-fat renderings. More than eighty thousand miles of fiber optic cable produced at Tyco's Simplex Technologies in Newington has been shipped down the Piscataqua and paid out across ocean bottoms around the world for telephone communications. Tons of tallow collected from deep-fat fryers all over New England are shipped from Sprague Energy, the terminal farthest upstream in Newington, bound to Europe and South America for cosmetics and animal feed.

The vitality of the working port is important to the region but with it comes the certainty of environmental impact and the risk of environmental disaster. Area residents got a wake-up call in 1996 when

the tanker *Provence* broke loose from the Schiller Station power plant in Newington while off-loading oil. The ship grounded at high tide across the Piscataqua on the Eliot shore with her tender belly teetering on a submarine ledge. Quick work by harbor pilots, tug crews, and Coast Guard personnel got her off while the tide was still full. The spill from parted hoses was limited to several thousand gallons, unanimously considered more than enough, but the incident demonstrated the need for the spill-response planning that had begun decades earlier.

In 1971, after years of informal meetings, terminal operators along the Piscataqua formed a cooperative to address local oil-spill prevention and clean-up strategies. The co-op evolved with better funding and technology following the Oil Pollution Act of 1990 (OPA 90), which requires all U.S. ports handling oil to have equipment and a plan to mitigate spills.

The Piscataqua River Cooperative has matured into a spill response partnership of the river's oil terminals—Sprague Energy, Irving Oil, Public Service of New Hampshire, and the Portsmouth Naval Shipyard. The co-op also works with the U.S. Coast Guard, the Maine and New Hampshire Departments of Environmental Services, and the University of New Hampshire. They maintain a fleet of specialized equipment, conduct biannual exercises with "spills" of popcorn or cornhusks to test gear and crews, and train personnel at the terminals to promote awareness and reduce the chances of human error.

Most of the people working on the Piscataqua's commercial waterfront also live in the area and it is reassuring that terminal operators here began working on spill prevention and response plans thirty years before federal laws forced them to. Recognition of the essential relationship between the quality of the natural environment and quality of life generally will ensure the continued health of the Piscataqua's estuaries, rivers, and coastline, even as the historic port retains a working waterfront. –NBB

Sources: Resource Guide to Worldwide Commerce (Portsmouth, NH: New Hampshire Port Authority, 1994); *The Responder* (Portsmouth, NH: Coastal Oil Spill Action Committee, Fall 2000); Interviews with New Hampshire Port Authority General Manager Geno Marconi and Piscataqua River Harbor Pilot Capt. Richard Holt Sr., Nov/Dec 2000.

MACPHEADRIS-WARNER HOUSE

INLAND JUST TWO BLOCKS from the swirling Piscataqua River, the Macpheadris-Warner House evokes historic seafaring commerce and the preservationist impulse that keeps people connected to the local past. A National Historic Landmark, it is a stunning site that speaks to both the light and the dark of eighteenth-century life.

Over the years home to a royal governor, several ship captains, at least ten black slaves, several wealthy merchants, and one of Portsmouth's customs collectors, as well as to the white wives and daughters through whose hands the house often passed, the stately home was occupied for more than two centuries before it became a historic site. Owned and operated today by the Warner House Association, which thoroughly understands the multifaceted importance of historic preservation, the house is open to the public from June to October.

An aristocratic merchant who once commanded ships between Boston and Barbados, Captain Archibald Macpheadris of Portsmouth appreciated the good things in life and the abundance around him. In 1717, as his sumptuous new brick mansion was under construction, he wrote a merchant friend overseas, "The river that leads through ye land, where all ye shipping lays, is full of Salmon, that in ye season you may take 1000 tuns here." A leading member of the "codfish aristocracy," Macpheadris capitalized on maritime opportunities. By age thirty-six, when he glowingly described the annual salmon runs, he owned at least six ships. Their profits, in addition to earnings from land speculation and timber sales, allowed him to import the tasteful furniture and silver he considered appropriate for a gentleman of his refinement and standing.

Macpheadris-Warner House. Lithograph by Stow Wengeroth (1906-1978). Courtesy of the Currier Gallery of Art, Manchester, NH.

Now almost three hundred years old, and known as the Warner House because it was owned by Jonathan Warner (another leading merchant, who married Macpheadris's daughter and lived there from 1759-1814), this opulent home is one of the crown jewels of early American architecture. With its original cupola still commanding a view of the Piscataqua River, and its famous interior murals of Indian chiefs, European noblemen, and Old Testament scenes—the oldest wall

Murals in the Macpheadris-Warner house. Photograph by Ralph Morang, 1993. Courtesy of the photographer.

The Macpheadris-Warner House interior is simultaneously urbane and old-Yankee, a mellow fusion that makes it one of the most exquisite colonial homes in New England. Although master builder John Drew constructed it to resemble fashionable brick mansions in London and Boston, it has become a symbol of provincial Piscataqua's gentility, entrepreneurship, and craftsmanship. A mecca for architectural historians and preservationists, the house itself is testimony to stewardship.

Of course, it is also a marker of loss. Without the commercial exploitation of natural and human resources—including timber, fish, and slaves—the Atlantic maritime economy could never have created such monuments. Organically connected to the sea by the Atlantic commercial system, the Macpheadris-Warner House—and other historic house museums in this region—speak to a time when concern for natural resources and human equality were not

paintings in America—it has endured great change in a way that Piscataqua salmon could not. Almost demolished in 1931 to make room for a gas station, the house was saved by preservationists who, despite the Depression, raised the necessary funds. By then the salmon about which Macpheadris had written eloquently were long gone. Just thirty-three years after he lauded their abundance, a visitor named James Birket noted that salmon had forsaken the Piscataqua River because of sawdust from the mills that were turning pine trees into profits.

as important as they are today. Enduring as it has, however, it connects us to a three-hundred-year epic story with a particular poignancy that reinforces the value of stewardship. —WJB

Sources: Gladys Montgomery Jones, "The Macpheadris-Warner House, Portsmouth, New Hampshire," in *Early American Homes* XXXI (August 2000), pp. 44-52; C.F. Jackson, *A Biological Survey of Great Bay, New Hampshire* (Durham, NH, 1944); *Portsmouth Black Heritage Trail Resource Book* (Portsmouth, NH: 1996), pp. 41-44.

THE PORTSMOUTH NAVAL SHIPYARD

The Sails to Atoms *logo of the Portsmouth Naval Shipyard, 1962. Courtesy of the Milne Special Collections and Archives Department, University of New Hampshire.*

ON JUNE 10 AND 11, 2000, the Portsmouth (New Hampshire) Naval Shipyard celebrated its bicentennial with a gala open house. The event drew 100,000 visitors—from toddlers who may ultimately seek careers at the shipyard to the secretary of the navy. The open house "met all of our wildest expectations," commented the event's chief organizer.

In like manner, the Portsmouth Naval Shipyard has exceeded the original aims and goals of the United States Navy. From its modest beginnings in 1800 to the present day, the shipyard has fulfilled its obligations to national defense. Through the vicissitudes of war and peace, fluctuations in appropriations, changing techniques and materials, Base Realignment and Closure (BRAC), commission decisions, and even closure orders, the shipyard has been an invaluable component of the navy team, invariably delivering surface ships, submarines, and inventions. Its succinct motto, "Sails to Atoms," attests to its pledge to employ the latest scientific technology. In recent years, the adoption of state-of-the-art technology has also meant close cooperation with federal and state agencies to make the shipyard environmentally safe.

The strategic geographical location of the Piscataqua River was a determining factor in the government's decision in 1800 to site the Portsmouth Navy Yard (as it was originally called) on an island in that waterway. As the oldest and northernmost government yard on the Atlantic coast, the Yard had (and still has) the advantages of access to open sea, an ice-free river, adjacent military defenses, ample natural resources,

a skilled Yankee workforce, and excellent land, water, and air transportation. Over time, the Yard expanded to three nearby islands, now joined by landfill, to comprise a contiguous, 288-acre industrial plant.

The Yard gradually developed into a self-sufficient "company town" protected by a security perimeter, with industrial shops, building ways, dry docks, a hospital, officers' quarters, a fire station, food services, a bank, a commissary, a chapel, a cemetery, recreational fields, gym facilities, and even a prison (now closed). Such thoroughness has

Launching of the Seadragon*, a submarine constructed at the Portsmouth Naval Shipyard, 1959. Courtesy of the Milne Special Collections and Archives Department, University of New Hampshire.*

Aerial view of the Portsmouth Naval Shipyard, circa 1960. Official photograph of the United States Navy. Courtesy of the Milne Special Collections and Archives Department, University of New Hampshire.

served the facility well; by 2000, the Portsmouth Naval Shipyard was one of only four remaining government yards (the others are Norfolk, Virginia; Puget Sound, Washington; and Pearl Harbor, Hawaii). Shipyards whose missions weren't matched to current needs were phased out and closed following World War II.

Charged with the primary responsibility of national defense, the Yard has provided war matériel for all the nation's conflicts from the War of 1812 to the 1990-91 Gulf War. The Yard is not strictly a military installation, however, continually preoccupied with supplying the sinews of war. During its two centuries of operation, the Portsmouth Naval Shipyard has rendered roughly 171 years of peacetime service—developing inventions, improvements, and concepts. These scientific breakthroughs—initiated, developed, tested, or otherwise implemented under actual emergency conditions for the first time at the Yard—have included life buoys, the Momsen Lung, the McCann Submarine Rescue Chamber, the submarine test tank, and the Planning and Engineering for Repairs and Alterations (PERA) program.

On the diplomatic front, the Yard hosted one of the twentieth century's most important peace conferences when President Theodore

Roosevelt sought help in ending the Russo-Japanese War. With the Yard ensuring the necessary security and privacy, the diplomats of these two nations met in the General Stores Building in 1905 to negotiate and sign the Portsmouth Peace Treaty, thus restoring order in the volatile Far East.

As the Yard entered the twentieth century, the Age of the Submarine revolutionized naval warfare. Dissatisfied with the performance of private yards, Secretary of the Navy Josephus Daniels in 1914 selected the Portsmouth Navy Yard to construct the first government-built submarine. During the next fifty-five years, the Yard delivered 134 submarines to the United States Navy, seventy-nine during the World War II era. The evolving design and power plants of increasingly sophisticated postwar subs stimulated the Yard's ingenuity in producing the USS *Swordfish*, the first nuclear-powered submarine built in a government yard; the USS *Albacore*, a whale-shaped submarine designed for underwater speed; and the USS *Dolphin*, an experimental deep-diving sub. Since launching its last submarine in 1969, the Yard has concentrated on repairing, overhauling, and refueling these craft, an assignment sometimes more complicated than their construction.

With environmental issues coming to the fore since the 1970s, the Yard has worked to comply with federal and state air- and water-quality standards in curbing the hazards of nuclear waste and other pollutants. In 1982 the Yard purchased a boat skimmer in order to be prepared for oil spills on the river. Endorsing the 1992 Earth Day principles, the Yard has practiced the three R's, "Reduce/Reuse/Recycle," in its daily operations. In 2000 the Yard converted its power plant from oil to natural gas, thereby reducing pollution emissions and cutting energy costs.

Economic, political, and demographic aspects of the Yard's long history are also significant. Appropriating billions of dollars over the years, the federal government has provided jobs for generations of local workers. Employment at the Yard peaked at more than 20,000 jobs during World War II and stabilized at 3,500 at the turn of the twenty-first century. From a political perspective, legislators from Maine and New Hampshire endeavor to keep the Yard busy with defense contracts for the First Congressional (or "Navy Yard") Districts in those two states.

Demographically speaking, the Yard has attracted many workers from the seacoast region, throughout New England, and indeed from the entire country. Many naval retirees have remained in the area, often working in civilian capacities at the shipyard. Such a constant influx of new people, along with their families, has enriched the area's cultural and social life.

Two centuries of hard work culminated in the June 2000 open house, when thousands attended the dedication of Shipyard Workers Memorial Park. Addressing the vast crowd, Vice Admiral George "Pete" Nanos, commander of the Naval Sea Systems Command, observed that the future of the four navy yards was bright, with the highest workload in twenty years. "Without naval shipyards," Nanos continued, "we would be totally captive to industry. There would be no competitive prod...the [Portsmouth Naval] shipyard, the Submarine Fleet, and the Navy are joined at the hip and will be for millennia to come." Accepting the Installation Excellence Award from Nanos, the shipyard commander, Captain Vernon "Tom" Williams, told the employees the award was all theirs. After some years of downsizing, Williams had instigated the Yard's resurgence. Pioneering the concept of "outleasing" underutilized shipyard buildings to the private business community, Williams was successful in reducing overhead costs to foster a more economically competitive operation. "We have reinvented the naval shipyard for the twenty-first century," concluded Williams. "It is our opportunity and it is our choice."

The Portsmouth Naval Shipyard is poised to charge ahead as an active workhorse military base. Without the shipyard's role in its history, the Piscataqua River estuary would not have reached its full economic and industrial potential. Such steadfast commitment, supported by a heritage of two centuries of service, should ensure the Yard's vitality for the next hundred years and beyond. –REW

Sources: Richard E. Winslow III, *"Do Your Job!" An Illustrated Bicentennial History of the Portsmouth Naval Shipyard, 1800-2000* (Portsmouth, NH: Portsmouth Marine Society and Peter E. Randall, 2000).

THE MOFFATT-LADD HOUSE AND GARDEN

North End. The Moffatt-Ladd House is the second house from the right, and is flanked by trees. Note that the photographer altered the image, removing power lines, antennas, automobiles, and a prominent modern building. Photograph by Scott Sulley, 2001. Courtesy of the photographer.

AT 154 MARKET STREET, diagonally across from Granite State Minerals' landmark salt pile, the majestic Moffatt-Ladd House still has an unimpeded view of the Piscataqua River. Here on this historic property, which includes the site of John Moffatt's original wharf and waterfront, Portsmouth's maritime history comes into focus.

Built between 1760 and 1763, during a time when hostilities with France made transatlantic trade uncertain, the Moffatt-Ladd House was the work of some of Portsmouth's most talented artisans. In addition to erecting this magnificent home, builder Michael Whidden III and ornamental carver Ebenezer Dearing also created elaborate woodwork and figureheads for Moffatt's ships. Moffatt, a native of England, came to the colonies in the 1720s and amassed a fortune through land speculation and shipping. He traded primarily in timber, fish, furniture, and cloth, but two documents reveal that he also traded slaves. In 1756 one of his ships, the snow *Exeter* (a two-masted ocean-going square-rigger) carried sixty-one slaves in addition to coins, gold bars, textiles, and an elephant's "tooth" weighing 39 lbs. Moffatt was still improving wharves

and building warehouses in the 1780s, and at the time of his death in 1786 he owned interests in several large vessels as well as gundalows for transporting goods via the region's shallow inland waterways.

It is not clear why John Moffatt commissioned such a grand house at the advanced age of seventy-two, but he spared no expense, and the plan was a bold one. The first three-story dwelling in Portsmouth, its massive stairhall occupies more than a quarter of the ground floor. Early letters refer to "the ball at Moffatts"; undoubtedly these balls took place in this impressive space. Whidden's bill mentions "Bringing ye frame from ye warf," indicating that the house was framed inland or along the coast near a source of timber, and then transported to Portsmouth by water.

John Moffatt's eldest son Samuel, who married Sarah Tufton Mason in 1764, was the first of the family to live in the house. A merchant like his father, Samuel unfortunately did not share his father's acumen for business. In 1768 he fled the British colonies—sailing to St. Eustatius in the Dutch West Indies—to avoid imprisonment for debt, and remained in the islands for the rest of his life. John Moffatt still retained ownership of the house, and after his wife died in 1769 he decided to abandon his old home on what is now State Street, and move with his daughter Katharine into this grand mansion.

Katharine married William Whipple about 1770, and the couple lived with her father in the Moffatt-Ladd House. Whipple was an ardent patriot, a delegate to the Continental Congress, a brigadier general in the New Hampshire militia, and one of New Hampshire's three signers of the Declaration of Independence. According to family legend, Whipple planted a horse chestnut tree, a European variety then known only in the Philadelphia region, as a memorial to that proclamation of freedom. The 225-year-old tree still towers majestically over the Moffatt-Ladd House. In spite of his clear ideas concerning freedom and independence, Whipple owned slaves, one of whom, Prince, fought beside him at the Battle of Saratoga and also accompanied him during the Rhode Island campaign. When Prince Whipple returned from military service in 1779, he and one of John Moffatt's slaves, Windsor, joined with eighteen other "natives of Africa now forcibly detained in slavery" in petitioning the New Hampshire legislature for their freedom. Windsor died a slave, but Prince and William Whipple's other slave, Cuffe, received their freedom in 1784. Whipple died the next year and was followed a year later by his father-in-law. Katharine Moffatt Whipple continued to live in the house for sixteen more years and purchased an adjoining lot for the use of Prince and Cuffe and their wives. Prince and Cuffe's house became the site of Portsmouth's first African school, and Prince's wife, Dinah, its first teacher.

John Moffatt's house passed to his grandson, Samuel Robert Cutt Moffatt, and from S. R. C. Moffatt to his sister Mary Tufton Moffatt Haven and her husband. The Havens gave the house to their daughter Maria and her husband Alexander Ladd. The Ladds moved into the house about 1817 and immediately began updating its interiors. They remodeled and redecorated the dining room, hung scenic wallpaper in the Great Hall and stairway, and in 1832 built a Counting House adjacent to the mansion. Alexander Ladd owned ships in partnership with his brother Henry, was a partner in the Portsmouth Pier Company, and with his sons Alexander Hamilton Ladd and Charles Haven Ladd underwrote several whaling voyages. Seeing an opportunity to expand on these ventures, A. H. and C. H. Ladd started a whale oil refinery known as the Portsmouth Whaling Company, which they continued until 1838. The brothers also became heavily involved in the cotton trade and established a trading house in Galveston, Texas. Like other Piscataqua merchants who transported southern cotton to northern textile mills, the Ladds indirectly accrued some of their wealth through slave labor, even at the height of the abolitionist movement.

The Ladds experienced firsthand the decline of the port of Portsmouth. After his mother's death in 1861, Alexander Hamilton Ladd and his family moved into the old home commissioned by his great-great-grandfather. A. H. Ladd and his wife added a bathroom, modernized the kitchen, and extensively redecorated, but did not alter the essential character of the house. By then Portsmouth's maritime fortunes had long since ebbed. After his wife died in 1865, Ladd's children tried to persuade him to move out of the city's deteriorating North End. He instead transformed his garden into a retreat from urban decay. He died in 1900, and in 1911 the family conveyed the house to The National Society of the Colonial Dames of America in the State of New Hampshire. The Society has operated it since 1913 as an historic house museum. –BMW

Sources: Richard M. Candee, *Building Portsmouth: The Neighborhoods & Architecture of New Hampshire's Oldest City* (Portsmouth, NH: Portsmouth Advocates, 1992); Nancy Douthat Goss, *Families of the Moffatt-Ladd House* (Portsmouth, NH: The National Society of The Colonial Dames of America in the State of New Hampshire, 1993); Kenneth R. Martin, *"Heavy Weather and Hard Luck": Portsmouth Goes Whaling* (Portsmouth, NH: Portsmouth Marine Society, 1998).

GUIDEBOOKS TO THE PISCATAQUA REGION

JOHN F. SEARS, IN *Sacred Places: American Tourist Attractions in the Nineteenth Century* (1989), argues that people react most strongly to places connected with stories or historical events. Guidebooks and the historical buildings, events, and characters they portray were integral to the promotion of the historic Piscataqua region as a tourist destination. They early guidebooks of the 1870s expressed the same nostalgic view of the area as the writers and artists who visited and brought many sightseers in search of an escape from city life. Samuel Adams Drake began *The Pine-Tree Coast* by describing Portsmouth as an "historic vestibule" through which all travelers should pass. As the majority of summer visitors to the Piscataqua changed from wealthy urbanites to the middle class, the region's guidebooks began to focus less on fine examples of architecture and more on natural features and sites associated with sensational stories such as the Nubble Lighthouse, the Old Gaol, and the "Devil's Kitchen," a rock formation along the shore in York.

As early as 1839 Portsmouth had turned to tourism as a source of income to supplement its waning shipping industry. In that year the *Portsmouth City Directory* claimed that the city's quietness, proximity to the sea and neighboring beaches, and delightful surrounding countryside made it a remarkably pleasant summer resort. Year after year Portsmouth's absent sons and daughters returned to visit their home during the summer. Throughout the nineteenth century, as nostalgia for Portsmouth's glorious past grew, real estate agents and promoters of tourism began to capitalize upon the city's historic landmarks that became just as important to visitors as the beaches.

In 1876 Joseph Foster, a local printer and bookseller, published his daughter Sarah's *Portsmouth Guide Book* which described a series of walking tours around the city. The *Portsmouth Daily Chronicle* for June 10, 1876, reported that the book "is a neat volume of 150 pages, bound in flexible covers, and of a handy size to carry in the pocket. The author's preface is signed with the initials of a lady of culture, taste,

talent, and marked ability as a writer." It was written for "strangers" but also for sons and daughters who "return[ed] to see the houses of their forefathers." The format of the book was based on European guidebooks that focused on convenient walks past historic sites. Foster was

"Wentworth Mansion and Mouth of the Piscataqua." From Samuel Adams Drake, The Pine-Tree Coast *(1891), a popular guide book at the turn of the century. Courtesy of Milne Special Collections and Archives Department, University of New Hampshire.*

also influenced by Charles W. Brewster, who published *Rambles About Portsmouth* in 1859 and 1869. Brewster had intended "to collect the incidents of unwritten history and to connect incidents and localities" so that readers, as they passed through the streets, might "at the turn of almost every corner be reminded of some early historical event." Through Brewster, and later Foster, buildings became visible links to a seemingly better time.

In 1896 Sarah Haven Foster republished *The Portsmouth Guide Book.* On the cover she placed a quotation from the Bible (Psalms 48:12-13) which symbolized to her the importance of Portsmouth's historical edifices: "Walk about Zion and go round about her; tell the towers therof. Mark ye well her bulwarks, consider her palaces; that ye may tell it to the generation following." In an addenda she discussed Portsmouth's progress during the last quarter century and mentioned the improvements to the Navy Yard, new parks, and the opening of the electric railroads which had increased trade.

In 1902 Caleb Stevens Gurney entered the field with *Portsmouth Historic and Picturesque.* Although Gurney was heavily influenced by Foster, he did not focus primarily on Portsmouth's historic sites. Instead, he created a complete photographic record of Portsmouth, including scenes of older, residential streets as well as views of more modern commercial buildings such as the Eldredge Brewery. Contemporary events such as the blizzard of 1898, numerous parades, and the arrival of the Spanish-American War prisoners were also included. Gurney was one of Portsmouth's earliest photographers. In 1892 he established the Acme Portrait Company, and five years later he organized the "Company International de Belles Artes." His photographs and glass-plate negatives provide one of the earliest and most complete portraits of the city. Gurney's choice of the more straightforward medium of photography corresponded to a less romanticized view of the city.

Although guidebooks to York exhibit a similar change from discreet discussions of history to more sensational depictions of the town's sites, from the beginning they seem to have been commercially oriented and aimed primarily at potential tourists. In 1873 Alex Emery, a native of York and a schoolteacher, published the *Ancient City of Gorgeana and Modern Town of York* with the intention of interesting "the thousands who will be brought to know it [York] through its associations [and] as a place of summer residence." Emery's book is arranged chronologically, beginning with early explorers and ending with a discussion of seaside resorts. Unlike Foster in *The Portsmouth Guide Book,* Emery does not focus his guide on historical sites; instead he provides a thematic history of such subjects as early schools, commerce, and religion, as well as more sensational issues such as earthquakes, haunted houses, and witches. In 1896 the York Bureau of Information further commercialized the book by condensing the historical sections and including information on train schedules and places to stay.

Tourism played a powerful role in America's invention of itself as a culture. The Piscataqua's guidebooks were crucial to the promotion of the area as an important cultural region through the use of key images of the colonial revival. Garrison houses, churches, and other historical sites are illustrated in the Piscataqua guidebooks and drew increasing numbers of visitors to the area. As the region moved from a place dedicated to those of genteel taste to catering for tourists, the commercialization of the region through guidebooks increased. Guidebooks transformed the Piscataqua's historic and natural sites into a commodity for tourists, often creating romantic historical myths, which to this day are drawing cards for the region. –SGR

Sources: John F. Sears, *Sacred Places: American Tourist Attractions in the Nineteenth Century* (New York: Oxford University Press, 1989); Samuel Adams Drake, *The Pine-Tree Coast* (Boston: Estes and Lauriat, 1891); *Portsmouth City Directory* (Portsmouth, NH: Joseph M. Edmonds, 1839); Sarah Haven Foster, *Portsmouth Guide Book* (Portsmouth, NH: Joseph N. Foster, 1876 and 1896); Charles W. Brewster, *Rambles About Portsmouth* (Portsmouth, NH: C.W. Brewster & Son, 1859); Caleb S. Gurney, *Portsmouth Historic and Picturesque* (Portsmouth, NH: Strawbery Banke, 1982[1902]); George Alex Emery, *Ancient City of Gorgeana and Modern Town of York* (Boston: G. Alex Emery, 1894[1873]); *York, Maine, Bureau of Information and Illustrated History of the Most Famous Summer Resort on the Atlantic Coast* (1896).

PISCATAQUA FISHING AND LOBSTERING

SIXTEENTH-CENTURY NORTHERN EUROPEANS were familiar with cod. They knew how to catch it, salt it, and dry it. They knew how to sell it. And they understood a good day's catch. But those who first sailed into the Gulf of Maine during the 1500s and early 1600s were flabbergasted by the abundance of cod on this side of the Atlantic. This was a fisherman's paradise. For centuries thereafter, racks for drying cod in the open air dotted the landscape in Kittery, Newcastle, Portsmouth, and the Isles of Shoals. Commercial fishing is the oldest sustained dimension of the Piscataqua region's economy and culture. But today the region's fishery is in flux.

Shortly after the American Revolution, the Piscataqua River fishery employed 250 men sailing from twenty-seven schooners and twenty boats. In 1791 they landed just over 2.5 million pounds of fish, considered an "uncommonly good" season. Most of the landings were cod. The local fleet grew to nearly 125 sailing vessels in the years during and immediately following the Civil War. They fished for halibut and cod with longlines, and seined mackerel, taking some other species as well. But ultimately Boston and Gloucester eclipsed Portsmouth as a major fishing port, due in part to strong legislative support in Massachusetts. By the early twentieth century, total landings in the Piscataqua had dropped substantially. The region was no longer central to New England's fishery, even though fishing remained important to some local families.

The Piscataqua River is still home to New Hampshire's primary fishing fleet. A recent survey suggests there are approximately 157 boats fishing from Portsmouth, Seabrook, Hampton, Rye, and Newington. Most are of moderate size, in the 45-foot range, and constructed of fiberglass. A few wooden boats remain from an earlier era. Two-thirds of the fleet set traps for lobster; the others trawl or set gillnets for finfish. Commercial fishing provides much of the color that makes the waterfront attractive. The state fishing pier at Peirce Island lies adjacent to Strawbery Banke's historic buildings and to taverns and restaurants that tout the past. Tourists and schoolchildren walking on the commercial fishing pier absorb the hustle and bustle of an authentic working waterfront.

Commercial fish pier, Portsmouth, New Hampshire. Photograph by Ralph Morang, 1999. Courtesy of the photographer.

New Castle Fishermen. *Pen and Ink drawing by Abbott F. Graves from John Albee's* New Castle: Historic and Picturesque, *1884. Courtesy of Milne Special Collections and Archives Department, University of New Hampshire.*

All of the necessities for maintaining a fishing fleet and selling its catch are still here. The region has lobster bait houses, boat builders, and fish processors, along with marine contractors, haul-out facilities, and marine surveyors. Today at least three hundred households directly depend on commercial fisheries and another four hundred are indirectly dependent. A well-integrated and comprehensive infrastructure supporting the fishing industry has been a historical constant of the region. Unfortunately, a sustainable supply of fish has not been so constant.

Two active co-ops serve the fishermen of Piscataqua River communities. The first, Portsmouth Fisherman's Cooperative, was established in 1979 and has twenty-six members. It handles fish from both gill-netters and trawlers. The second, Yankee Fishermen's Cooperative at Seabrook and Hampton, merged with Newburyport Cooperative in 1997 and now has fifty-nine members. Fishermen land many more species today than they did in previous eras. As stocks dwindled, species

once considered "trash" fish became valuable. Lobsters, for instance, are no longer used routinely to bait eel traps or to feed the indigent as they were in the seventeenth century. Today fishermen seek cod, dabs, winter flounder, yellowtail flounder, haddock, weakfish, pollock, red hake, halibut, grey sole, whiting, shrimp, squid, herring, mackerel, bluefin tuna, striped bass, dogfish, monkfish, tilefish, scallops, sea urchins, slime eels, and conch. In addition to finfish, Yankee Fishermen's Cooperative handles lobsters and shrimp. Both cooperatives rely on fees tied to pounds landed, so each suffered during the 1980s and 1990s when regulations diminished finfish landings. In addition to buying fish from fishermen, the cooperatives also sell ice, bait, and chandlery supplies.

Contemporary commercial fishermen do not agree on the condition of the fishery. Some credit the decline of fishing as much to poor management and over-regulation as to smaller stocks of fish. Others suggest that late twentieth century declines have dramatically reversed and that the economic condition of the industry is now "good." Even those who acknowledge a scarcity of fish argue about who or what is responsible. Blame is variously attributed to commercial fishermen who take their income in the present rather than conserving for the future, recreational fishermen with their sonar and fast boats, pollution and uncontrolled development in coastal areas, limited understanding of the biology of fish populations, and the intervention of politics into marine fisheries.

The United States government and the Canadian government closed vast areas of their northwest Atlantic fishing grounds during the 1990s to allow decimated fish stocks to rebuild. After the government closed Georges Bank to most fishing in 1994, New England fishermen flocked to the Gulf of Maine where Piscataqua boats typically fished. According to scientists, this increased fishing effort rapidly depleted the gulf's fish stocks, and the government responded by closing inshore areas of the Gulf of Maine to fishing in 1999. Fishermen from Portsmouth and Hampton with small vessels in the 22- to 45-foot range were forced to take long trips to offshore areas in more dangerous waters. With inshore areas closed by regulation, smaller vessels continue to take bigger risks. In one case, a 25-foot trawler run by a solo fisherman was caught in a deadly storm. The captain stuffed a mattress into the wheelhouse to prevent himself from being battered to death by the boat's violent motion.

Many fishermen believe that government assessments are overly pessimistic and that the stocks are improving faster than anticipated. This was evident in the controversy over the 100-pound daily catch limit on cod imposed in 1999. That policy forced commercial fishermen routinely to throw back hundreds of pounds of already dead cod, because more than 100 pounds could not legally be landed. The political upheaval over this policy resulted in changed regulations that raised the daily catch limit to 400 pounds. Of course, a modern trawler equipped with a diesel engine, polyester nets, and expensive electronic navigation gear cannot pay its bills by landing only several hundred pounds of fish per day. That amount would have been a good catch for colonial fishermen hand-lining from open boats.

Against this backdrop of a crisis in fin fishing, the lobster fishery represents a unique dilemma for fishery managers and fishermen. Scientific advice suggests that lobsters are over-fished and that lobster mortality should be reduced. Research suggests that the industry is catching too many lobsters the first year they shed their shells to become the legal size, and that in most areas a high percentage of the lobsters harvested have not had a chance to reproduce before being caught. Lobster fishermen question the advice from scientists and point out that landings are at record levels. They believe the catches suggest that lobster populations are very high, and that most areas have sufficient numbers of juvenile lobsters in the population to provide a healthy fishery in the near future. Scientists, however, attribute the high recruitment and population levels to higher water temperatures, decreased predation, and other factors that are neither understood nor controllable. This debate has caused some fishery managers and lobstermen to become concerned that the current abundance of lobster is creating a false sense of security, and that this fishery—the most prominent one in the region—could crash.

Management of the lobster fishery dates to 1890. New Hampshire Fish and Game Commissioners recognized the need to limit the size of lobsters being caught. They sought to standardize trap construction to

LOBSTERMEN'S COVE   *Kittery Point, Maine*

This is a carefully staged photograph illustrative of calendar art, circa 1947. There was no "Lobstermen's Cove" in Kittery Point: the scene is the public boat launch area of Pepperrell Cove. Moreover, the traps and buoys in the foreground are arranged for visual effect, not convenience. Note the Sir William Pepperrell House in the background. Private Collection.

allow undersized lobsters to escape, and to impose restrictions on taking egg-bearing lobsters. Many of these management tools are still in effect, and lobstering has been economically healthy for more than a century.

Today many commercial fishermen have an optimistic view of their future in the industry, particularly if management improves. The 1990s forced fishermen to tighten their belts and to adapt to problems by targeting more species and more valuable species. Many area fishermen now actively participate in Fishery Management Council meetings and seek to develop new markets for specific fish stocks. As one commercial fisherman noted, some controls are necessary and "we have to learn to live with controls that make sense. I have to learn to come in with less fish and make more money per pound on quality." The days of boats sagging with fish are over. Dedicated fishermen hope to weather what they perceive to be a rough time so that when cod, haddock, and flounder come back, they will be here to catch them.

Fishermen also believe that they have considerable knowledge to share, but that management has consistently ignored them. Commercial fishermen contend that the ground fish fishery is in much better condition than managers claim, and that the drastic closures that put small-scale family fishermen at risk are no longer necessary. A new program, Northeast Consortium, was created in 1999 to encourage and fund effective, co-equal partnerships among fishermen, researchers, and other stakeholders as active participants in collaborative research and monitoring projects. Ultimately this may lead to significant changes for the better in the management of New England's fisheries.

Fishermen are the last market hunters in our society, a group with special skills and knowledge who until recently had a relatively open season on much of what lived in the sea. Their story draws attention not only to their skill and courage, but also to the relationship of capitalism and nature. It suggests that market forces alone simply will not ensure the sustainability of natural commodities like fish. But with luck and stewardship the fishery will endure as the longest uninterrupted commercial activity in the Piscataqua region. –RAR and MHA

Chris Dyer, PhD, an anthropologist with Human Ecology Associates, and Tracy Fredericks, the Special Project Coordinator at the Seacoast Science Center in Rye, NH, contributed to this article.

Sources: David Dobbs, *The Great Gulf: Fishermen, Scientists, and the Struggle to Revive the World's Greatest Fishery* (Washington, DC: Island Press, 2000); Mark Kurlansky, *Cod: A Biography of the Fish that Changed the World* (NY: Walker and Co., 1997); National Research Council, *Sustaining Marine Fisheries* (Washington DC: National Academy Press, 1999).

Seabrook Harbor. Photograph by Peter E. Randall, circa 1990. Courtesy of the photographer.

THE PORTSMOUTH ATHENÆUM

MOST NEWCOMERS TO Portsmouth cannot resist peering through the panes of the tall windows flanking the entrance to the slender Federal style building opposite the North Church in Market Square. They will catch a glimpse of the equally elegant high-ceilinged interior, filled with portraits of people and ships, a gilded figure with outstretched arm, ship models, a reading table, and books.

The Portsmouth Athenæum is closely connected to the maritime heritage of the Piscataqua. The building it has occupied since 1823 is the centerpiece of a row of brick commercial buildings finished in 1805 in the wake of a devastating fire, and is listed in the National Register of Historic Places. It was built for the New Hampshire Fire and Marine Insurance Company. The records of the insurance company, which vacated the building in 1822, are part of the Athenæum's collections and contain insurance policies for many Piscataqua vessels. The destruction of one, the *Eudora*, is documented in two pictures currently located on the first floor.

The Athenæum was founded in 1817 as a proprietary library patterned after the Boston Athenæum. It originally was intended to meet the needs of the city's "most intelligent and affluent citizens," whose wealth often originated with maritime enterprise. After moving into 9 Market Square in 1823, the Athenæum

The Portsmouth Athenaeum. Photograph by Douglas Armsden, 1946. Courtesy of the Portsmouth Athenaeum.

continued to use the first floor as a reading room and installed its library upstairs. Remnants of its early museum have survived, including items donated by seafarers returning from all parts of the world. Among the prints, paintings, maps, and models are a remarkable plank-on-frame model of the Piscataqua-built warship *America* constructed in 1749 for the Royal Navy, a model of a gundalow, and dozens of nineteenth-century half-hull lift models of vessels built at Piscataqua shipyards.

In the mid-1990s the Athenæum expanded into adjoining space on the two upper floors at 6-8 Market Square and opened the Joseph P. Copley Research Library for Portsmouth and Piscataqua history for the use of its members, scholars, and the general public. The Athenæum regularly sponsors lectures and exhibitions on local history. –JP

Sources: Michael A. Baenen, "The Portsmouth Athenæum: The First Decade" (brochure, 2000); Richard M. Candee, *Building Portsmouth* (Portsmouth, NH: Portsmouth Advocates, 1992); Lawrence R. Craig and James L. Garvin, "The Portsmouth Athenæum" (A sesquicentennial history published by the Athenæum, 1966); James L. Garvin, "Academic Architecture and the Building Trades in the Piscataqua Region of New Hampshire and Maine, 1715-1815" (PhD dissertation, Boston University, 1983).

JOHN PAUL JONES, HIS MUSEUM, AND THE *RANGER*

JOHN PAUL JONES is arguably the most famous person who ever resided in the Piscataqua region. Born in Scotland, reviled as a traitor and pirate in England, honored in France, disgraced in Russia, and charged with murder in the West Indies, he is entombed today at Annapolis and identified to the dismay of some as the "father of the American Navy." Despite all that, and despite the hundreds of books and articles written about him, Jones died obscure and alone in Paris at age forty-five. Everyone knows his name, but few know what he did, much less his Piscataqua connections.

Born in 1747 as John Paul, he left home for a sailor's life at thirteen. Intelligent and determined, by age twenty he was owner of his own ship. A fiery 5'6" Scotsman with sandy hair and prone to wearing military style uniforms, John Paul was twice accused of killing a crewman. Despite pleading self-defense, he caught a ship from the West Indies to Fredericksburg, Virginia, in 1774 to avoid a prolonged trial. As the American Revolution began, he changed his name to Jones and was accepted as a captain in the pitifully small Continental Navy.

Never satisfied with his rank or status, Jones quickly distinguished himself aboard the ships *Alfred* and *Providence*. While other captains played it safe, Jones consistently sailed in harm's way against British ships along the North American coast. Jones favored plans to take on the world's largest Navy in its own home waters, which he knew well. He

Captain John Paul Jones. *Engraving by Jean Micel Moreau. Official photograph of the United States Navy. Courtesy of the Milne Special Collections and Archives Department, University of New Hampshire.*

was also the only naval officer able to write and speak fluent French at a time when France was considering joining the American cause. Jones arrived in Portsmouth in the summer of 1777, initially to co-command the French ship *Amphitrite* on a journey to Europe. When that plan fell through he was given command of the *Ranger*, then being completed at Rising Castle in Kittery, Maine, now known as Badger's Island, just across the Memorial Bridge from downtown Portsmouth.

Jones' arrival in Portsmouth came just after the death of Captain Gregory Purcell, a merchant ship owner who had left his wife and at least eight children in debt. Sarah Purcell was the niece of the former Royal Governor Benning Wentworth. With the Loyalist members of her family decidedly out of favor in Portsmouth, legend says, she was required to rent rooms in her house on Middle Street to a gentleman border named J. P. Jones and his steward.

Jones' historic guerrilla raid on the British Isles as commander of the Portsmouth-built *Ranger* was a public relations masterpiece. With authorization from Congress to pick his own targets, Jones conducted bold attacks on his childhood homeland, burning a single boat at Whitehaven and absconding with the Earl of Selkirk's family silver in nearby Scotland. These terrorist attacks by the American pirate—greatly exaggerated in the telling—panicked the British. Before returning to France, and then home to Portsmouth, the *Ranger* crew captured HMS *Drake*, an incomprehensible affront to the Royal Navy. A year later Jones returned under the American flag with the *Bonhomme Richard*, and in one fierce and bloody battle against the *Serapis*, came to symbolize the colonial determination for independence.

Jones returned to Portsmouth a conquering hero in 1781 and settled back into the Purcell house while outfitting another ship. The ship of the line *America* was then the largest warship ever built in North America. But after a masterfully complex launch into the swift running Piscataqua, the *America* was given to France. Crushed after a year of planning and preparation, Jones slipped out of Portsmouth and out of the country for which he had fought so ferociously. After a stint with the French and service under Catherine the Great in Russia, Jones died in 1792. Largely ignored by the new United States, he was buried in a leaden coffin and placed in an obscure Protestant grave in Paris. Meanwhile, people continued to live in the Purcell House, which changed hands occasionally.

In 1905 John Paul Jones' body was returned from Paris to the United States. Amazingly well preserved, it was exhumed for reburial with full military honors, 114 years late. President "Teddy" Roosevelt used the occasion to promote his new naval White Fleet. Jones's popularity rating, already high in the nineteenth century, went through the roof. Biographies for children and adults flew off the shelves. Paul Jones whiskey, cigarettes, cigars, and "middy" sailor clothing became popular as America prepared for a new war at sea. At that moment, at the height of the "Colonial Revival" era, the gambrel-roofed house in Portsmouth where Jones had stayed came on the auction block; a local "antiques" dealer planned to dismantle and sell off the old home to make way for a brick insurance building. Loud protest and $10,000 from Woodbury Langdon, a grandson of John Langdon's brother, saved the old building in the nick of time. In 1917, just four years after Jones's body was finally re-interred in the chapel at Annapolis, the John Paul Jones Museum was born in Portsmouth. It has been open since.

Jones' ship *Ranger*, like its famous captain, is now on the verge of a second coming. In 1999 the Ranger Foundation was organized as a

Artist's rendition of the Ranger. *Courtesy of the Ranger Foundation.*

nonprofit agency with a stirring mission of its own—to raise money to reconstruct a Piscataqua tall ship. No building plans exist for the *Ranger*, but its lines were taken when the ship was later captured by the British and renamed *Halifax*. *Ranger*, however, was a sister ship to the *Raleigh*, also built at John Langdon's yard and currently featured on the New Hampshire state seal.

Ranger Foundation members believe the reconstructed ship will reinvigorate recognition of the "real" John Paul Jones, a self-described "citizen of the world." Once described as "a perfect jewel," its presence in Portsmouth Harbor will remind visitors and residents alike of a time when Piscataqua ships roamed the world, and when the Piscataqua was primarily a maritime region. –JDR

Sources: Samuel Eliot Morison, *John Paul Jones: A Sailor's Biography* (Boston: Little Brown, 1959); Joseph Sawtelle, *John Paul Jones and the Ranger* (Peter E. Randall, 1994); Clara Ann Simmons, *John Paul Jones, America's Sailor* (Annapolis: Naval Institute Press, 1997).

ATLANTIC HEIGHTS

ATLANTIC HEIGHTS IS A GARDEN SUBURB in Portsmouth built during World War I for shipyard workers at the adjoining Atlantic Corporation. This private shipyard, like the Shattuck Shipyard in Newington, was created to revive America's shipbuilding industry prior to World War I. The Atlantic Corporation occupied a defunct paper mill, established after 1902 at Freeman's Point, and remodeled it as a steel shipbuilding facility in 1917 and 1918. When the United States entered the First World War the federal government created the quasi-public Emergency Fleet Corporation to fund the massive shipbuilding program and emergency housing needed to sustain those yards. The Atlantic Corporation took advantage of this government funding to both renovate the shipyard and build Atlantic Heights.

The key figure in Atlantic Heights's unified design was Boston architect Walter H. Kilham (1868-1948). An 1889 graduate of M.I.T., Kilham became as deeply involved with the study of historic architecture as he was with reforming house design for working people. In partnership with James C. Hopkins after 1901, the firm of Kilham and Hopkins became well known for the design of schools, town halls, suburban homes, and workers' housing. In this work the firm was engaged in what Greer Hardwicke has called the "culture of recall," an ideology that sought to restructure the landscape using architectural symbols of community and civic values often drawn from colonial sources. On the basis of the firm's earlier reform housing efforts in Massachusetts, Kilham was invited in April 1918 to design and plan a million-dollar residential development for the Atlantic shipyard in Portsmouth. In only ten days the village plan was created and several house designs were submitted to the government agency for approval. Construction began that May and, despite the need for design approval for all stages and building materials shortages due to the war, the project was substantially completed within the year.

Located along the Piscataqua River, a mile beyond the city core, Atlantic Heights contained 278 family houses in 150 permanent individual structures, eight dormitories, a store, a cafeteria, and a school laid out as a self-contained "village" according to ideals promoted by the English Garden City movement. Streets conformed to topography, winding around trees and rocks and were all named for famous Portsmouth-built ships. No curbing was used for the road, nor any garages originally planned, as it was assumed no worker would have an automobile.

Kilham had sketched Portsmouth's historic buildings as a student and wrote about the city's important colonial and Federal period brick homes in 1902. His first step in planning this new addition to the port city was to photograph old buildings whose form or details might be adapted to the houses his firm had already built elsewhere. Gambrel roofs, simple Federal style fanlights set in brick arches, and triangular Georgian pediments over doorways of the city's old homes provided particular models. One reporter concluded that the architects had followed as far as possible the colonial lines of the city, "many of the houses having reproduction[s] on a smaller scale of some of the best of the colonial doorways." Using these different ornamental doorway details, brick bonding patterns, or occasional clapboard walls on seven different basic house plans not only provided variety but evoked symbolic association with local and regional building tradition. Public buildings, set around what was conceived as a New England town common at the head of the only road into the project, included a proposed village recreational hall with connected shops "of old-fashioned type" to be built in "colonial red brick with white trimming" to look not unlike a miniature Independence Hall. Such architectural symbols were designed, literally, to install civic pride and harmony through their colonial style.

This shipbuilders' housing program was the first use of federal funds for housing. In an era and a region suspicious of government intervention in the private market, reformers tried to win acceptance of this radical idea by wrapping the two dozen American war housing

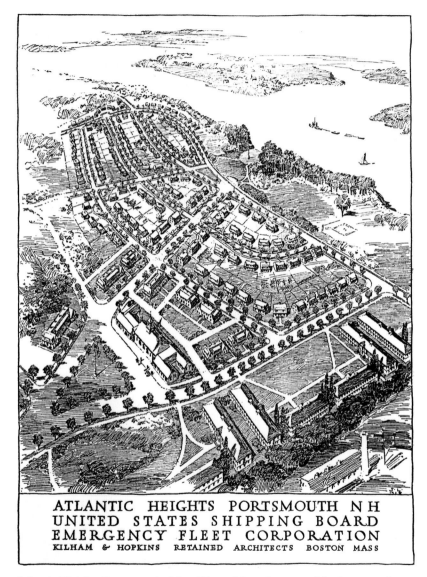

ATLANTIC HEIGHTS PORTSMOUTH N H
UNITED STATES SHIPPING BOARD
EMERGENCY FLEET CORPORATION
KILHAM & HOPKINS RETAINED ARCHITECTS BOSTON MASS

Atlantic Heights Portsmouth, New Hampshire. *Courtesy of the Portsmouth Athenaeum.*

projects in colonial garb. The architects and planners wanted to demonstrate that improved housing could be competitive with speculative forms of worker housing. They argued that such projects might also improve the nation's social order and that such stylistic associations could help avoid labor strife by inculcating American values among ethnic workers.

Nevertheless, Congress canceled the program immediately after the war, and the government sold all of the housing it had financed during the war. The houses at Atlantic Heights were sold to private owners in 1925 after the Justice Department won a suit against the Atlantic Shipyard over its shipbuilding contracts. The town added a school designed by Robert Coit of Boston in 1924, one dormitory became a church, and several new homes have since been added to those originally built. When the I-95 bridge was erected, the remaining dormitories and a few homes were removed from the eastern edge of the village.
–RMC

Sources: Richard M. Candee, *Atlantic Heights: A World War I Shipbuilders' Community* (Portsmouth: Portsmouth Marine Society, 1985); Richard M. Candee, *Building Portsmouth: The Neighborhoods and Architecture of New Hampshire's Oldest City* (Portsmouth, NH: Portsmouth Advocates, Inc., 1992); Greer Hardwicke, *Town Houses and the Culture of Recall: Public Buildings and Civic Values and the Architectural Firm of Kilham, Hopkins, & Greely, 1900-1930* (PhD dissertation, Boston College, 1986).

NEWINGTON

SHIPBUILDING

EXCEPT FOR SUBMARINE REPAIRS at the Portsmouth Naval Shipyard and the construction of an occasional lobster boat or yacht, shipbuilding does not exist in the Piscataqua today. What a change. Shipbuilding in this region was as old as the English settlements, and for centuries fishing vessels, cargo ships, and warships were launched into the river and its tributary streams. Badger's Island in Kittery, Swasey Parkway in Exeter, and the town landing in Durham are just a few of the local spots in which shipwrights plied their craft. Rightly famous as one of the centers of wooden ship construction in North America, the Piscataqua lost its competitive edge as shipbuilding evolved from artisans' work to industrial production.

One of the earliest arguments for settling New England was the availability of shipbuilding materials—a case made by Capt. John Smith in 1614, and again by Christopher Levett in 1628. English settlers relied on vessels and began to build them immediately. An inventory of goods shipped to the region in 1631 for Capt. John Mason and Sir Ferdinando Gorges included "Carpenters tooles, clinch nayles etc., for the Pinace." Governor John Winthrop mentioned a Piscataqua-built pinnace in his journal as early as September 16, 1632, and two months later he recorded that Piscataqua had sent two shallops and two pinnaces eastward against the fisherman-turned-pirate Dixie Bull.

Shipbuilding was too important to be left unregulated. In 1644, three years after Massachusetts seized New Hampshire, the General Court passed legislation to promote New England shipbuilding in Europe. It required officially designated shipwrights to inspect all ships under construction. By the second decade of settlement, local shipbuilding was well underway. Documents reveal that in 1647 an English merchant directed his New England factor to build a hundred-ton vessel on the Piscataqua under the direction of Mr. Shapleigh, a Kittery merchant. Two years later Sampson Lane of Strawbery Banke also had a hundred-ton ship on the ways.

Over the remainder of the seventeenth century a number of shipwrights settled along the river; among them was John Bray, future father-in-law of William Pepperrell, founder of the greatest Piscataqua merchant shipping house. Shipbuilding was fundamental to local economic growth from the late seventeenth century to the early nineteenth century, and it would remain an integral part of local life until after World War II.

Most early shipyards were not established directly on the Piscataqua itself, but on small coves such as North Millpond, South Millpond, and Puddle Dock, or on small tributaries such as Sagamore and Spruce Creeks, or near the head of tide on larger streams—the Salmon Falls, Cocheco, Oyster, Squamscott, and Winnicut Rivers. Here the yards were accessible to ox teams bringing timber from the back country, as well as to seagoing vessels bringing naval supplies from the southern colonies and Europe. Here also yards were not subject to the great currents that disrupted navigation on the river itself, and they were sheltered from bad weather. According to surviving customs house records (by no means complete), Piscataqua shipyards produced eighty-eight vessels totaling 7335 tons between 1690 and 1714. Collectively these yards turned out hundreds of vessels before the War of 1812.

Shattuck Shipyard, circa 1919. Courtesy of Old Berwick Historical Society, South Berwick, Maine.

Shipbuilding was a way of life on the Piscataqua. It was also a craft industry and livelihood that local men took seriously. In 1766 a growing wage differential between rural and urban shipbuilders created such competition for work that local ship carpenters went on strike against Portsmouth shipyards. The angry workers vandalized ships on the ways, and vowed more trouble if the yards continued to employ cheaper rural labor.

During the colonial era, Piscataqua yards built several warships for the British Navy, including the first built in America for that service. Some of these ships performed well, although the Admiralty voiced considerable contempt for New England ship timber. During the Revolutionary War and the War of 1812, Piscataqua shipbuilders sent many privateers to sea and built warships for the Continental Congress and the United States government. John Paul Jones' *Ranger* was built here, as was the *Raleigh*, now on the New Hampshire state seal. The *General Sullivan*, built in 1777 on a farm in Lee five miles from navigable water may have been the most unorthodox. According to the chronicle, "Ten men of Lee, including Captain Parker, worked on its construction, each man owning one-tenth of the ship. When it was completed and all the timbers numbered, it was taken apart, loaded on wagons drawn by oxen, hauled to [the] Newmarket shipyard, put together again and launched there."

Following the War of 1812, Piscataqua shipyards increasingly built vessels for merchants from larger seaports to the west. As the Industrial Revolution spread northward from Boston, it had a three-fold effect on the outlying yards around the Piscataqua. The first was the growing scarcity of timber created as farmers clear-cut their woodlots to create pasture for sheep and cows. Meat and milk made more immediate profits than did ship timber. The second, largely a consequence of deforestation, was growing siltation of the tributary rivers. This made navigation increasingly difficult and ultimately isolated outlying yards from most deepwater commerce. And finally, ships increased dramatically in size. A Piscataqua-built ocean-trader might have displaced eighty tons in 1690, and two hundred tons in 1790, but by 1850 it routinely displaced over five hundred tons. Many exceeded one thousand tons. Such vessels consumed whole woodlots in one hull and required especially deep water for launching. Shipbuilding had become a corporate industry, outgrowing the small-scale artisan capitalism that had driven the Piscataqua economy since 1631. The yards around the fall line disappeared one by one through the first half of the nineteenth century, victims of industrial modernization. The last square-rigged vessel slipped down Exeter's ways in 1806, Stratham's in 1811, Somersworth's in 1818, Durham's in 1831, Berwick's in 1833, Newmarket's in 1836, and Dover's in 1841.

As the ships grew larger, shipyard work became concentrated on the main river in Eliot, Kittery, and Portsmouth. From the mid 1840s to the great depression of 1857 that crippled shipping, a number of large clipper ships were built in Fernald and Pettigrew's shipyard on Badger Island, in George Raynes's yard on North Millpond, and in a few others. They were among the fastest sailing ships the world has ever seen, and a handful made it into the record books. The 1600-ton Kittery-built *Typhoon* crossed the Atlantic in less than two weeks on her maiden voyage, and the *Witch of the Wave* made a splendid winter passage to San Francisco in 121 days. For a brief time in the 1850s local people shared the national craze for clipper ships, but with a slight difference: Piscataqua people knew the men who built them.

Lacking local coal and iron resources, few Piscataqua yards made the transition from timber to steel. Eliot produced its last square-rigger in 1852, Kittery in 1872, and Portsmouth in 1877. Some yards continued to build smaller vessels for the coasting and fishing trades, but except for submarine construction at the Portsmouth Naval Shipyard, the last hurrah of Piscataqua shipbuilding occurred during World War I. In Newington, L. H. Shattuck's shipyard geared up to build freighters for the war effort. At their peak of operation more than eight thousand men worked round-the-clock, and in one grand flourish they launched three ships simultaneously on the

The 147 ton ship Pallas, *built in South Berwick in 1800, is shown leaving Marseilles, France. Watercolor by Honore Pellegrin, 1829. Courtesy of the Peabody Essex Museum.*

Fourth of July in 1918. Constructed entirely of Douglas Fir imported from the West Coast, these ships were anachronistic and poorly built. The last of them was abandoned before completion.

Today only an occasional bronze plaque or a rusting bolt in a tangle of weeds reminds Piscataqua-area residents that for centuries local shipwrights built vessels that connected their towns to the wider world. –WBL

Sources: W. B. Leavenworth, "The Ship in the Forest" (PhD dissertation, University of New Hampshire, 1999); New Hampshire Historical Society Series, *Colonial and State Papers*, vols. 1-40 (Concord, NH, 1867-1943); *Calendar of State Papers, Colonial Series*, vols. 1-43 (London: HM Stationery Office, 1860; Kraus Reprint, 1964).

Bridges of the Piscataqua Region

Although most freight and passenger traffic in the Piscataqua region during the eighteenth and early nineteenth centuries was waterborne, the region has long been noted for its bridges. Extending inland in irregular patterns, the region's many rivers and estuaries demanded that any highway network linking the tidewater villages would be a system of bridges as well as of roads. As early as the 1700s some spans in the Piscataqua region were celebrated as engineering masterpieces. Crucial to commerce and travel, the numerous bridges of the Piscataqua have long been part of the local landscape.

Providing private capital to build such bridges required incentives. Private companies received government charters empowering them to build bridges and then collect tolls for passage over them. The first such bridge in the Piscataqua region was built over the York River by Major Samuel Sewall and his assistant, Capt. John Stone, in 1757. Two hundred and seventy feet long, Sewall's Bridge was supported by wooden piles driven into the bed of the stream, and had a draw span to allow vessels to pass upriver. This was the first pile drawbridge built in the colonies, and won Sewall the contract to design a similar bridge over the Charles River in Boston in 1786. Much renewed and improved over the years, Sewall's Bridge still spans the York River.

Another bridge built without public funding was the Stratham-Newmarket Bridge. First authorized by a law of 1747, this span over the Squamscott River between Stratham and South Newmarket

Before completion of the Memorial Bridge in 1923, the fastest passage between Portsmouth and Kittery was by ferry. Beginning in 1895, the Portsmouth, Kittery, and York Street Railway operated this paddlewheel steamer between the Spring Hill landing on Ceres Street in Portsmouth and Badger's Island. Undated photograph. Courtesy of the Society for the Preservation of New England Antiquities.

(today Newfields) finally opened about 1775. The Province of New Hampshire found it necessary to authorize lotteries to finance, and later maintain, the span. The crossing later became a toll bridge, and remained so until 1907. The crucial need to keep the river open for

The tugboat Portsmouth *guides the oil tanker* Mobilight *under the raised drawspan of the Interstate Bridge (completed in 1940) and now known as the Sarah Mildred Long Bridge on the Route 1 bypass. This aerial photograph is from the early 1950s, shortly after the Socony-Vacuum Company opened a Newington terminal to receive 16,000-ton tankers. Photograph by Paul E. Marston. Courtesy of Portsmouth Athenaeum.*

navigation to Exeter required the first bridge and each of its many replacements to have a movable span until 1955 when the swinging mechanism was welded shut.

The first local span to attract international attention was the Piscataqua Bridge, constructed by a private company in 1794. The bridge extended 2,363 feet from Fox Point in Newington to Goat Island, and from Goat Island to Cedar Point in Durham. Its mighty fabric consumed 8,000 tons of stone, 3,000 tons of oak, 2,000 tons of pine, 20 tons of iron, and 80,000 four-inch planks. Most of the structure was a pile trestle, but a draw span on the Durham end gave tall vessels access to Great Bay and all its tributaries. The most impressive

part of the bridge stood on the Newington side of Goat Island; this great timber arch with a 220-foot clear span was designed by Timothy Palmer of Newburyport, who received a United States patent for arched bridge trusses in 1797. The bridge survived until 1855.

In 1822 another private toll company secured a charter to bridge the main channel of the Piscataqua River. Their 1,600-foot wooden crossing ran from Rindge's Wharf at the upper end of Market Street in Portsmouth to Noble's Island, then crossed to the Kittery shore along the alignment now taken by the steel Interstate Bridge. Most of the bridge was a pile structure, some piles standing in more than sixty feet of water. Scoured by some of the fastest currents on the East Coast, the rocky bottom of the Piscataqua River denied the pile bridge a secure anchorage. Over the years, spring tides and ice pushed the bridge as much as six feet out of alignment despite the placement of hundreds of tons of boulders around the feet of the wooden piles. In 1859, local newspaper editor Charles W. Brewster penned an arresting description of the audacious trestle: "How would the head swim, in looking down the dizzy distance, were all the water to be removed, leaving the traveler elevated between sixty and seventy feet above the ground!" The bridge stood until 1940, used in its later years mostly by the Boston & Maine Railroad.

In 1919, Maine and New Hampshire, in partnership with the federal government, decided to build a modern span to supplant the old wooden Portsmouth Bridge. To span the river and yet provide a 150-foot vertical clearance above mean high water, authorities adopted a design drawn in 1920 by the New York office of eminent engineer and author John Alexander Low Waddell. One of the most accomplished engineers of the early twentieth century, Waddell had built the first important vertical lift bridge in the United States in Chicago in 1892.

The Piscataqua River Bridge (soon named "Memorial Bridge" to honor the fallen veterans of the Great War) is a classic Waddell design. It has two concrete piers supporting three steel truss spans, each 297 feet long. The two fixed outer spans have vertical towers aligned with their piers. The central span, weighing 100,000 pounds, is lifted along the inner faces of these two towers by cables wound on drums driven by electric motors. As in all vertical lift bridges, the movable span is counterbalanced by two massive weights connected to the span by their own sets of cables.

Completion of Memorial Bridge in 1923 routed all traffic on U.S. Route 1 through the center of Portsmouth. Almost immediately, the city began to experience monumental traffic jams whenever the draw span was raised for a ship, especially during the summer when the coastal highway was crowded with tourists. The idea of supplementing Memorial Bridge with a second crossing became the topic of ever more strident discussion during the 1930s.

Meanwhile, in 1929, the state legislature created a commission to study the feasibility of bridging Little Bay somewhere in the vicinity of the former Piscataqua Bridge. Such a crossing would return the old First New Hampshire Turnpike (Route 4) to its historical status as the main route between the Piscataqua and Merrimack Rivers, or between Portsmouth and Concord. After an intense debate lasting several sessions, the legislature ultimately decided to construct the new bridge, not where the old Piscataqua Bridge had stood, but between Bloody Point and Dover Point. Designed by engineers Fay, Spofford, and Thorndyke of Boston, the General Sullivan Bridge opened in 1934. It has curved top and bottom chords that give it a distinct resemblance to the arch of the Piscataqua Bridge of 1794 and provide a vertical clearance of fifty-three feet at low tide.

To relieve traffic pressures in downtown Portsmouth, the states of Maine and New Hampshire created an interstate bridge authority

The three steel spans of the Memorial Bridge between Portsmouth and Kittery were built on shore and floated into position on barges. Here, the ebbing tide lowers the northern (Badger's Island) span into place at noon on July 8, 1922. Courtesy of Strawbery Banke Museum.

in 1937, empowering that body to construct a new toll bridge across the Piscataqua River. Consulting engineers Harrington and Cortelyou of Kansas City designed a vertical lift bridge on the alignment of the Portsmouth Bridge of 1822. To conduct traffic around Portsmouth to this crossing, the engineers devised a bypass highway that veered around the city in a great curve. Opened in 1940, the Interstate Bridge has a lift span that is raised by independent but synchronized electric motors at the tops of each of its two towers, a technology that had been introduced around 1935.

Completed in 1934, the General Sullivan Bridge opened a direct highway from Portsmouth to Concord through Durham, a route that had fallen out of use when the Piscataqua Bridge of 1794 collapsed in 1855. This photograph was taken in 1961, five years before a parallel span was built to carry northbound traffic. Photograph by Douglas Armsden. Courtesy of the Old Berwick Historical Society, South Berwick, Maine.

Interstate Bridge, just below Spinney Creek in Kittery. The largest bridge ever constructed in New Hampshire or Maine, this massive structure carries traffic 135 feet above mean high water, allowing ships to pass beneath it with no lift span. To achieve this height, and to span the full width of the river, engineers Hardesty and Hanover of New York designed the bridge as a great arched truss, with its roadway suspended from the arch. The steel arch weighs 10,000 tons and rises to a height of 250 feet above the river. In 1973, the Piscataqua River Bridge received an Award of Merit from the American Institute of Steel Construction as the most beautiful steel bridge built in 1972. In 1974 the bridge was named the most outstanding new bridge in the United States.

For centuries the Piscataqua has been a region of bridges. Built to spare travelers the inconvenience of confronting rivers, bridges today are vantage points from which drivers and their passengers watch the cross-grained and wily waters. –JLG

By the early 1950s, a new interstate highway, Route 95, had pushed north from Boston and joined the Portsmouth bypass near the Interstate Bridge, creating the Portsmouth Traffic Circle. The merged traffic from these two highways eventually overwhelmed the capacity of the 1940 bridge. It was apparent that a third bridge was needed over the Piscataqua River.

The new high-level Piscataqua River Bridge on Interstate 95 opened in 1972. It stands at the Narrows, half a mile north of the

Sources: Woodard D. Openo, *The Sarah Mildred Long Bridge: A History of the Maine-New Hampshire Interstate Bridge from Portsmouth, New Hampshire, to Kittery, Maine* (Portsmouth, NH: Peter E. Randall, 1988); Elaine M. Peverly, *Bridge Over the Piscataqua in Text and Pictures* (Sanford, Maine: Wilson's Printers, 1974); Robert A. Whitehouse, and Cathleen C. Beaudoin, *Port of Dover: Two Centuries of Shipping on the Cochecho* (Portsmouth, NH: published for the Portsmouth Marine Society by Peter E. Randall, 1988).

THE FIVE FACES OF NEWINGTON

A BIRD'S EYE VIEW OF NEWINGTON reveals a distinctive mosaic. From the air, or from a car or a boat, one cannot help but be struck by the five faces of Newington. Virtually sealed from each other, but all within town bounds, lie a historic community, a riverfront industrial zone, a tradeport, a wildlife refuge, and many malls. More than in any other Piscataqua town, the past, present and future of land-use patterns are boldly inscribed here, providing considerable food for thought.

"There may have been some better places than Newington in the world of the 1920s to live out one's boyhood," observed one townsman sixty years later, "but it would be hard to convince one fortunate enough to live there of such an unlikely place. With its miles of tidal shores, fragrant pines where huts could be built, ponds, brooks, and grassy pasturelands where the berry bushes grew, the salt air of the river, and the changing tides of the Piscataqua, the town had everything to offer." When, however, the Air Force began to clear land for a huge bomber base in 1952-1953, Newington changed in a hurry. No other Piscataqua town was forced quite so dramatically into the twentieth century.

To most people in the region today, Newington appears first and foremost as the corridor for the Spaulding Turnpike and the site of malls and giant warehouse stores. It is a town full of jobs, and its shopping centers are a hub for the region's automobile culture. Newington is thus an incarnation of many of the land-gobbling, mall-building, automobile-driving forces that propel the American economy at the turn of the twenty-first century. Ironically, Newington was one of the first four towns in New Hampshire to adopt a zoning ordinance and establish a planning board. That, like the beginning of the Pease Air Force base, came in 1952. Today the percentage of land in town that remains developable is one of the smallest in the region. Taxes are low, but Newington has learned some hard lessons about planning, pollution, and the limits of local control.

Mall in Newington. Photograph by Peter E. Randall, 2001. Courtesy of the photographer.

A fertile peninsula, Newington is surrounded by Great Bay and Little Bay to the west and by the Piscataqua River's Long Reach to the east. Known initially as "Bloody Point," it is one of the oldest settlements in New Hampshire, and one in which residents quickly learned to cope with the wily waters of the Piscataqua estuary. By 1640 a ferry crisscrossed the entrance to Broad Cove, carrying passengers and livestock from Bloody Point to Dover Point. The ferry was also licensed to cross the Piscataqua to Maine, and to run downstream as far as Strawbery Banke.

Although ferries and small boats were long part of local life, farming was predominant. Residents changed the town's name to the more decorous "Newington" in 1714. But they did not really change the way they used the land until the outbreak of World War I. Lacking substantial waterfalls, Newington never industrialized like Newmarket,

The "Old" Parsonage still stands on Nimble Hill Road in Newington. Built by Richard Pomeroy in 1699 as a dwelling, it was purchased by the town fathers in 1765. It has also been a tavern, a town farm, a public school, and a rented residence. Photograph circa 1912. Courtesy of Newington Historical Society.

Dover, and other towns that built water powered textile mills. So Newington remained a quiet country throwback of fields, roads, woodlots, and marshes. Agriculture reigned, even as farm commodities changed through the generations. Mixed cereals in the eighteenth century gave way to dairy in the nineteenth century, and to turkeys and Newington's renowned apples in the twentieth century.

Yet Newington was never isolated from the larger world. Its strategic location attracted travelers to the place where they could cross Little Bay at its narrowest spot, whether by ferry or bridge. The road from Portsmouth to Concord went that way, and in 1794 a group of private investors erected the famous Piscataqua Bridge from Fox Point in Newington to Cedar Point in Durham via Goat Island. The railroad

came to town in 1873, and another bridge went up connecting Dover Point to Bloody Point. The tracks ran north-south along the Piscataqua in what is today the industrial section of town.

With sufficiently deep water in the Piscataqua River and railroad access, the eastern section of town became well suited to development as a shipbuilding facility in World War I. The Shattuck Shipyard built fifteen large wooden freighters (3,500 tons each) for the U.S. Shipping Board during the war, attracting thousands of workers who arrived *en masse* and took up residence in the surrounding fields. While the shipyard did not endure long beyond the armistice, it paved the way for development of a heavy industrial zone along the banks of the Piscataqua. Nevertheless, most of Newington remained quiet, residential, and agricultural. Like much of the region, it weathered the Great Depression with old Yankee skills and old Yankee stoicism, and during World War II it watched, with the rest of the region, as the Portsmouth Naval Shipyard increased both workforce and production.

Nothing prepared residents, however, for the announcement in 1951 that the Air Force was planning to build a base on more than 4,000 of the town's acres. Military planners saw the land as strategic for national defense. Acrimonious arguments erupted at town meetings between neighbors who had divided into pro-base and anti-base factions. Some envisioned a windfall; others, the end of their way of life. Despite all the talk, the government wasted little time. Buying land or seizing it by eminent domain, they unleashed bulldozers and built a two-mile long runway, along with workshops, housing, offices, and bunkers. Pease Air Force Base opened in 1956. It literally cut the

Schiller Station and Newington Station, the two electrical generating plants run by PSNH in Portsmouth and Newington. The town boundary is between the plants. Photograph by W. Jeffrey Bolster, 2001. Courtesy of the photographer.

economic development zone, has risen from its ashes. But the legacy of a splintered town continues, although now the divisions are largely geographic.

Besides the economically flourishing tradeport, Newington is also home to a typical American commercial "strip," as well as a zone of heavy industry along the banks of the Piscataqua that includes TyCom, (formerly the Simplex Wire and Cable Company) and Public Service of New Hampshire's Newington Station. There is still a remnant old New Hampshire community of farmland and houses, with the occasional summer cottage shoehorned into the northern quarter of town. And to the west, clinging to six miles of intertidal shoreline, the impressive Great Bay National Wildlife Refuge occupies more than 1,000 acres carved from the former Pease Air Force Base. Newington's juxtapositions are stunning; its transitions bold.

A rare slice of the colonial New Hampshire vernacular landscape still exists. The town's old parsonage was built in 1699. Newington's elegantly proportioned Town Meeting House, which dates from 1712, is the oldest Congregational Meeting House in the United States still in continuous use. Each year they attract a modest number of sightseers who drive down Nimble Hill Road, cameras at the ready. More visitors, however, walk through the wildlife refuge's forested uplands, open grasslands, and shrub, or skirt its wetlands and saltmarsh. The refuge was established to encourage and protect the natural diversity of plants, fish, and wildlife species, and to enhance the water quality of both local aquatic habitats and Great Bay itself. Residents and visitors alike recognize it as an antidote to the surrounding sprawl, as well as an avenue to the shore.

town in two, and for decades children from the southern part of Newington were forced to ride their school bus twenty-one miles around the perimeter of the base to get to a schoolhouse only one mile away as the crow flies. Military protocols and Cold War paranoia kept the U.S. Air Force from building a through-route, and the town remained physically divided for more than twenty years. Some residents supported the base and worked there. Others fumed. "The federal government came into Newington and raped and pillaged the land, burned the houses and evicted the townsfolk," remembered one resident nearly fifty years after the fact.

The base is gone now, closed in 1991 amid concerns about regional economic decline. The Pease International Trade Port, an

Newington's waters have changed with the rest of the town. Shoal spots in Long Reach that had long plagued mariners became a thing of the past when the federal government dredged the Piscataqua River upstream of Portsmouth for a channel 35 feet deep and 400 feet wide. Today it is buoyed. Local pilots and tugs maneuver cable-laying ships to TyCom's pier, and take oil tankers to terminals just south of the General Sullivan Bridge and to Public Service of New Hampshire's Newington Station. They don't worry about tide rips at Boiling Rock, for it is no longer there, and the end of Gosling Road is no longer called Boiling Rock Road. There is less public access to the water for boat launching in Newington than formerly, but it is still possible for town residents to launch a boat at the Newington Town Landing on Long Reach, or for customers to use the launching ramp and docks at Great Bay Marine. Anyone can stroll the shore of the wildlife refuge.

A protected natural area on Fox Point owned by the town complements the open space of the Great Bay National Wildlife Refuge. But Newington also has more than its share of toxic Superfund clean-up sites. The military was a serious polluter. Cleanup and remediation has occurred at several spots on the former air base, including Paul's and McIntyre Brooks, which had elevated concentrations of pesticides, metals, and other contaminants. Today diffuse storm water runoff is more threatening to the estuary than is military or industrial pollution. McIntyre Brook, for instance, flows from the runway at Pease into the Great Bay Estuary, carrying with it residual waste from aircraft washing, painting, fueling, and de-icing.

Newington is a town of extremes. Its five faces represent economic growth, historic preservation, suburban sprawl, and environmental protection. Ironically, the most dramatic preservation of open space, the Great Bay National Wildlife Refuge, was an

Built in 1712, this sanctuary, which is the oldest Congregational Church in the nation in continuous use, links Newington's past to its present and future. Photograph circa 1912. Courtesy of the Newington Historical Society.

unintended consequence of military base building, a silver lining in the cloud of base construction and base closure. Had the federal government not taken that land out of private hands for military use fifty years ago, developers probably would be building on it now, to the detriment of Newington and the entire Great Bay watershed. —WJB

Sources: John Frink Rowe, *Newington, New Hampshire: A Heritage of Independence Since 1630* (Canaan, NH: Phoenix Publishing, 1987); *The Newington Neighbor* vol. 28 (Winter 1999), p. 8; Stephen H. Jones, ed., *A Technical Characterization of Estuarine and Coastal New Hampshire* (Durham, NH: Jackson Estuarine Laboratory, 2000), pp. 70-73.

GREENLAND

GREENLAND AND THE WINNICUT RIVER

THE WINNICUT RIVER—whose Abenaki name has been translated as "beautiful place" and "where water pours out"—formed the western boundary of Greenland, a part of Portsmouth, in 1653 when the area was still part of the colony of Massachusetts. The banks of the river and the Great Bay shoreline, which had been popular Native American camping spots, became favorite homesites for Greenland's first English settlers, who found the branches of the Piscataqua system convenient highways on which to transport their household furniture and other heavy goods. And, of course, there was timber.

Greenland's first sawmill was built near the ford by which the Portsmouth-Exeter road crossed the Winnicut, in or just before 1670, by Philip Lewis of Greenland and Isaac Cole of Hampton. By 1685, Lewis had built a gristmill in the same area. Nathaniel Huggins built a sawmill nearby in 1689 for the widow Mary Haines. In 1697 the Portsmouth selectmen authorized Samuel Weeks of Greenland and Tobias Langdon of Strawbery Banke to build another sawmill on the upper Winnicut near the mouth of Winniconic Brook, later operated by the Davis and Simpson families. An early sawmill where the road to Hampton crossed Norton Brook, a second Winnicut tributary, was said to have been "lately burned down" in 1706, while another in that location was established by Nathaniel Berry around

Tide Mill area and the town landing, Greenland, circa 1900. Courtesy of Paul F. Hughes.

1710. Sawmills were the heart of the seventeenth-century town.

Greenland, like every other town in the estuary, began as something of a lumber camp. In 1670, the Portsmouth selectmen authorized Philip Lewis to cut 2000 feet of lumber from the town's common land near the Winnicut, and deliver it "near the meeting house for the use of the school" to be built on Great Island (New Castle). The customary means of delivery was to float the boards to "the Banke" (as Strawbery Banke was then called) via Great and Little Bays and the Piscataqua, a route that was followed by many lots of timber from Greenland's Bayside area for the next two hundred years.

Development of settled societies in the wilderness required other amenities: burial grounds, landings, roads, and bridges. The English settlers, quite conscious of their manipulation of the environment, considered these "improvements." A 1671 Portsmouth town meeting set aside "about one Acre of Land for a burying place forever joyneing to Tho[mas] Avery and Leonard Weeks Land,...between said Avery and Weeks Land and Winnicot River." This was Greenland's first burial ground, on a site described in the Haines genealogy as a "bold promontory jutting a little into the Winnicut, thirty or forty feet above the river—a beautiful, quiet spot, now covered with a wooded growth."

A landing existed at the burying ground. Another one, which eventually would become the chief landing for the town, was established at the end of today's Tide Mill Road by Captain Walter Neal, a Portsmouth militia officer whose garrison house stood nearby on the highest point of John Heard's Neck. Several early deeds refer to "Captain Neal's landing," suggesting that it was a well-known and important place in early Greenland.

A committee appointed to lay out "a convenient country way" between Exeter and Greenland in 1700 recommended a route ending at "Mr. Philip Lewis's mill pond; and we do apprehend great necessity of a float" (or pontoon) "bridge to be maintained over said mill pond." This was never built, and it was only in 1711 that a Portsmouth town meeting voted that a conventional bridge be erected at the site.

A tide mill near the Winnicut's mouth was authorized by a Greenland meeting in 1756, at which residents voted "that John Johnson and others may build a Mill upon the River against the lower landing place so called... and Join their dam to said landing place."

Greenland, New Hampshire: The Veteran's Memorial park points northward to the Winnicut River, Great Bay, Newington, Little Bay and the Piscataqua River. Photograph by Arthur A. Peterson (1891-1978). Courtesy of Paul F. Hughes.

An artist's conception of this mill appears in M. O. Hall's *Rambles About Greenland in Rhyme* (1900). Various proprietors operated it until it burned about 1854. By 1823 at least six mills operated on Greenland's portion of the Winnicut: a sawmill, four gristmills, and the Burleigh clothing mill. Theodore Burleigh of Newmarket had obtained permission to build and operate "a fulling mill and napping machine for developing cloth" near the Winnicut bridge in 1821. Burleigh ran the mill for forty years before selling it to members of the Brackett family in 1861. By the time Burleigh built his fulling mill, all of the big timber was long gone, but the river remained crucial to Greenland's economy, although it never was navigable by any vessel larger than a gundalow.

Small boys found the Winnicut stimulating to their imaginations. Captain Nathaniel G. Weeks, who later commanded vessels that carried ice to India, and who crossed the Atlantic Ocean fifty-three times in his career at sea, had grown up on the river's western bank. He recollected, "I attempted at the age of eight years [in 1822], to cross the broad bosom of the Winnicut River on a plank. When about half seas over, either I or the plank (I suspect it was the plank) lost its balance and precipitated me into my destined element." After more successful experiments involving two- and three-plank craft and a dugout canoe, Weeks recalled that in 1828, "our boat was duly provisioned for a long voyage, and the Winnicut was fearlessly navigated to its very mouth, and our Canoe was fairly launched upon the bitter waters of that celebrated inland Sea called in modern times the 'Great Bay.'"

One mill after another ceased operation during the late nineteenth and early twentieth centuries until the last sawmill, located on the river's east bank near the bridge, closed in the early 1940s and its dam collapsed. At the dedication of a new dam in 1957, locals expressed hope that it would bring increased recreational opportunities to the area. Newspaper accounts said that the dam "includes a fish way that will enable salt water fish, if Great Bay is ever cleansed of pollution, to travel upstream and spawn." In the same year the Piscataqua Fish and Game club, whose breeding pools near today's Route 33 had been rendered useless by the lowering of central Greenland's water table in the 1940s, bought thirty acres on the Winnicut near Tuttle Lane. A clubhouse was built in 1961-2, and the club provided fishing facilities and instruction in safe hunting. Nearby, Camp Gundalow, operated by the Portsmouth YMCA, has offered recreational opportunities to area children for over forty years. Unfortunately, the Winnicut's once-prolific smelt and alewife spawning grounds are no longer productive, and there is no telling whether they will ever revive. –PFH

Sources: Thomas V. Haines, *Deacon Samuel Haines…and his Descendants in America* (Boston: Stanhope Press, 1902); Micajah O. Hall, *Rambles About Greenland in Rhyme* (Boston: A. Mudge & Son, Printers, 1900; reprinted with additional material, 1979); Capt. Nathaniel G. Weeks's autobiography (manuscript at New York Historical Society).

South Berwick, Maine. Gundalow loaded with coal below Portsmouth Manufacturing Co. There is a second gundalow without a rig tied inboard. Berwick Academy's Fogg Building is in the background. Circa 1896. Courtesy of the Old Berwick Historical Society, South Berwick, Maine.

GUNDALOWS

GUNDALOWS WERE THE TIDEWATER TRUCKS of the Piscataqua region from the 1600s through World War I. The word first appears in writing in 1669 as "gondola," a pronunciation that still survives among some native watermen. The earliest of these craft were simple lighters, undecked, without sailing rigs. They were rowed short distances between the Portsmouth shore, which lacked wharves, and ships anchored in the stream. Their job was to unload the ships newly-arrived from England, carrying their cargoes of manufactured goods to shore and then to reload the ships with the furs, timber, and dried fish being produced by the new colony.

As upriver settlements in South Berwick, Dover, Exeter, and elsewhere developed, freight service to Portsmouth was needed. The gundalows became larger and more numerous, with the addition of decks for ease of loading and sailing rigs to save rowing as trade grew. These vessels were well suited to the shallow rivers. They were flat bottomed, allowing them to float in a minimum depth of water and to "take the ground" at low tide, sitting comfortably until the flooding tide refloated them.

The real key to the success of gundalows, though, was the speed of the tidal currents in the Piscataqua region. The main channel of the river in Portsmouth is judged to be the second-fastest navigable tidal river in the continental United States, surpassed only by the Columbia River on the West Coast. This current essentially acts as an engine for a riverboat, a natural resource to be harnessed just as mills harnessed wind or falling water. A skipper simply timed his moves to the tide, riding upriver with the incoming or flood tide and floating seaward on the ebb. There was always the sail to help when the breeze was favorable, and long oars to get into a tricky cove, but day in and

The reproduction gundalow, Capt. Edward H. Adams, *docked at Prescott Park near Strawbery Banke Museum, circa 1995. Photograph by Paul C. Dustin. Courtesy of Nicholas B. Brown.*

Gundalow loaded with wood underway on the Squamscott River. Courtesy of the Exeter Historical Society.

day out the power of the tidal currents gave gundalows on the Piscataqua an ease of movement envied by barge and scow operators from the Penobscot to the Chesapeake.

The final unique aspect of a Piscataqua River gundalow was its triangular lateen sail, hung at an angle from a pivoting yard. Counterbalanced correctly, the peak of this yard could be quickly pivoted to the deck, reducing the overhead clearance needed from fifty or sixty feet down to twelve or sixteen, depending on the exact dimensions of a given vessel. This proved to be a tremendous advantage in passing under the low fixed bridges typically built on the smaller rivers.

Gundalows were usually owner-operated, and quite often the skipper was a part-time waterman, being also a farmer or mechanic of some sort. One high-seas captain said that, lacking the glamour of their blue-water brethren, "a man that would sail a gundalow would rob a churchyard." Rivermen were known for their fondness for strong drink and strong language. In 1811 after a trip upriver from Portsmouth to Dover, itinerant Baptist minister Enoch Hayes Place wrote in his journal, "If the people in Sodom and Gomorrah was given to the practice of Swearing as much as they are here in this packet I do not wonder at Lot's being willing to leave the place."

The last gundalow to operate commercially was the *Fanny M.*, launched from Adam's Point in Durham in 1886, abandoned on

"Gundalow men" - Captain Edward Adams (on the right) and his son, Cass. Photograph by Clyde Waterhouse, circa 1935. Courtesy of the Old Berwick Historical Society, South Berwick, Maine.

Dover Point circa 1920, and totally lost during the spring ice-out in 1926. In 1982 a reproduction of the *Fanny M.* was launched and named the *Captain Edward H. Adams* in honor of the last gundalow skipper. The *Adams* travels throughout the Piscataqua region conducting school programs in environmental and maritime history of the Piscataqua region. –MG

Sources: Richard E. Winslow III, *The Piscataqua Gundalow: Workhorse for a Tidal Basin Empire* (Portsmouth, NH: Portsmouth Marine Society, 1983); William G. Saltonstall, *Ports of Piscataqua* (Cambridge, MA: Harvard University Press, 1941); D.F. Taylor, *The Piscataqua River Gundalow* (unpublished typescript, Historical American Merchant Marine Survey, Smithsonian Institution, 1937).

ICE FISHING

FEW FISH STILL CREATE AS MUCH FUSS in the Piscataqua region as the rainbow smelt, *Osmerus mordax,* a slender, pale green fish with a silver belly and a broad silvery band along its sides. Six to nine inches long, and only a few ounces in weight, the lowly smelt arrive in the estuary each fall, wintering over until river temperatures rise sufficiently in the spring for them to swim upstream and spawn. Driven by an ancient biological clock, these hordes of hungry fish thus inhabit Great Bay and its tributaries in the season of ice.

From a smelter's perspective, "black ice,"—four to six inches of nearly transparent ice with strength like steel—is the best surface for sliding a five-hundred-pound shanty into a favorite spot. Hundreds of shanties (also called shacks, or bobhouses) sit on the ice in Greenland Cove and up the Lamprey, Squamscott, and Oyster Rivers in winter. Like weatherproof sentry boxes, they shelter the smelters who cut holes in the ice beneath them with a chisel and an ice saw or perhaps a power auger. A cold winter gives ice fishermen a season of two-and-a-half months, from early January to mid March. Warmer weather drastically limits the season, cutting short the satisfaction smelters find when huddled together around a Coleman lantern at night on the ice, or when alone, with a short pole and bobber, in the glinting stillness of a sunny winter day.

Smelt fishing is primarily a recreational activity, but it has a commercial history. In Maine, ice-caught smelt may be sold commercially without any permit or fee. New Hampshire fisherman must spend $25 for a commercial license that allows them to sell to local fish markets. The limit is generous—ten liquid quarts in New Hampshire, and no limit at all in Maine—and the right fisherman on the right night can limit out. Usually the fishing is slower, with only five or six fish caught per hour. Total catches in the Great Bay estuary are highly variable, ranging from about ten thousand fish in 1980 to half a million in 1989. As of 2000, fisheries biologists did not yet have sufficient data to chart discernible trends.

Ice fishermen, Great Bay, Newington. Photograph by Peter E. Randall, circa 1977. Courtesy of the photographer.

During the Great Depression smelters sold their catch for forty cents a pound, and as one remembered, "the change came in handy," even if the catch was only two or three pounds. The commercial smelt fishery on Great Bay, albeit always small in scale, seems to have begun around the middle of the nineteenth century according to a letter to the editor in the Portsmouth *Daily Chronicle* on January 1, 1859. Most of the tens of thousands of dedicated smelters withstanding cold feet and groaning ice since the 1850s have been sport fishermen.

During the 1930s and 1940s many Portsmouth Navy Yard workers were avid fishermen. Men at the Yard worked around the clock, sometimes getting off the night shift at seven-thirty in the morning and heading out to their shacks as soon as they got home. The best fishing was always on the incoming tide, from half-tide to flood, though sometimes a few stragglers were hooked on the early ebb tide.

Bobhouses in Exeter. Photograph by Ralph Morang, 1996. Courtesy of the photographer.

the channels from trapping the sled when it froze. Smelters wind-proofed their portable shacks "with cheesecloth, which was covered with molten wax applied by a brush." In those days, Mr. Hughes remembered, "there were perhaps a couple of hundred fishermen on the bay, most of them on the Newington side." He generally fished the Winnicut River side, near the tide mill early in the season, and then at "the Elbow," a bend in the channel just west of Daniels Point. Ice fishermen had names for their favorite sections of channel in the bay, such as "Simpson's Ebb," "John Stone Junction," and "the Elbow." Clusters of shanties marked each spot.

Some aspects of ice fishing have changed through the decades. Elaborate bobhouses are considerably warmer than an empty keg perched on a kerosene lamp ever was. Snowmobiles have replaced sleds to move the houses from place to place. But much remains the same. Standing far from shore on a dark night with the incoming tide producing groans and cracks, ice fishermen know from tugs on their lines that despite the lifeless appearance of the landscape, a huge mass of fish are feeding beneath their feet. The pleasure of starry nights and the prospect of fried smelt dinners continue to attract local men and women willing to make a fuss over smelt. –MG

The permanent shacks so prevalent on the ice today were not used regularly until the 1950s. Paul C. Hughes, who died in 1989, fished the bay throughout much of the twentieth century and remembered that smelters often fished in the open during World War I. They "carried their gear in a nail keg, suspended by a rope from one shoulder," and frequently carried a kerosene lantern "not for light, but to place in the keg while fishing." Draped in long coats and seated on the keg, they remained sufficiently warm, at least by smelters' standards. By the 1930s and 1940s fishermen were likely to have portable houses "made of four sections, which folded up and were stored atop a sled, which also carried a built-in box for the fishing gear, kerosene stove, and other necessities." After each use the house was disassembled, stored on the sled, and pulled off the channels and onto the flats where it was tied to a stake. This precaution prevented water flooding

Sources: Frederick T. Short, ed., *The Ecology of the Great Bay Estuary, New Hampshire and Maine: An Estuarine Profile and Bibliography* (NOAA-Coastal Ocean Program, 1992); Paul C. Hughes, "Memoir on Smelt Fishing" (Unpublished manuscript in possession of Paul F. Hughes, 1979); Michael Mariano, "Rainbow Smelt," (New Hampshire Fish and Game Department and Great Bay National Estuarine Research Reserve pamphlet, 1990); Interviews with Doug Grant, New Hampshire Fish and Game, January 2001, and Warren "Junior" Sawyer, Newmarket, January 2001.

Color Plate I. The Province of Mayne, *1650. Courtesy of Baxter Rare Maps Collection, Maine State Archives.*

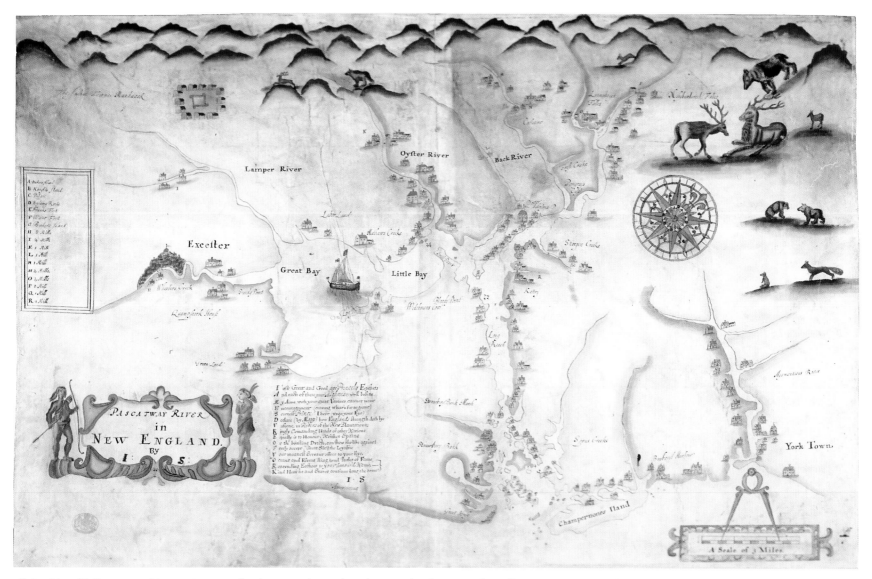

Color Plate II. Pascatway River in New England, *circa 1670. Ink and watercolor, by I. S. (John Sellers). By permission of The British Library.*

7559 FORT MC CLARY. KITTERY POINT, ME.

July 25, 1908, arrived here safely & found quite a number of friends. Very pleasant room overlooking the beach. Slept finely & am all settled for a good rest. With love to you both, W. L.

Color Plate III. Postcard view of Fort McClary, Kittery Point, Maine. Photograph by Detroit Photograph, 1904. Courtesy of Society for the Preservation of New England Antiquities.

Color Plate IV. Durham, New Hampshire, waterfront at the falls, circa 1822. Original mural at the Community Church in Durham, New Hampshire. Oil on canvas, by John W. Hatch, 1954. Photograph by Gary Samson. Courtesy of Marianna Hatch.

Color Plate V. The Piscataqua River from New Castle to Seavey Island, 2001. This multibeam sonar image of the Piscataqua River was produced by the combined efforts of the University of New Hampshire's Center for Coastal and Ocean Mapping (C-COM), and the National Oceanic and Atmospheric Administration (NOAA) through the Joint Hydrographic Center in Durham, New Hampshire. The center, founded in June of 1999, is developing and evaluating a wide range of state-of-the-art ocean mapping technologies, and training a new generation of hydrographers and other ocean scientists for public and private sector endeavors in the marine environment. Note that the multibeam sonar was deployed only in the main shipping channel, and that many shallow areas of the harbor (such as Pepperrell Cove) are displayed here as they appear on the conventional navigational chart. The multibeam sonar image is color-coded for depth, but it also reveals dramatic bottom features such as Cod Rock, north of Fort Constitution, and the remnant of Henderson's Point, south of Seavey Island. Courtesy of the Center for Coastal and Ocean Mapping, University of New Hampshire.

Color Plate VI. Painting lobster buoys. Photograph by Peter E. Randall, circa 1977. Courtesy of the photographer.

THE GREAT BAY COAST WATCH

"THE TIDE WAITS FOR NO MAN." That adage was familiar to generations who worked on the water. Today, few people make their living on Great Bay and its rivers, and for the most part only recreational boaters and fishermen keep tabs on the tides, along with marine scientists and river pilots. But they are not entirely alone. Volunteers in the Great Bay Coast Watch, a group monitoring water quality, are sampling water temperature, pH, salinity, dissolved oxygen, transparency, and fecal coliform bacteria at twenty-one sites throughout the region. Armed with buckets, salinometers, and secchi disks, they sample at high and low tide on the weekday closest to the new moon every month from April to November. Coast Watchers are gathering data crucial to the effective management of the Piscataqua ecosystem. Like the old-timers who kept an eye on the tide, these students, retirees, and other volunteers are learning the bay's moods and its ways. And they are making a difference.

The Great Bay Coast Watch was founded in 1990 as part of the University of New Hampshire Cooperative Extension/Sea Grant outreach. Its mission is to protect New Hampshire's coastal and estuarine resources far into the future through monitoring and educational programs. In addition to water quality sampling, Coast Watchers also conduct shoreline surveys, looking for sources of pollution and characterizing shoreline habitats. In 1998 the Watch began a new project to monitor harmful algae blooms in Seabrook, Hampton, and Rye Harbors; in New Castle; and at Dover Point. Water quality data gathered by Coast Watchers is included in annual reports and a long-term database that currently includes information from nearly four thousand monitoring visits. Many have access to this data, including state and federal agencies, local governments (including planning boards and conservation commissions), scientists, educators, and the volunteers themselves.

The Coast Watchers work in places known to generations of Piscataqua region residents. Monitoring sites include the Exeter Town

Kathy Pierce and Ruth Larkin, eighth-grade teachers at Portsmouth Middle School, recording data from water quality sampling in South Mill Pond, Great Bay Coast Watch Site #20, 2001. Photograph by Ann Reid. Courtesy of the photographer.

Docks, the mudflats at the Sandy Point Discovery Center, Fowler's Dock on the Lamprey River (the only freshwater site), Cedar Point (the north shore of Little Bay between the mouths of the Oyster and Bellamy Rivers), the Dover Footbridge, Patten Yacht Yard in South Eliot, the Maplewood Avenue Bridge on Portsmouth's North Mill Pond, and the UNH Coastal Marine Lab in New Castle. Many of these sites have rich maritime histories. In the future they also will be seen as instrumental to the marine science that is currently redefining this region's waters.

"Muckin' with Mussels." Students with the Great Bay Coast Watchers collecting mussels on South Mill Pond in Portsmouth, 2001. Photograph by Ann Reid. Courtesy of the photographer.

The Great Bay Coast Watch can boast a long series of accomplishments. Their shoreline surveys helped to reopen clam-flats in Hampton and Great Bay. By implementing procedures in ten local schools for water monitoring, they not only taught "hands-on" science, but also influenced some students to select conservation and natural science as college majors. The Watch has coordinated phytoplankton-sampling volunteers to work in the U.S. Food and Drug Administration's National Shellfish Toxicity program, and it has supplied data to the Great Bay National Estuarine Research Reserve

on horseshoe crab populations in Great Bay. Coast Watch volunteers are making history, as surely as the weir fishermen, gundalow skippers, and brick-makers who preceded them on the bay.

The Watch's findings offer good news in addition to cause for concern. "Despite years of human impact," according to their year 2000 report, "much of the Great Bay remains a pristine, healthy, and vital natural ecosystem." Given the numerous estuaries in New England that have been compromised or destroyed, Great Bay is a remarkable example of a large estuary in good health. In the past, threats to the ecosystem included particulate pollutants such as sawdust, and toxic discharge from single points such as factory waste pipes. Fortunately, those problems are resolved. In the future looms the threat of increasing residential development guaranteed to strain the estuary and decrease its resistance to human pollution and destruction of natural habitats.

Stewardship involves caring enough about something to put that care into action. The members of the Great Bay Coast Watch (more than three hundred volunteers over ten years) personify that kind of stewardship through dedication and hard work. Their efforts are making Great Bay and Piscataqua waters healthier and more appreciated. In the future, the Watchers' impact will be regarded as historic, a marker of these wily waters' rejuvenation in the late twentieth century. As in generations past, those who actually get their feet wet know most about the bay. –SM

Sources: R. Konisky, W. Pagum, A. Reid, J. Schloss, and D. M. Burdick, *Great Bay Coast Watch 1990-1999: A Ten Year Report on the Volunteer Water Quality Monitoring of the Great Bay Estuarine System* (University of New Hampshire Cooperative Extension/Sea Grant Technical Report UNH MP-AR-SG-00-12, 2000).

STRATHAM

THE STUART FARM

THE 270-ACRE PROPERTY NOW KNOWN AS STUART FARM is one of the best-preserved examples of the prosperous coastal farms that once were a hallmark of the Piscataqua region. Located on the tidal Squamscott River in Stratham, Stuart Farm—still in operation—was determined eligible for the National Register of Historic Places as "an important example of the evolution of a large and productive coastal New Hampshire farm, reflecting the accomplishments of a number of significant owners." Its rich and colorful history tells of generations of stewardship and of continual change and evolution. Owners over the centuries have redefined the farm and adapted to changing agricultural trends.

People long made their living from the rich natural resources of the estuary. Artifacts reveal Native American sites along the Newfields and Stratham shores of the Squamscott. After Europeans settled near the river, generations of the farm's owners lived in a Stratham that was far more bucolic than today. Long an agricultural town, it lacked even a village center. While earlier inhabitants never envisioned the twenty thousand vehicles per day that the New Hampshire Department of Transportation recently counted passing the farm, it is located on what has always been an important route around the southern end of Great Bay. The earliest known Squamscott River ferry crossed the river where it bends around the farm. Later, the state's first toll bridge was built at the site of the Route 108 bridge. As late as the 1960s, a large, peeling sign listing the tolls remained on that shore, a relic from the early twentieth century.

Stratham town founder Capt. Thomas Wiggin bequeathed this section of the town to his son Andrew (c. 1635-1700). The main part of what is now the Stuart Farm stayed in the Wiggin family until 1875,

The Stuart Farm, in Stratham, New Hampshire, is one of the last remaining dairy operations in the Piscataqua region. Photograph by Lorraine S. Merrill, 1997. Courtesy of the photographer.

although several generations of daughters changed the names to Smith, Clark, and Robinson. Abendigo Robinson built the Italianate-style main house in 1867 (the oldest house on the farm dates to about 1700). According to 1870 census records, this was one of the five most valuable and productive of the 131 working farms in Stratham. The December 12, 1873, *Exeter News-Letter* reported the "big story" of Robinson winning a $100 prize for his record-breaking potato yield.

But by the 1870s farms all over New England, especially hill farms on thin, rocky soils, were failing or being abandoned, unable to compete with cheap agriculture from the West. The depression of 1873 hit many farmers hard. Whether because of that depression, or for other reasons, the Robinsons sold the farm to Benjamin Whitcomb, Boston's Fire Commissioner and an avid breeder of racehorses, in 1875. After two hundred years of producing both for family subsistence and market sales, the farm became something of a "gentleman's farm" for the next half century or more.

Whitcomb was a hard-racing and hard-drinking man, about whom many wild tales have been confirmed. He was said to have planted the silver maples that line the long, gravel driveway to guide his horses safely home on those occasions when he could no longer drive. His friend, the impressionist painter Childe Hassam, often visited the farm, where he painted several landscapes that can be seen at the Currier Gallery and the Museum of Modern Art.

Benjamin Whitcomb, and then his son Charles, kept fifty to sixty horses at the farm through the 1890s and early 1900s, including the nationally famous stud "Wildfire." Edwin "The Boss" Baker, a successful Boston businessman raised on a Vermont farm, acquired the farm when the Whitcombs were foreclosed in 1919. The Boss, always seen with a big cigar, drove around town in a Pierce Arrow car.

With an eye for fine dairy cattle, The Boss developed a nationally famous herd of registered Holsteins. He converted the two big horse barns to dairy barns, and built a third to house his two hundred Holsteins—a very large herd for the time. Milk was bottled at the farm and sold throughout the Exeter area. Single male employees lived in a dormitory over the milk plant. After The Boss died in 1937, his son Willis A. "Bill" Baker returned to manage the farm. Having inherited his father's love and talent for selecting and breeding cattle, he won top prizes in the show ring. When the farm was sold in 1944 to settle Baker's estate, dairymen regarded it as a history-making dispersal of the herd. The cattle commanded high prices, with many going to other big-name herds of the day. The bull Dunloggin Woodsman topped the sale at $5,000, and the top-selling cow, Joy's Delight of Baker Farm, went for $3,500.

Andrew Christie, a national and international leader in chicken breeding, then purchased the farm as the flagship of his six-farm poultry operation. His trademarked slogan proclaimed that the Christie strain of New Hampshire Reds had "Spizzerinktum." To house ten thousand chickens, he converted two cow barns into three-story poultry houses with service elevators. The poultry market crashed in the late 1950s, with the chicken meat business declining along with the region's textile and shoe industries. The dual-purpose New Hampshire Reds, bred for both meat and egg laying, fell out of favor in the increasingly specialized and competitive poultry industry. Again, the farm was for sale.

Simultaneously, construction of Route 495 forced the Stuart family of Massachusetts to relocate their dairy farm to New Hampshire. Since 1961, three generations of Stuarts have continued to adapt the Stuart Farm for modern dairying. Alfalfa, grass, and corn are grown to feed the herd of up to two hundred milking-age registered Holstein and Brown Swiss cows, plus young stock. Following the tradition of previous owners, the Stuarts have cared for this historic farm so that it continues to be productive farmland and vital wildlife habitat.

With prime agricultural soils of national significance and soils of statewide significance, the farm in 1981 became one of the first to be protected by the state with a conservation easement. In 1993 the U.S. Fish and Wildlife Service's "Partners for Wildlife" program helped restore a twelve-acre salt marsh on Mill Brook. UNH Jackson Estuarine Lab researchers have studied this restoration, and often bring classes here for fieldwork. The farm's owners have worked with federal and state agencies to minimize its impact on estuarine water quality.

Despite changes in ownership and uses—from horses, to dairy, to poultry—Stuart Farm has nevertheless remained a productive farm. As development rapidly consumes open land in the Seacoast region, especially near the waterways, working farms play a key role in conserving fields, woodlands, and wetlands in the estuarine watershed. Agriculture helps to preserve the rural and traditional character of the region, while protecting groundwater and surface water, providing habitat for wildlife, and enhancing the quality of life for all. –LSM

Sources: Lisa Mausolf, *Historical Resource Survey* (Concord, NH: New Hampshire Division of Historical Resources, 1996); Interview with the late W.A. "Bill" Baker, 1986; Handwritten notes from the late Margery Brooke of Newfields, a Wiggin descendant.

DEVELOPMENTAL PRESSURES IN THE PISCATAQUA REGION

RESIDENTS OF THE PISCATAQUA REGION now take growth for granted. New houses are sprouting like weeds from fields and woods, schools are overcrowded, and towns that did not even have a traffic light twenty-five years ago currently confront traffic jams. Rockingham County, which includes Exeter, Rye, Hampton, Portsmouth, New Castle, and Newington, among other towns, is expected to grow by an astonishing 53 percent between 1998 and 2020. That means a population of 265,000 will balloon to 401,000.

It was not always so. Historian Dona Brown explains that when Yale University's President Timothy Dwight toured the region in 1810, he found parts of it desolate. York had been virtually clear-cut, and it appeared "naked and bleak" with an aura of "stillness and solitude." Following the War of 1812, as New England's maritime economy faltered, Portsmouth and other towns fell into serious decline. Shipping dried up and jobs evaporated. Local writers reflected the sense of gloom: "The crazy old warehouses are empty; and barnacles and eel-grass cling to the piles of the crumbling wharves," wrote Thomas Bailey Aldrich in 1868 in *The Story of a Bad Boy*, set in Portsmouth. To Sarah Orne Jewett, South Berwick seemed equally somnolent: "From this inland town of mine," she wrote in 1881, "there is no sea-faring any more, and the shipwrights' hammers are never heard now. It is only a station on the railway, and it has, after all these years, grown so little that it is hardly worth while for all the trains to stop."

In fact, half of the counties in Maine and New Hampshire made no population gains between 1860 and 1880, and many towns saw outright declines as families moved west and south to obtain cheap land under the federal government's Homestead Act. Out-migration and its ills prompted New Hampshire's governor, Frank Rollins, to

Open space is rapidly being developed in the Piscataqua region. Photograph by W. Jeffrey Bolster, 2000. Courtesy of the photographer.

introduce "Old Home Week" in 1899. Designed to lure former residents back to their hometowns, even if just for a vacation on which they would spend money, Old Home Week publicly acknowledged New Hampshire's faltering economy and population loss.

The region has come full circle. During the 1990s, as Connecticut and Rhode Island actually lost population, and as the United States as a whole grew by only 0.9 percent, New Hampshire was the fastest growing state in the Northeast, with a 6.8 percent growth rate. And the bulk of New Hampshire's population growth has been in the southeast corner of the state—right here. Housing starts are booming and population density is increasing. All Rockingham County communities, except

Newfields and Hampton Falls, are told to expect growth rates above forty percent between 1998 and 2020. It certainly introduces a whole new set of concerns to the region.

The challenge for Piscataqua towns is to channel the inevitable growth so that it results in a landscape with which we can live. Planners like to think in terms of "smart growth," or economic and population expansion without sprawl, but that can be an exasperatingly elusive goal. Local planning and zoning ordinances often are not sufficiently far-sighted to prevent a town from losing its sense of place in the face of rapid and large-scale development. And within the rules for site plan and design review that exist at any given time, market forces prevail. Developers easily find capital to purchase open land. Leapfrogging development, whether it jumps beyond the periphery of densely settled areas or fills in the gaps in a once sparsely settled place such as Durham Point Road, is consuming forest and field at an alarming rate. The pattern is obvious in much of Maine's York County and New Hampshire's Rockingham and Strafford Counties.

Sprawl has not been charted or analyzed consistently across the state, according to Jeffrey H. Taylor, Director of New Hampshire's Office of State Planning. But population and development data (which together indicate sprawl) has been examined for one section of the Piscataqua region—the towns of Exeter, Stratham, and Greenland. Comparison of data from 1974 and 1992 revealed that during those eighteen years the three towns' population rose by 76 percent and their developed land rose by 110 percent. That, in a nutshell, indicates sprawl. Our society is currently consuming more land per person than did previous generations. Our roads are wider, our parking lots larger, our homes and businesses more expansive. The town of Stratham, on the southern shore of Great Bay, not only increased its population a dramatic 172 percent in those eighteen years, but increased its developed land 221 percent. Sprawl threatens wetlands and lands that supply critical water supplies for residents; it threatens forests and biodiversity; it threatens the very landscape that residents and visitors alike associate with the Piscataqua.

According to a report called *New Hampshire's Changing Landscape*, prepared by the Society for the Protection of New Hampshire Forests and The Nature Conservancy, the greatest loss of forestland in New Hampshire during the next generation is forecast to occur in the southeastern corner of the state. Predicted losses of wooded lands in municipalities are especially striking. Tiny New Castle is expected to lose 22 percent of its remaining forest cover between 1993 and 2020. Portsmouth is expected to lose 19 percent; Seabrook, 18 percent; and Newmarket, 10 percent.

Countervailing the forces of development is an increasing consciousness of the importance of protecting land. Some parcels were protected long ago. In 1710, for instance, Newington set aside land as a town forest, initiating the public protection of land at the local level. Essays in this book explain the creation of Prescott Park in Portsmouth and the preservation of Wagon Hill Farm in Durham. But the price of land with proximity to the coast has skyrocketed. Citizens' groups will never have enough money to buy all the land that they would like to save. The result is that a relatively small percentage of land in the Piscataqua is currently protected—whether by conservation easements, deed restrictions, or outright ownership by public agencies or private organizations dedicated to preserving land from development.

The Great Bay Resource Protection Partnership, a joint initiative of New Hampshire's Fish and Game Department and The Nature Conservancy, supports land acquisition efforts within the Great Bay estuary. Theirs is an excellent example of a public/private partnership dedicated to conservation. In December of 2000 the state accepted a donation of 154 acres in the estuary to protect critical wildlife habitat. This included the 75-acre Pearson conservation easement on land adjacent to Great Bay in Durham and Newmarket; 50 acres and approximately 1,000 feet of frontage on the Cochecho River in Dover; and 29 acres and 1,150 feet of frontage on Great Bay in Greenland and Newington. Such protection is no longer cheap: the combined value of those lands and easements was about two million dollars.

Fortunately the federal government is willing to purchase land in the Great Bay estuary, or to help buy the development rights to it through conservation easements. "Great Bay is the crown jewel of New Hampshire's unique coastal area, and it is important to preserve critical areas to ensure that it is not overdeveloped," said Senator Judd Gregg in June of 2001 as he announced a federal government grant of $7.8 million for the Great Bay Resource Protection Partnership. So far that partnership has acquired about 3,000 acres, approximately 2,400 acres of it through public funding. Of course, thousands of acres in the Piscataqua region *outside* the Great Bay estuary also need protection. While private land trusts are doing an admirable job of convincing landowners to put conservation easements or deed restrictions on undeveloped property, the costs associated with preserving large tracts of land (or especially significant parcels) are monumental. Market values—meaning both the dollar value of land and the cultural value that people put on land as wealth—encourage the consumption and development of the Piscataqua's shrinking open space.

Rampant population growth probably will not endure forever. A historical perspective shows how cycles of development have ebbed and flowed in the region. But it is obvious that the Piscataqua will be more densely populated in twenty years than it is now. It is also clear that government will be instrumental in preserving open space and historical sites in the future. Government at the local and state levels must strengthen zoning, planning, and design standards, and work with citizens' groups so that planning boards are understood primarily as protectors of the common good, not as obstacles to individuals' desires. And the federal government must continue to make funds available for the acquisition of open space, especially for critical habitats such as wetlands.

For centuries the distinctive landscape of the Piscataqua consisted of estuaries, forests, farms, mill sites, and working waterfronts. It evolved its signature shape under private ownership and market forces. Today, however, market forces and free enterprise are making the Piscataqua look more like the rest of America—a land of subdivisions, sprawl, and endless asphalt. So while the stereotypical old Yankees who once populated the region were loath to accept governmental assistance, fearing that it would compromise their cherished independence, contemporary residents of Piscataqua know that without alliances of

Scamman Farm in Stratham, New Hampshire. Photograph by Ralph Morang, 1984. Courtesy of the photographer.

private organizations and governmental agencies dedicated to preservation, developmental pressures will overwhelm what remains of the Piscataqua's essential mix of nature and heritage. –WJB

Sources: Dona Brown, "Purchasing the Past: Summer People and the Transformation of the Piscataqua Region in the Nineteenth Century," in *"A Noble and Dignified Stream": The Piscataqua Region in the Colonial Revival, 1860-1930*, eds., Sarah L. Giffen and Kevin D. Murphy (York, Maine: Old York Historical Society, 1992); Dan Sundquist and Michael Stevens, *New Hampshire's Changing Landscape: Population Growth, Land Use Conversion, and Resource Fragmentation in the Granite State* (Concord, NH: Society for the Protection of New Hampshire Forests and The Nature Conservancy, 1999); "Great Bay Gets More Support," *Foster's Daily Democrat* (June 16, 2001).

Sandy Point Discovery Center and Great Bay National Estuarine Research Reserve

During the autumn of 1973, Great Bay estuary narrowly escaped becoming home to the world's largest oil refinery. The Greek shipping tycoon Aristotle Onassis had covertly acquired purchase options on one-quarter of the town of Durham. Joined by New Hampshire governor Meldrim Thompson, Onassis's agents dreamed of a supertanker terminal at the Isles of Shoals with a pipeline for crude oil to Durham. Had Onassis prevailed, smoke stacks and storage tanks would have dominated the skyline and shore. The night would have been lost to ambient light, the swift tidal waters dirtied, and the estuary's biological productivity seriously compromised. Luckily, a group of passionate and dedicated seacoast residents led by the late Evelyn Browne fought Onassis and won. This victory spurred awareness and support for Great Bay that eventually led to its federal designation as a National Estuarine Research Reserve.

Acquired through land purchases and conservation easements, the Reserve became part of a national network of protected sites in 1989. It consists of approximately five thousand acres of tidal waters and wetlands, together with over a thousand acres of coastal upland. The uplands and wetlands acreage is neither contiguous nor all publicly owned, and encompasses a variety of habitats. The Adams Point/Cromment

Skiff and gundalow, Sandy Point, Stratham, New Hampshire. Photograph by Ralph Morang, 1994. Courtesy of the photographer.

Creek component features open fields, salt marsh, and woodlands. The Lubberland Creek/Moody Point component includes marshes, riparian land, and forested uplands, while the Squamscott River

Wetlands component consists of salt marsh, farmland, and riparian land. Other components of the Reserve include vernal ponds, mudflats, rocky promontories, and small coves. Much of the estuary that Onassis coveted is now safe from development.

The Reserve promotes informed management of the estuary through linked programs of stewardship, public education, and scientific research. Funding is provided by the National Oceanic and Atmospheric Administration (NOAA) and the New Hampshire Fish and Game Department. The Reserve is also supported by a non-profit friends group called the Great Bay Stewards.

During the decades that have passed since Durham residents made it clear that they did not want an oil refinery in their backyard, the estuary's health has continued to improve. Most of the egregious single-point sources of pollution in the Bay have been addressed, such as factories that dumped chemicals and towns that dumped untreated sewage. Measures are being taken to reduce pollution carried by run-off surface water. The estuary is probably healthier in many respects today than it has been for the last 250 years. Nature has helped in the cleansing process; the shape of the estuary accentuates tidal flushing, and the average flushing time for water entering the head of the estuary is only twenty-five or twenty-six days, depending on river flow.

The Reserve is home to many endangered species. Great Bay estuary supports one of New England's largest winter populations of bald eagles, who spend the winter feeding on waterfowl and roosting in trees in the Reserve. Several pairs of osprey have nested successfully in the Reserve, and many migratory birds such as the Pied-billed Grebe and the Northern Harrier forage in the Reserve as they pass through the Piscataqua region. Rare plants such as robust knotweed and lined bulrush, and rare amphibians such as four-toed salamanders and the hog-nosed snake also inhabit the Reserve.

Much of the flora and fauna thriving in the Reserve is not officially endangered, although it could be without the habitats that the Reserve provides. Two hundred and eighty-one species of birds use the Reserve. Harbor seals are observed frequently. Whitetail deer, red fox, woodchuck, muskrats, chipmunks, gray squirrels, cottontail rabbits, mink, otter, and beaver live in various parts of the Reserve.

Lobsters are fished commercially in the estuary, as are American eel, smelt, and alewives. Altogether, fifty-two species of finfish have been identified in the estuary, many of which are sought by recreational anglers. Without the protection from development provided by the Reserve, the Great Bay estuary would be ecologically impoverished.

Geologists call the estuary a drowned valley. The weight of the glacier that covered this region until about ten thousand years ago depressed the crust of the earth by about forty feet. Once the glacier melted, the crust rebounded. But the uplift was not uniform throughout the region; Great Bay and Little Bay are a low-lying area in which the crust sagged, and later filled as the sea level rose. Present sea level was reached approximately three to five thousand years ago.

Current residents and visitors interested in the complex interactions that have made and defined the Great Bay estuary are invited to visit the Sandy Point Discovery Center, which was constructed in 1993. Located in Stratham on the shores of Great Bay, it serves as the conservation education headquarters for the Reserve. A universally accessible trail and boardwalk allow visitors to explore a variety of habitats including upland hardwood forests, freshwater wetlands, salt marsh, and mudflats. Visitors can stand on the deck of a nineteenth century gundalow replica, or wander through the native gardens surrounding the center. Inside, children can plunge their hands into an estuarine touch tank as they learn about lobsters, horseshoe crabs, mud snails, and other inhabitants of the Bay. Interactive displays interpret salt marsh farming, salmon migration, the role of plankton, and tidal flow in the estuary. The Sandy Point Discovery Center is a far cry from the Olympic Refinery envisioned by Aristotle Onassis and Governor Meldrim Thompson. As part of the Great Bay National Estuarine Research Reserve, the center is crucial to preserving the integrity of the Piscataqua maritime region. –KM

Sources: Frederick T. Short, ed. *The Ecology of the Great Bay Estuary, New Hampshire and Maine: An Estuarine Profile and Bibliography.* (NOAA, Coastal Ocean Program Publication, 1992); Stephen H. Jones, ed. *A Technical Characterization of Estuarine and Coastal New Hampshire* (Durham: Jackson Estuarine Laboratory, 2000), 4-7, 10-19, 161-164.

EXETER

EXETER WAS A SEAPORT

EXETER WAS A SEAPORT. Today it is difficult to imagine that the marshy, silty banks of the Squamscott River were the edges of a busy tidal water that in the eighteenth and nineteenth centuries floated schooners, wherries, and gundalows back and forth to the Atlantic Ocean. But it began even longer ago than that.

The Squamscott River begins at the Great Falls in the heart of downtown Exeter, where the fresh stream-fed waters of the Exeter River meet the tidal saltwater coming in from the Piscataqua River basin and Great Bay. "Squamscott" (properly—though not commonly—pronounced "swamscott") gets its name from the Algonquin sub-tribe, the Squamscott Indians, who called it *Msquam-s-kook*, translated as "at the salmon place" or "big water place." Plentiful game, vegetation, and an abundance of fish supported northeast Native Americans who inhabited the region until English settlers displaced them in the early 1600s. The northern stretches of the river—salt marsh wetlands that grip the edges of dense woodlands—look somewhat as they did thousands of years ago.

Exeter was settled in 1638 as one of New Hampshire's first townships, along with Portsmouth (Strawbery Banke), Dover, and Hampton. The town's Puritan founder, the Reverend John Wheelwright, purchased land from local Algonquin sagamores for a village. Those natives who did not perish from confrontation or disease eventually migrated to Canada or assimilated into the colonial population. Today over 2,000 members of northeastern tribes reside in New Hampshire.

After 1638 the lower falls of the Squamscott River were harnessed for a gristmill and soon rocky ledges upon the freshwater

Exeter River and the falls were peppered with water-driven industries: sawmills, gristmills, mills for pressing linseed oil from flax seed, a fulling mill for napping woolen cloth, a carding mill, a snuff mill, an iron slitting mill, starch mills, paper mills, chocolate mills—even New Hampshire's first gunpowder factory. Exeter's most memorable mill, the Exeter Manufacturing Company (its brick buildings still a prominent part of the river's northern banks), was incorporated in 1827 for the production of cotton cloth. By the early 1880s these mills contained 20,000 spindles and 452 looms and produced four million yards of cloth annually.

Before the railroad arrived in 1840, tradesfolk relied on the river's currents to bring in their merchandise and take out locally manufactured products. Local physician and historian William Gilman Perry reminisced about the shipping process of the 1830s: "The merchants went to Boston in the spring and fall and bought goods to last them through the following months. They spent two or three days in selecting their stock, shipping it to Portsmouth to be reloaded on Captain Furnald's packet for Exeter. Quite a time it took to get the goods here, and a lively day it was, and very interesting for us boys, when the packet discharged her cargo."

The wide tide-washed basin below the lower falls held the turn-around for seagoing vessels to and from Exeter. Along the shoreline, now Swasey Parkway, stood the wharves and docks where ships as large as five hundred tons were built; as many as twenty-two in a single season. Eighteenth-century ships built in Exeter and Newfields carried tons of wood products south to Virginia, to the West Indies, and across the Atlantic, bringing back whale oil, rum, sugar, molasses,

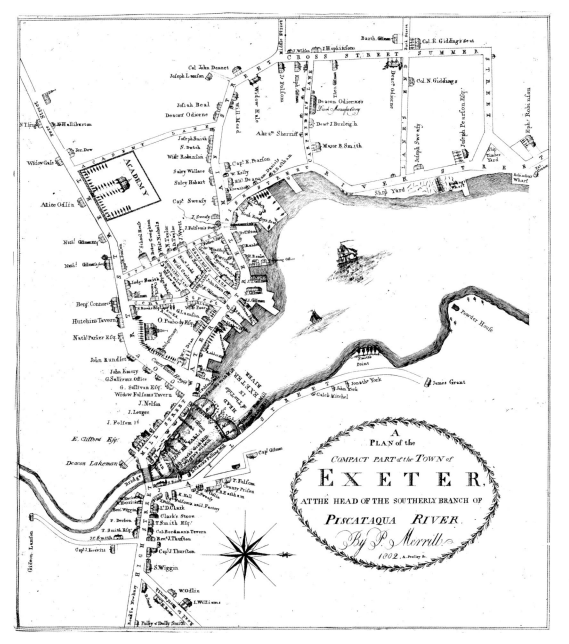

A PLAN of the

COMPACT PART of the TOWN of

EXETER,

AT THE HEAD OF THE SOUTHERLY BRANCH OF

PISCATAQUA RIVER.

By P. Merrill

1802.

cloth, and manufactured goods. Barges continued to carry bulk cargoes, especially bricks and coal, in and out of Exeter until the 1930s. So what happened to the seaport?

In the mid-1600s when early colonists established their farms and homesteads along the waterways off Great Bay, the only way to cross the Squamscott River at Newfields was by fording at low tide, or by ferry. By 1746 a "permanent and substantial" bridge across the river between Stratham and southern Newmarket (now Newfields) was proposed. Hearings and petitions in favor of a permanent crossing ensued from area residents. At a meeting of the "freeholders & inhabitants" of Exeter (upriver), however, held at the town house on January 19, 1747, a new group of petitioners passionately objected to the bridge:

"For that the building of such a bridge would in Great measure Stop the Course of the Fish Especially the Bass which Providence hitherto greatly supplyd us with great Quantitys of to the Support of our Selves and Towns above us, and many Poor Familys if the Course of the Fish be Stopped will Likely thereby to be Great Sufferers...For that whereas the said river having been Free Ever since the settling of Exeter...For the passing and repassing of Vessels from hence to Portsmouth & Boston and other Ports, and there being Generally water sufficient for...Any vessel of one hundred Tons Loaden whereby this Town as well as other Towns above it have reaped great

A Plan of the Compact Part of the Town of Exeter at the head of the southerly branch of Piscataqua River. *Phineas Merrill, 1802. Reprinted from the original plate by the Exeter Historical Society.*

Squamscott River looking towards Fort Rock Farm, the Swasey Homestead, circa 1900. This photograph was made prior to the construction of Swasey Parkway. The wharves and crane were vestiges of Exeter's days as an active port and shipbuilding town. Courtesy of the Exeter Historical Society.

the Narrow Passage of Thirty foot. For the Straitening of the river must of Consequence Cause the Current to run very swift and Rapid and thereby Greatly Endanger the Lives of the People as well as the Loss of their Vessels Lumber and Gundelows."

Exeter won that round. But about thirty years later a wooden lift toll bridge was finally completed and vessels could pass through the manually operated opening. By 1792 each person was charged two cents to cross the bridge while a person with a horse paid six cents. The bridge was rebuilt in 1806 and again in 1838. Exeter merchants, such as Henry W. Anderson who owned the Exeter Coal Company, relied on the river. Five schooners in Anderson's coal fleet shipped cargo up and down stream. On weekends, sightseers and townsfolk headed downstream on his "well-scrubbed coal schooners" and in Capt. George W. Furnald's gundalow, *Alice*. The return trip to Exeter was on Trefethen's barge until street-cars were brought to town in the 1890s.

On a rainy day in 1902, the barge *Merrill* was launched onto the Squamscott River. Henry W. Anderson, coal merchant and barge owner, named the vessel after his five-year-old son. Designed to carry freight, the *Merrill* made its first trip to Boston on June 25 that year with sixty five cords of wood and about 8,000 feet of elm planks to be used for horse stalls. She was the last vessel launched in Exeter.

Silting became an obstacle to efficient vessel traffic in the tidal river, and dredging took place in 1880, 1900, 1911, and 1930. One of the state's few oxbows, visible from NH Route 101, was cut through in 1880 to create a straight channel for shipping. During subsequent dredging of the river, the oxbow was filled with river mud and sludge.

A new steel bridge with swinging span replaced the original eighteenth century wooden bridge by 1926. Then came time for a bridge

advantages By means of Transporting their Lumber and by having return'd to them by the same Vessels The Provisions and Necessaries for the Support of Life & For Commerce and Trade with Each other; Which the building of aforesaid bridge would greatly hurt if not Totally Stop, & also Prevent Carrying on the building of vessels in the Town of Exeter which they have as Just a right to do as any other Towns in the Province…For that the Free use and Privelege of That river to the head thereof was the Principal reason and cause of Peoples settling so far into the Country and Defending their Settlements in such Dangerous & Difficult times as have been since the Settlement of the Same. . . .For that the building the aforesaid Bridge would be a great Impediment to the conveying Down to Portsmouth the Mast Trees which are Yearly Procured in & brought to the Town of Exeter for his Majestys use, and would make it very dangerous to pass with Vesells rafts & Gundelows in

The tug Iva *towing the two-masted schooner* Ada J. Campbell *from Great Bay to Exeter, circa 1900. Courtesy of the Exeter Historical Society.*

over Great Bay between Newington and Dover. The *Exeter News-Letter* in a May 5, 1933 editorial decried:

"Shipbuilding that was once the glory of the Squamscott can never come again. At Newmarket, Durham, Greenland, Newfields and Exeter, in times past, hundreds of vessels were built and launched and sent down the river to the sea. The industry can never be revived, for the new steel bridge that is to span Great Bay shuts off all passage to the Ocean. There is to be no draw in the new bridge, so the towns named might as well be located on Mud Creek. They are to be forever barred from access to the ocean. This looks like cunning work, for we are sure the great outlay for this bridge would never have been authorized had this fact been known. The matter calls for investigation…Citizens of Exeter, Newmarket, Newfields and Durham should attend the public hearing before the War Department engineers, to be held at the Council

Chamber, City Hall, Portsmouth on May 8…and protest against losing river rights of their towns that have been maintained for three hundred years. We believe a great wrong has been perpetrated in the attempt to build this bridge as a permanent obstacle to navigation. The government has spent thousands of dollars to make the Squamscott navigable, and opened great possibilities for Exeter, which someday will be of greatest value."

The frustrated communities, tied together by their rivers, gained only ten feet additional clearance over the channel in the new General Sullivan Bridge over Great Bay. "The whole matter of this new bridge has been a high-handed affair," decried the *Exeter News-Letter* again on May 19, 1933, "and the *News-Letter* has no hesitation in saying that, considered in all aspects, a more iniquitous measure was never enacted by the New Hampshire legislature." Their complaints were for naught.

After the Depression, bridge rules on the Squamscott River changed to reflect the dwindling river traffic. Freight and cargo once carried by river vessels switched to trucks. As early as 1935 the swing bridge was operated by a bridge tender who needed nine hours' notice to have the bridge opened for a vessel. In 1954 the Boston & Maine railroad bridge, upstream towards Exeter, was changed from a swing span to a low fixed span. At that point, Exeter was blocked off from the sea, and river traffic could only move between the railroad bridge and Great Bay. By the next year the swinging mechanism on the Stratham/Newfields Bridge carrying NH Route 108 was welded shut. Automobiles reigned, and few drivers missed the old watery ways. Exeter's days as a seaport were over. –CWA

Sources: James Hill Fitts, *History of Newfields, New Hampshire, 1638-1911,* ed., N. F. Carter (Concord, NH: Rumford Press, 1912); Charles B. Nelson, *The History of Stratham, New Hampshire, 1631-1900* (Somersworth, NH: New Hampshire Publishing Co., 1965); Olive Tardiff, *The Exeter-Squamscott: River of Many Uses* (Rye, NH: CGC, 1986).

American Independence Museum

Located twenty-five miles upstream from Portsmouth Harbor, the inland seaport of Exeter long relied on shipbuilding and maritime trade. Exeter historian Charles Bell noted that as early as 1651 Edward Gilman "had upon the stocks a vessel of about 50 tons burden." Two hundred and fifty years of shipbuilding in Exeter ended in 1902. Although Swasey Parkway has replaced the town's old wharves and shipyards, the homes and stores of many merchants and captains remain. Some, such as the Ladd-Gilman House and the Folsom Tavern (which together are now known as the American Independence Museum) provide a direct link between visitors and the Piscataqua's maritime past.

Ladd-Gilman House of the American Independence Museum, Exeter, New Hampshire. Photograph by Carol W. Aten, 1999. Courtesy of American Independence Museum.

When the Ladd-Gilman House was first built in the 1720s, the view from its hilltop perch was that of a small, bustling waterfront clustered with wharves, clapboard-sided shops and houses, and in-town plots of land with the odd small barn and a cow or two. Exeter, already nearly a century old, had over one thousand residents participating in a sophisticated and integrated economy dependent on maritime commerce. Shipbuilding, milling, leather tanning, iron working and silversmithing were all part of that economy, as was the production of clay pots and clothing. After Daniel Gilman purchased the house in 1752 from Nathaniel Ladd, he "modernized" it. Gilman's son Nicholas, a shipbuilder and merchant who owned a wharf on the Squamscott River, and who played a key role in the political and economic growth of Exeter, moved in.

The American Revolution destroyed many mercantile families throughout the colonies, but the Gilmans in Exeter were able to weather the storm. They consolidated both their financial clout and political power in the early years of the new nation. Nicholas Gilman's eldest son, John Taylor Gilman, inherited the house in 1783, along with two warehouses and the wharf. He prospered in the molasses trade, and later served as state treasurer of New Hampshire, then governor for fourteen discontinuous years. Throughout his career he was centrally involved in Piscataqua shipping and banking, which were often linked. Gilman partially financed construction of the privateering brigantine *General Sullivan* in 1778. He owned shares in the schooner *Adventure*, and was part owner along with Gilman Leavitt and Daniel Conner of the *Hampshire*, built in 1801 by Joseph Swasey. A Federalist merchant, Gilman believed that both the prosperity of Exeter and the stability of the new American republic depended upon profitable maritime commerce.

His younger brothers Nicholas, Nathaniel, and Daniel also invested in shipbuilding and international trade. Nicholas had an interest in the *Frances*, a 259-ton ship built in 1803 by Daniel Conner. Nicholas and Daniel owned in part the 331-ton *Roxana*, built in Exeter in1806 by John Page. Daniel Gilman spent much of his time at sea, handling the family business in trade.

The Gilman family home, still with its view to the water, and the nearby Folsom Tavern (c. 1775), which served captains and townsfolk during Exeter's heyday as a port, preserve and interpret part of the Piscataqua's maritime past. Visitors to the American Independence Museum can savor exquisite domestic architecture and material

Postcard of the Ladd-Gilman House, circa 1910. Private Collection.

objects from the era in which Exeter was a seaport, and in which the Piscataqua's wealthiest and most politically powerful families followed the sea. –CWA

Sources: Charles H. Bell, *History of the Town of Exeter* (Bowie, MD: Heritage Books, 1979[1888]); Ray Brighton, *Port of Portsmouth Ships and the Cotton Trade 1783-1829* (Portsmouth, NH: Peter E. Randall, 1986); William G. Saltonstall, *Ports of Piscataqua* (Cambridge, MA: Harvard University Press, 1941).

EELS AND EELING

FISHING FOR EELS DURING THE 1860S AND 1870S was part of many local farm families' subsistence strategy. Born to one such family in 1855, Francis Drew Winkley grew up in Barrington along the shores of the Isinglass River. He would later reminisce that his father preserved "several small barrels" of eels each year. A tributary of the Piscataqua, the Isinglass flows from Bow Lake in Center Strafford through Barrington and Dover, where it joins the Cocheco River. A small dam and millpond that powered a sawmill, gristmill, and fulling mill abutted the family farm. The Winkleys caught eels in several ways, but when they wanted a real haul, they set an eel pot downstream of the sluice-gate in the dam, which they opened after dark. Often, Francis remembered, they successfully trapped "a mass of squirming eels." As a boy, it was his job to shift those slippery eels from the trap to wicker baskets.

For centuries people fished for eels throughout the Piscataqua estuary and on all of its tributaries. On Broad Cove during the 1870s and 1880s, eels were caught by the light of pine knot torches or speared through holes in the ice. In 1876, fisherman William Rodman caught two hundred pounds of eels in the Squamscott River in Stratham in just three hours. Eels, locals knew, were a peculiar creature that lived in both fresh and salt water.

The American eel (*Anguilla rostrata*) is a catadromous fish.

Paul Morrisette of Exeter holds up two American eels at Swasey Parkway, February 2000. Morrisette provided eels for the eel and smelt fry at Exeter's Winterfest, 2000. Photograph by Emily Reily, © Seacoast Newspapers, *2000.*

Spending most of its life in fresh or brackish waters where it is known as a "yellow eel," it spawns in the deep sea. Moreover, the sexes remain largely segregated during much of their lives. For the most part, males remain in the estuaries' brackish waters, while females migrate upstream to live in freshwater rivers like the Isinglass, or in lakes and ponds. Their breeding is very mysterious. Once in their lives, during the autumn, a group of sexually mature females (called "silver" eels because their yellowish hue becomes silver on the belly and bronze-black on the back) begin to swim downstream. Entering the estuary, females are joined by males. All then head for the Sargasso Sea, a vast area east of Bermuda, where the ocean is about three miles deep. There they mate and spawn at depths of one thousand feet, and die soon after. Within a few weeks, hundreds of millions of tiny eels rise to the surface to obey an impulse that bids some of them to swim to America, while others—presumably the offspring of European eels that have bred in the same waters—head for Europe. The American eels reach fresh water in a year, while those bound for Europe will travel for up to three years before reaching the estuaries and rivers in which they will live.

The tiny immatures are called "glass" eels because of their transparency, which may protect them against predators during their long journey. Once the eels enter coastal bays and rivers, humans are among those predators. By now cloudy gray and called "elvers," young eels become very valuable from time to time on international food markets. If the elver survives to reach its new home, it will mature into a "yellow" eel and remain that color until its final year of life. Males typically reach sexual maturity after three years; females are four to seven years old when they turn silver and strike out for the Sargasso Sea. Considered a delicacy in Europe and Japan, elvers are caught in a fyke net, a long bag net held open by a series of hoops and placed in a narrow tidal stream. Today, a good market price may be $300 per pound or more. That pound consists of thousands of elvers that must be collected at the right tidal moment (even if inconveniently at two o'clock in the morning), and then kept alive until sold. If the price drops to $100 per pound, fishermen will not bother to catch them. New Hampshire banned elver fishing in 1978, but as of 2001, it is still legal in Maine.

Most Americans today shy away from eating eels, but to early English colonists in the Piscataqua, eels were familiar and comforting, much more desirable than that unfamiliar, menacing creature, the lobster. In 1634 William Wood, an early promoter of settlement in New England, wrote: "There be a great store of saltwater eels, especially in places where grass [eelgrass] grows. To take these there be certain eel pots made of osier [strips of wood], which must be baited with a piece of lobster, into which the eels entering cannot return back again….These eels be not of so luscious a taste as they be in England, neither are they so aguish [trembling], but are both wholesome for the body and delightful for the taste."

A few Great Bay-area fishermen still trap eels in the warm months, primarily for use as striped bass bait. In the winter, fishermen with spears seek eels to eat. As the first ice forms along river banks, eels "go into the mud" in the eelgrass beds, but are not truly hibernating. At half-tides they raise their heads clear of the bottom and feed on worms, clams, and any small fish within reach. Nevertheless, they are sedentary and often bunched together. Under these conditions, a man may begin spearing eels from a boat in early December, switching to spearing through holes in the ice as the rivers freeze solid. The shaft of an eel spear can be twelve, sixteen, or twenty feet in length. Made to order by blacksmiths, spear heads exist in a variety of configurations; often there is a flat spatula-shaped center prong with two, three, or four light tines on each side of it. The light tines might be round, square, or flattened, but regardless of shape, each has a barb on its inner side.

Today eel spears are more likely to be found hung on a wall than at the business end of a shaft. But there are still some long-time eelers like Paul Morrisette of Exeter, who learned the secrets of spearing eels from his dad a half-century ago. "We lived on eels in the winter," Morrisette recollected in an interview in 2000. "You have to know the right spots. You probe three or four inches into the mud, holding the tines broadside to the current. If you hit something wrong, like a limb or stump, you move. When you feel something like rubber, you push. In a couple of good spots you can get twenty-five, thirty-five, even forty pounds in two or three hours. Now it seems to be a dying art but I don't know why—everytime you go you'll get eels."

Spears and eel pots were not the only methods used in the Piscataqua region for hunting eels. Bobbing was a common method that is now obsolete. The Winkleys bobbed for eels on the Isinglass River at the time of the Civil War. Old timer Ken Mathes remembered bobbing on boyhood visits to Durham in the 1920s. "You thread earthworms onto a length of coarse twine and then roll it into a ball about four inches across, tucking the loose end into the ball, or bob," according to Mathes. "You tied a line to the bob and dropped it overboard, letting it sit on the bottom for a bit. The eels' teeth would catch in the twine and you could haul in several at a time. You had to be careful not to let them touch the side of the boat or they'd let go. If you swung them aboard correctly they would spring loose of the bob when their tails touched the boat bottom. You could get a boatload in an hour."

Eels look like snakes, and are covered with mucous. Thus the expression, "slippery as an eel." Today most eel aficionados use paper towels to pick up eels, but old-timers had their own methods. "Use your first three fingers," says Ken Mathes. "Raise the middle finger up, slide the eel onto the tops of the first and third finger, positioning them on the eel's 'neck' just behind his head, then clamp down that

One of Paul Morrisette's old eel spears. Photograph by Michael Gowell, 2002. Courtesy of the photographer.

Eels are still found on occasion in local fish markets, particularly from Thanksgiving to Christmas, but most go to ethnic markets in urban areas for old-world celebrations. The price frequently exceeds that of haddock, a prized food fish. Locally, eels are often smoked after soaking in a brown sugar-lemon juice brine, though many people favor pan-frying or deep-frying. The eel is cut into chunks, sometimes soaked or parboiled, often breaded or battered, and finally fried. Most people brave enough to try eel find it a wonderfully sweet, light flesh. An opportunity to taste two traditional winter fish comes early each February during Exeter's "Winterfest." The town Fire Department sponsors an "Eel and Smelt Fry" (with chicken, chowder, and burgers available for the faint-hearted). –MG

middle finger. He can't move. Slap the tail against a rock, slit the throat, break the backbone at the neck, and strip the skin down. We dried the skins in the barn and used them for horsewhips, to tie up boats, and to tie up the tops of burlap bags." Eels were once part of everyday life in the Piscataqua region, a ubiquitous source of food, cash, and horsewhips.

Sources: Francis Drew Winkley, *A Yankee's Soliloquy* (Madison, WI: Democrat Printing Company, 1940); Clyde L. MacKenzie, Jr., "The Eel Fishery of Martha's Vineyard," *Dukes County Intelligencer* (Edgartown, MA; February, 1995); Interviews with Paul Morrisette, Exeter, January 2001; Ken Mathes, Schenectady, NY, January 2001; Doug Grant, New Hampshire Fish and Game, December 2000.

EXETER'S ALEWIVES

THE WORD ALEWIFE (*Alosa pseudoharengus*) may be a corruption of the seventeenth-century *aloofe*, thought by some to be a Native American name translated as "bony fish." The fish was an important source of food and bait to the Wampanoag and Squamscott Indians who inhabited the Piscataqua thousands of years ago, as it was to early colonists who settled Exeter in the 1630s. Closely related to herring, the alewife is also known as branch, blear-eyed, big-eyed, wall-eyed, freshwater, glut, gray, or spring herring; golden or green shad; the bang, ellwife, gaspereau, grayback, kiak, kiack, kyak, mulhaden, racer, sawbelly, seth, skipjack, and spreau. Alewives, who eat tiny zooplankton, are in turn consumed by striped and smallmouth bass, salmonids, eels, perch, bluefish, weakfish, terns, eagles, ospreys, great blue herons, and gulls.

Longer than people have lived along the banks of the Squamscott River, alewives have run its waters, headed upstream each spring during the vernal equinox when daylight and darkness are evenly split. Anadromous fish, they fulfill their ancient migration ritual, leaving the salt waters of the ocean and bay to spawn upstream of the falls in the fresh water of the Exeter River. Male alewives first enter the river during daylight hours. Females spawn at night, laying as many as 200,000 eggs, only three of which might survive. After spawning, many alewives die. Those that live return to the ocean within a few days. The eggs hatch and the young remain in the fresh water until they are up to six inches long; in late summer or autumn they wind back over the falls and spill into the Squamscott River, riding the tide to the Atlantic Ocean, where they will spend the majority of their adult life. At three to five years old, when approximately a foot in length, spawners return to the rivers of their birth to start the cycle over again. Alewives spawn in rivers as far north as Newfoundland and as far south as the Carolinas; their numbers plummeted in the twentieth century, however, as did the numbers of rivers to which they successfully returned.

Measuring the spring alewives during their annual migration upriver, May 2001. Photograph by Carol Walker Aten. Courtesy of the photographer.

Historically, the alewives' journey has been far from easy. As early as 1640, the town of Exeter ordered that "all creeks are free; only he that makes a weir therein is to have in the first place the benefit of it in fishing time; and so others may set a weir either above or below, and enjoy the same liberty." The weir, an elegant array of several hundred hardwood stakes, stretches partially across the river as a fence, herding smelt, alewives, and other unsuspecting fish into its trap. Fish swim along the weir's nets, which extend from the riverbed to the water's surface, until caught in its terminal pocket. Thousands of years ago, native inhabitants trapped fish in weirs on New Hampshire's tidal rivers in similar fashion.

Within the first decade of European settlement on the falls of the Exeter River, mills were built to harness waterpower. Dams dotted the rocky outcrops of the river, shaping the waterflow to human needs, but inhibiting the seasonal springtime passage of many fish. By 1888, Charles H. Bell noted in his *History of the Town of Exeter, New Hampshire*, that "the salmon, for the excellent reason that they can no longer pass the dams to breed their young in the fresh water above, have long deserted the Squamscot [*sic*]; but the alewives still frequent the river, though probably not in such profusion as formerly."

As the nation industrialized, alewives faced more than physical obstacles. Mills, changing from water-driven power to coal-powered steam, escalated industrial production. Pollution from oil and chemicals increased as well. Yet fishing remained a seasonal occupation for many townsfolk, even during the new era of industrialization. Although not as abundant as before industrialization, the fish still came. S. Roswell Peavey was among the best-known fisherman in the area at the end of the nineteenth century. According to Nancy C. Merrill, "In early April several tons of salt were stored in [Peavey's] fish house for the coming alewife catch. The fish were packed in barrels and…taken downriver for sale in Boston, New York, or the West Indies. In 1895, Mr. Peavey formed a fisheries partnership with John Brewster of Stratham. When the alewife season was at its height, the partners caught seventy bushels or more at a single tide, using as many as six weirs."

Concern over degradation of water quality in the Exeter and Squamscott rivers grew through the end of the nineteenth century. Exeter's increasing population, coupled with ancient plumbing systems that emptied straight into the rivers, meant escalating human pollution. The editor of the *Exeter News-Letter*, reacting to the noxious quality of the tidal river, called for the appointment of a sewerage committee in 1892. Despite political inaction, the alewife remained a revered river creature—so much so that it became the sole star of Exeter's first town seal, designed by Albert N. Dow, who explained his choice in the March 28, 1930, issue of the *Exeter News-Letter*: "The fish on the seal is the alewife, typifying one of the town's most profitable natural resources. The alewife is allied to the herring

Gillnetting alewives on the Squamscott River for use as lobster bait. Undated photograph from the Exeter News-Letter. *Courtesy of the Exeter Historical Society.*

and the shad, and the latter has no bones on the former. In Exeter's early days the alewife came up river in schools of countless numbers. It was caught in weirs and provided fertilizer for the cultivated lands of the new town, after furnishing all that could be utilized for home consumption. Salmon and bass were also plentiful in the Squamscott, but owing to the damming of the Fresh [Exeter] River, these fish come up no longer, but the alewife still makes its annual appearance in great numbers."

Sentimental regard for Exeter's favorite fish, however, was insufficient to galvanize water cleanup. Attempts to pass town warrants for new sewage treatment facilities were defeated in 1933, 1954, and again in 1959. A mandate from the state in 1961 finally forced Exeter to confront its sewer problem. Although scheduled to take two years, the cleanup actually spanned a decade; in 1965 the sewer lagoons were completed, and throughout the 1970s pollution in the river decreased, allowing new opportunities for recreational boating and fishing. The "new" sewage treatment plant was upgraded in 1990, and wastewater treatment projects no longer suffer at the mercy of voters—water quality is now a preventative initiative and budgeted annually. Good water quality must be maintained in the Exeter River, as it is the primary source of municipal water supply for the town. Meanwhile, the last working mill, the Exeter Manufacturing Company, ceased operations in 1981 and the historic brick structure was converted to fish-friendly residences. Yet according to the New Hampshire Fish and Game Department, alewife numbers remained extraordinarily low during the 1990s. Estimates suggest that only *hundreds* of alewives were ascending the fish ladders in Exeter, compared to tens of thousands on the Cocheco, Oyster, and Lamprey Rivers.

Fishermen, like fish, continued to follow ancient ways even though times had changed. As late as the 1970s and 1980s, lobstermen caught alewives using nets from String Bridge, filling fifty-five-gallon drums with the fish. They used alewives as lobster bait, but today most commercial fishermen buy their bait wholesale. The marked decrease in Exeter's alewife population noted in the late 1980s and early 1990s has begun to reverse, although the resurgence of striped bass means alewives have more predators with which to contend.

The restoration of several area fish ladders, including the Great Dam in downtown Exeter, allows more alewives access to their traditional spawning habitat. The Great Dam fish ladder, first constructed in the 1960s, was poorly designed: some fish species could pass through, but alewives had problems finding the entrance. Modifications over the past few years have increased the ladder's effectiveness. A permanent fish trap has been installed at the top, and the fish are counted electronically and monitored daily during the spring, eliminating the need for volunteers to count the fish manually.

In the year 2000, tens of thousands of alewives were counted below the dam, and up to two thousand of them were making it up over the falls, up from five hundred only a few years earlier. The shad count in Exeter has increased from only fifty or so to over two hundred and fifty, and fish populations traversing the ladder are expected to increase. The ongoing anadromous fish restoration effort for alewives, shad, and blueback herring will be supported by the fish ladders at Pickpocket Dam and Great Dam, permanently allowing these fish to reach upstream spawning and nursery habitats in the Exeter River. With luck, and barring catastrophe elsewhere, the alewives will continue along their route, which, as John Hay once wrote, "is being followed out with primal grace and power." –CWA

Sources: Charles H. Bell, *History of the Town of Exeter* (Bowie, MD: Heritage Books, 1979[1888]); John Hay, *The Run* (New York: W.W. Norton & Co., 1979); Nancy C. Merrill, *Exeter New Hampshire 1888-1988* (Exeter, NH: Peter E. Randall, 1988); Interview with George Olson, Town Manager of Exeter, November 2000; and Doug Grout, Marine Biologist, New Hampshire Fish and Game, November 2000.

NEWMARKET

DEFINING COMMUNITY

NEWMARKET IS A SMALL TOWN with a dramatic skyline. The giant brick and granite mill buildings that sprawl along the banks of the Lamprey River cast deep shadows across Main Street. Long rows of tall mill windows catch the late afternoon light. Inside, where half the population of Newmarket once labored to the pounding of the looms, residents of high-ceilinged condos now enjoy sweeping views of the river. Today, the town's mill workers are gone. The looms are silent. But the buildings themselves remain, testament to the hard-working history of this little town.

Newmarket's earliest English settlers built sawmills along the river's edge during the seventeenth century. A carding and fulling mill went up on the west bank during the eighteenth century. When the Newmarket Manufacturing Company came to town in 1823, funded by wealthy shipping merchants from Salem, Massachusetts, they brought with them an era of building and industry that established an international reputation for Newmarket.

Mills built of local granite on Lamprey River, Newmarket, New Hampshire. Photograph by Ralph Morang, 1995. Courtesy of the Photographer.

Over the years, the company built eight mill buildings, including three constructed from massive blocks of granite quarried from Newmarket's Lubberland Neck. The river was busy during these years. Flat-bottomed gundalows and, later, three-masted schooners ferried raw materials to the mills, arriving with the tide then departing laden with yards and yards of fabric. Over the years, Newmarket became one of the world's biggest producers of celanese, the shiny cloth used to line caskets.

With the textile mills came an influx of new residents: Yankee farm girls seeking a new, independent life and better wages; French Canadians who boarded the train, bringing with them their families and all their possessions; and, at the turn of the century, Eastern Europeans. A thriving Polish community soon developed, as well as a smattering of Russian, Italian, German, and Irish immigrants. Each new group brought their food, their music, and their traditions. And nearly all of them worked in the mills. The towering buildings on Newmarket's riverbanks shaped a quintessential American melting pot. No matter what their ethnic background, the residents of Newmarket were united in at least some way by their labor. Despite inevitable differences, Newmarket became a community defined by hard work, production, and useful lives.

Things changed in the early 1930s. Relations between union workers and mill managers deteriorated into bitter disputes, and the Newmarket Manufacturing Company moved south. Almost overnight, sixteen hundred jobs vanished from a town of about three thousand residents. The townspeople remained deeply divided; fights broke out in the bars and on the streets. And for the first time in a century, the massive mill buildings stood empty. The silence was deafening.

When the shoe industry arrived later in the 1930s, jobs began to return. There was even a small revival of the textile industry in one building where necktie cloth was woven. Then, in 1951, the Macallen Company moved its Boston operation to Newmarket, and suddenly the town was on the map again. One of the world's largest importers of raw mica, mostly from India, Macallen brought three hundred new jobs to Newmarket.

For the next three decades, employees in the brick and stone mills along the Lamprey transformed two million tons of mica chips a year into insulating material used in everything from electrical railway joints to toasters and microwave ovens. Like the cloth woven by an earlier generation, mica products manufactured in Newmarket's mill were shipped all over the world.

Today, evidence of Newmarket's industrious, multicultural heritage remains. The phone book offers a tongue-twisting mix of French Canadian and Polish names. Marelli's Fruit & Real Estate (est. 1909) remains a favorite landmark. Polish Babka bread is still sold at Easter. Recent town elections have added names like Caprioli, Adamczyk, and Pasquale to a roster that once included mostly old Yankee standards like Smart, Pickering, and Hamel. In the last decade, an influx of Laotian residents escaping political unrest in their native country has added another flavor to the cultural blend.

The town also attracts an eclectic mix of lifestyles and professions—college students and tradesmen, high-tech employees and

The Lamprey River at Newmarket Mills, circa 1900, during the heyday of the Newmarket Manufacturing Company. Coal for the mills, delivered up river by schooner, is piled on the wharf in the background. The overhanging warehouse and the derrick at the far left date from an earlier era. This summer outing featured Harry Varney, standing in the bow of his 16-horsepower naptha launch, and Charles Chipman, sitting in the stern of the other boat. Courtesy of the Newmarket Historical Society.

musicians, entrepreneurs and artists, young families and retired empty nesters. Newmarket has a sizable percentage of renters and low-income residents. It also has luxurious, waterfront homes. People who move here are drawn to, among other things, Newmarket's small-town character, its natural beauty, and its walkable downtown—a cluster of historic brick and clapboard buildings anchored by the mills themselves.

The mill whistle no longer blows at the end of each shift in Newmarket, and fewer and fewer people who grow up here stay to raise a family. Like all small towns, Newmarket has become bigger and busier. Community building is not as straightforward as it was a century ago when it was the inevitable result of working together on the weave room floor.

One thing hasn't changed, though. Newmarket residents still seek community and crave a sense of belonging. And they find it just as past residents did: by working shoulder-to-shoulder with friends and neighbors. These days the work takes place on committees, on baseball field, and at town council meetings. It can be found in volunteer beautification efforts, benefit fundraisers, and events like Olde Home Weekend and the newer Heritage Festival, which celebrates Newmarket's richly textured past with music, food, and storytelling.

And then there's downtown Newmarket itself, where people stand in line at the post office, eat breakfast at Joyce's Kitchen, chat with a neighbor on the sidewalk in front of Marelli's, and sip coffee at the Big Bean. The village area's eateries and structures are a bit worn around the edges, and businesses sometimes struggle to survive, but Newmarket is a town where you can still make your way on foot, among historic buildings that once provided goods and services to the mill workers themselves.

In the mid 1990s, the town's profile changed dramatically. A giant new cinderblock gas station built on the outskirts of the village was followed by a convenience store, a drugstore, and a fast-food restaurant. Suddenly, the commercial development that drains the life from town centers across America had arrived in Newmarket. It threatened to obliterate the town's character as quickly as the glare above the new gas pumps erased the stars. A citizen group formed in response, in part because residents cherished the past as much as they cared about the future. Their efforts to establish local guidelines for commercial development began because people valued what Newmarket is—and they feared what it might become.

Passion for the historic village gradually grew into a movement to revitalize citizen participation in town politics. Now a new generation of residents, people with little direct connection to Newmarket's past, has become committed to the town and its future. The issues, from taxes and development to education and the environment, are widely discussed and debated. Local politics are often heated. Voter turnout is gradually increasing, though broader participation in elections and other town events remains an ongoing goal.

Controversial commercial development comes to Newmarket in the 1990s. Photograph by Peter E. Randall, 2001. Courtesy of the photographer.

Above it all stand the buildings on the Lamprey River that first shaped this town, the mills where so many residents worked so hard. Their presence announces a pride in the past and a vision for the future. The same mills that once melded people of many backgrounds into a new community stand today as tangible reminders that, by working together, it becomes possible to achieve a sense of community, a place of belonging. –SC

With appreciation to Forbes Getchell, Sylvia Fitts Getchell, Priscilla Schanda, and Richard Schanda for sharing their knowledge of Newmarket history and their memories of life in this mill town on the river.

Sources: Nellie Palmer George, *Old Newmarket, New Hampshire; Historical Sketches* (Exeter, NH, The News-Letter Press, 1932); Sylvia Fitts Getchell, *Lamprey River Village: The Early Years* (Newmarket, NH: Newmarket Press, 1976); Sylvia Fitts Getchell, *The Tide Turns on the Lamprey: Vignettes In The Life of a River* (Newmarket, NH, 1984).

Sneak Floats and Market Hunting

DUCK HUNTING BOATS ARE AMONG THE MOST RADICAL small watercraft in the world. They are distinctive to highly specialized uses under very particular conditions. Like many small craft, their geographical origins are contained in their names—the Merrymeeting Bay Boat, the Plum Island Needlenose, the Hudson River Creeper, and the Barnegat Bay Sneakbox.

The Great Bay Sneak Float—usually just called a float by its owner—was coastal New Hampshire's waterfowling boat. It often carried an inside weight on a track so that when the water was calm the weight could be slid forward, submerging the narrow bow. "Grassed" with salt marsh hay in the early season or painted white in winter, it looked like insignificant flotsam rather than a boat. The float was "sculled"—propelled by a single bent oar worked through a hole in the stern by a hunter who lay in loose hay on the bottom of the float with only his head propped up for visibility. Done correctly, with consideration of the current, wind, sun (ideally all at the hunter's back), and

A sneak float photographed at Ducker's Day at Wagon Hill Farm in Durham, New Hampshire, circa 1994. Courtesy of Michael Gowell.

tide (low, when the birds are feeding, not high when they are heads-up and alert), the hunter could sneak up to a raft of dozens, even hundreds, of birds. The gunner then "flat-shot" the flock on the water, trying to kill a maximum number of birds without giving a thought to the niceties of sportsmanship or the art of wingshooting.

Punt guns were the firearms of choice for this style of hunting, usually single-shot and muzzle-loading. Hunters compensated for these limitations by turning the guns into virtual cannons, bored in very large sizes: eight, six, and four gauges. These guns were too heavy to shoot from the shoulder and so were mounted in frames called "wooden men" or "dead men" that sat in the cockpit of a float.

The four-gauge gun (shown on page 140) is illustrative of the pride of ownership taken in these formidable firearms. It is a double-barreled muzzle-loading gun built in Raymond, New Hampshire, and converted to a breechloader by Kirkwood Gunsmiths of Boston. The native origins of this gun were very unusual in an age when most large-bore guns came from Belgium or England.

The social history of this gun is equally interesting. It was originally owned by the Shute family of Newmarket, who market-hunted the Greenland and Stratham shores and are remembered for shooting swans whenever possible. They sold it to a worker in the Newmarket Mill (either a Weston or a Walcott—opinions vary). The worker's foreman, Herb Brackett, forced the resale of the gun to himself, and then Mr. Gallant, the mill owner, did the same thing to Brackett. It is now in the collection of the Newmarket Historical Society, a gift of Mr. Gallant's son Richard.

Great Bay is a magnet for waterfowl. Large expanses of water offer safety to ducks and geese wary of shoreline predators. The shallow depths and mixture of salt and fresh waters encourage the growth of eelgrass and other aquatic plants. The resultant wealth of waterfowl historically attracted subsistence hunters beginning with Native Americans and succeeded by early European colonists.

Waterfowl shot on Great Bay, March 28, 1912. Courtesy of the Milne Special Collections and Archives Department, University of New Hampshire.

Four-gauge gun with reloadable brass shell, once owned by the Shute family of Newmarket. Originally a muzzle loader, this gun was converted to a breech loader by Kirkwood Gunsmiths, in Boston. Owned by the Newmarket Historical Society. Courtesy of Michael Gowell.

Market hunting is the harvesting of wild protein—fish, birds, or animals—taken as a rural commodity and shipped to urban consumers. Typically, market hunting is a short-lived phenomenon because it quickly exhausts the resource base. This form of hunting must rely on specialized boats, specialized guns, and trains or trucks to quickly ship freshly shot game to an urban market in commercially viable quantities. The time frame can be very short—from a few decades for the American buffalo—to lengthy—a half-dozen centuries for the now-collapsing commercial fisheries of the world.

Market hunting in Great Bay arose during the mid-1800s, coinciding with the rural development of the railroads needed to carry game to city markets. At that time, the game of choice was ducks—highly prized fare for city banquets and hotel dining rooms—but men who relished the outdoor life of market hunting would be quick to turn a hand to tonging oysters or spearing eels if the season dictated. They usually worked regular jobs, particularly if they were married and had a house and family in town, but they spent long periods at their "oyster camps"—simple sheds alongshore.

Some of the most colorful market hunters became legendary: Louis "Loady" Herson of Newmarket, sometimes boat builder and sometimes policeman, who broke a strike at the Newmarket Mill by shooting the organizer; Forest Elmer "Hoddy" Atherton, who hunted grouse as well as ducks, stumping through the woods on one leg and a crutch; "Loady" Roberts, who carelessly jerked his punt gun out of his beached boat and blew his arm off; and Len Hill, "a real outlaw" according to several old gunners, who accepted a paycheck for his work as a game warden while simultaneously being paid by hunters to feed their "tollers"—(highly illegal) live ducks used to lure the wild birds within range. Piscataqua market hunters adopted two tools already traditional in British waterfowling—the specialized duck hunting boat and the long-barreled punt gun, and adapted them for local use. –MG

Sources: Interviews with Richard Atherton, Randy Dow, Bob Brophy, Dorothy Watson, David Watson, Peter Witham, David McConnell, Brad Connor, beginning 1991 and ongoing.

OYSTERING ON THE BAY

IN 1971 AN OLD-TIMER FROM PORTSMOUTH named Richard Pinkham reminisced about tonging from rowboats in the Oyster River, "my favorite spot for oysters." "I been up there when I could get two bushels of oysters half an hour at the outside," he continued, before adding pensively, "Of course, the bay has changed." Pinkham rattled off a list of nefarious influences: automobiles, traffic, and so many people that "they just ruined it up there dumpin' their sewerage and everything into it and polluting it a mile a minute." Then he caught himself with a glimmer of hope. "We're startin' to make a comeback. Goin' to take years, but it's a beginnin.'"

Pinkham had cause for both concern and optimism. During the last two hundred years, oystering in the Great Bay and Piscataqua estuary has been one aspect of local peoples' subsistence strategy, as well as a commercial enterprise and a recreational activity. Oyster populations have fluctuated dramatically, declining from pollution and overharvesting, but sometimes quietly rebounding after being

An oyster from Great Bay harvested by researchers from the University of New Hampshire's Jackson Lab, 1969. Courtesy of Milne Special Collections and Archives Department, University of New Hampshire.

ignored. In 1874, for instance, a U.S. Coast Survey team mapping channels in Great Bay found flourishing oyster beds that were "looked upon almost as an original discovery," even though natives, colonists, and citizens had been gathering oysters off-and-on for centuries.

Today large beds of Eastern oysters exist in Great Bay near Nannie Island and in the upper Piscataqua River. Smaller beds are found in the Bellamy and Oyster Rivers and in Greenland Bay. But most are off-limits. In 1985, 9,000 of the 12,599 acres of shellfish waters in the Great Bay estuary—that's 71 percent—were closed because of bacterial pollution, primarily from human feces. In 2000, 63 percent of New Hampshire's estuarine waters was closed to shellfishing. Over the years, sewage, sawdust, and siltation, as well as overfishing, have reduced oyster populations and kept people from harvesting those oysters that were left. But reopening shellfish beds has been a regulatory priority for a decade, and there is reason to believe that despite growing population pressure, shoreline development, and eelgrass die-off, Great Bay shellfish can rebound. The real cause for optimism is the relatively recent awareness of the importance of estuarine management. Monitoring programs coordinated through the University of New Hampshire's Jackson Estuarine Laboratory allow state regulatory agencies and the Great Bay Estuarine Research Reserve to create management and research priorities. Intelligent stewardship, including better sewage treatment, is necessary. It is the only alternative to decimated shellfish and a diminished estuary.

During the 1870s, Great Bay oysters were almost wiped out. It took only five years—a flash-in-the-pan fishery similar to the sea urchin boom on the Maine coast in the 1990s—when again, lack of regulation allowed catastrophic overfishing. An old Chesapeake oysterman named Albert Tibbetts lived in Newmarket when the Coast Survey team broadcasted its discovery of untapped oyster shoals. He sent to Providence for oyster tongs, and commenced raking commercially. By the next year approximately a dozen boats, each with two or three men, were tonging or raking every day, averaging about five bushels per man. Oyster fever prompted men in Dover to build a schooner in the spring of 1876 destined for Great Bay oystering. With prices good, not even ice slowed the harvest. Oystermen cut long holes in it, and systematically stripped the beds with horse-drawn dredges. Worst of all, they did not throw back the old shells and stones known as "clutch" to which the juveniles clung. Abandoned, the small ones froze to death. The *Exeter News-Letter* ignored those unsustainable practices when, in January of 1876, they commented buoyantly on a newly discovered oyster bed in Stratham between the railroad bridge and the Newmarket bridge. "Bivalves of large size, good flavor and in abundance are being taken."

But by the summer of 1879 only seven or eight men, lucky to take a bushel and a half per day, still raked oysters. By then the state had forbidden ice dredging, and imposed a closed season from June through August. It was too little, too late. Commercial harvesting never rebounded.

Today commercial oystering is forbidden in New Hampshire. The law allows residents (with a license) to take one bushel of unshucked oysters daily, by hand or hand tongs, with a closed season in July and August. Dredging and all forms of oystering through the ice are no longer allowed. With close monitoring and regulation, a sustainable recreational oyster fishery might long endure, and oysters will remain a vital part of the Great Bay ecosystem. –WJB

Sources: John P. Adams, *Drowned Valley: The Piscataqua River Basin* (Hanover, NH: University Press of New England, 1976), pp. 152-156; George Brown Goode, *The Fisheries and Fishery Industries of the United States*, sect. II (Washington, 1887), pp. 106-107; *The Ecology of the Great Bay Estuary, New Hampshire and Maine: An Estuarine Profile and Bibliography*, ed. Frederick T. Short (NOAA-Coastal Ocean Program Publication, 1992), pp. 127-129, 145-159.

THE LAMPREY RIVER

CALLED THE "LAMPREY," "LAMPERELL," "LAMPEREELE," and by other variations on early maps, English settlers named the Lamprey River after a bloodsucking eel. Generations later the circuitous river became compromised by industrialization and development. Today the Lamprey River is designated as a National Wild and Scenic River. A marvelous recreational resource, it is also a rich ecosystem in its own right, still home to sea lampreys and American eels.

The Lamprey River flows south out of the Saddleback Mountains in Northwood, making a great loop around Pawtuckaway Lake before turning northward and eastward to spill into the Great Bay at Newmarket, forty-seven miles from its source. Four minor rivers and smaller tributaries make up the rest of the Lamprey River Watershed, which drains the northwest corridor of the Piscataqua River basin. Stratified drift aquifers of sand and gravel deposited by the last glacier underlie much of the 212 square mile watershed, including the whole length of the river in the town of Raymond.

Excellent fishing attracted Native Americans to its shores at least eight thousand years ago, and long-vanished fishing camps beside the Lamprey's numerous falls still reward diligent searchers with occasional artifacts. The Squamscotts coexisted peacefully in the region with the English from the 1630s until 1672, when they moved en masse to Troy, New York. Bloodshed began a few years later when sixty white settlers were killed along the river during King Philip's War. Indian warriors killed twenty-one more English settlers in raids in 1690, and burned Wadleigh's Mill in 1712. The Pennacook and other Abenaki did not relinquish these lands and waters easily.

Yet fine natural pastures along the Lamprey River's shores lured settlers moving outward from Dover and Exeter, including Darby Field, the first Englishman to climb Mount Washington. Early residents caught alewives, and shipped barrels of salted fish from the Lamprey to Caribbean sugar islands. Timber proved more profitable. Extensive stands of tall white pines attracted the attention of royal mast agents who enforced the King's Broad Arrow policy, and local entrepreneurs, who resented it. During the 1730s rowdies dressed as Indians attacked David Dunbar, the Surveyor of the King's Woods, as he attempted to arrest pine poachers between the Exeter and Lamprey Rivers. Freetown (now Raymond) got its name because the King's agent never came that far upstream.

Mills, more than fishing or lumbering, came to characterize the river. In 1652 Valentine Hill built the first saw mill where Macallen Dam stands today in Newmarket, and Thomas Packer had a mill at the falls bearing his name in the 1660s. The rate of flow over the first falls is greater than that on the Squamscott or Oyster Rivers today: it averages 278 cubic feet per second, making the Lamprey difficult to harness. Mills and bridges in Newmarket washed out periodically. Nevertheless, sawmills and gristmills sprang up on nearly every stretch of the Lamprey's turbulent water during the early 1700s, followed by an iron works, carding and fulling mills, tanneries, and even a factory producing nuts and bolts. Clusters of houses were built around many of the mills, as clear-cut land along the river attracted farmers.

In 1823 Quaker Stephen Hanson bought Ebenezer Smith's sawmill near the foot of the falls in Newmarket. Eventually the Newmarket Manufacturing Company owned most of the mill sites below Pawtuckaway, controlling the flow of water downstream for their three cotton mills, sawmill, machine shop, blacksmith shop, dam, bridges, and canal. Newmarket became a company town and the Lamprey became a company river. This did not preclude other operations upstream. Epping had a brickyard that produced six million bricks a year as late as the 1940s. Small mills in Lee operated into the 1920s, when cheap electricity undercut waterpower, and when cheaper labor in the South lured textile mills away from New England. For almost three centuries, however, local residents harnessed the Lamprey River's moving waters to power machines.

Today, most of the dams have washed out and the millponds silted in. Farms have lain fallow for a few generations and tall trees once again stretch toward midstream. Time has scoured the river clean. In fact, the New Hampshire Fish and Game Commission recently designated the Lamprey the state's "most significant river for all anadromous fish." The river's abundant wildlife includes endangered species such as Blandings and Spotted Turtles, and the Brook Floater Mussel. The attractive scenery features 172 types of wetland and aquatic plants along a watercourse that varies from flat calm to Class III rapids—at least during spring runoff. Canoeing and kayaking along the thirty-six miles from Deerfield to Newmarket are popular in the spring, and the river is stocked with freshwater game fish. Public parks and conservation lands bordering the Lamprey, including Pawtuckaway State Park, attest to citizens' interest in preserving natural space.

In 1990 residents in Durham and Lee who feared that a private hydroelectric company was going to develop Wiswall Dam recommended that the Lamprey River be enrolled in New Hampshire's new State Rivers and Management Program. That led to the creation of the Lamprey River Advisory Committee and the Watershed Association. By 1996 they had arranged for the designation of eleven miles of the Lamprey River—from Lee through the Macallen Dam—as a National Wild and Scenic River. Later another twelve miles through Epping were included. That federal designation is helping to maintain land and water quality in the face of rampant development in southern New Hampshire. Stewardship seems to have prevailed.

But decisions about conservation work both ways. While many Raymond citizens are active in Bear Paw Regional Greenways, which supports private and voluntary conservation, the town welcomed the Wal-Mart Distribution Center, a twenty-seven acre building and fifty-five acre parking lot on a bend in the river. Excavation of sand

Snow on the Lamprey River. Photograph by Karen Alexander, 1994. Courtesy of the photographer.

and gravel reduces groundcover, and may affect water quantity and quality. It is no surprise, then, that a rain-swollen Lamprey inundated the hundred-year flood mark three times between 1995 and 2000. The Lamprey continues to change; what remains clear is that corporate, civic and individual decisions will determine the future character of a river remarkable for its beauty and resilience. –KA

Sources: Sylvia Fitts Getchell, *Lamprey River Village: The Early Years* (Newmarket, NH: Newmarket Press, 1976); Lamprey River Association and the Lamprey River Advisory Committee, *Lamprey River Watershed Guide* (1997); Lamprey River Advisory Committee, *River Story: The Lamprey River through History* [videorecording] (Portsmouth, NH: Ideaworks Productions, 1999).

DEFORESTATION AND SILTATION:
A HISTORICAL AND ECOLOGICAL LOOK

THE PISCATAQUA BASIN IS A STUDY IN MINIATURE of the landscape changes that occurred throughout North America following European colonization. During the four hundred years since trans-Atlantic explorers first mapped the Piscataqua region, its forests, soils, and waterways have been transformed. The environmental consequences of seventeenth and eighteenth century land use practices are still playing out in the contemporary landscape, and are now complicated by nineteenth and twentieth century changes. Soil erosion and silt deposition patterns that normally operate over decades (or even centuries) are closely linked in the Piscataqua to short-term ecological changes such as deforestation. Teasing out connections between human actions and long-term changes in any environmental processes is always challenging, but in the Piscataqua the historical record offers an opportunity to explore some of these links in unusual detail.

The Piscataqua Basin was recognized by Europeans as early as 1603 as a promising source of lumber. By 1650 a rapidly expanding forestry industry included skilled laborers, sawmills, and export facilities. A 1660 map of the region shows fifteen mills of various kinds on the four rivers flowing into Great Bay. By 1700 Portsmouth was a frontier boomtown that turned trees into money.

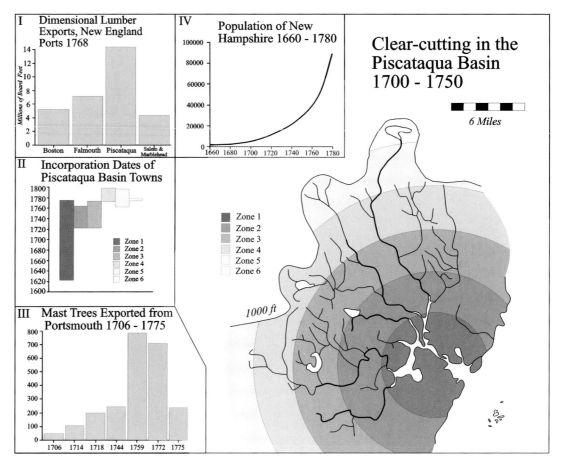

Graphics courtesy of Matthew Bampton

The key forest resource was the white pine, used for masts by the British Navy. The technology of masting had an enduring impact on the ecology and physical geography of the Piscataqua Basin. Significant collateral damage accompanied each pine cut. Felled in winter onto a prepared cushion of brush, the masts were trimmed and then hauled along cleared paths to the nearest waterway. All pines greater than 24 inches in diameter were supposedly reserved for the king. But mast trees claimed by the crown could be sold at higher prices on the open market. White pine made excellent clapboards and planks, and fierce competition existed for large trees. Pine boards wider than 24 inches survive today in roofing, flooring, and cabinetry in many older buildings, indicating that many trees technically reserved for the Royal Navy were illegally used by locals.

One historical map of the Piscataqua region drawn by Navy Board Agent Jonathan Bridger about 1698 illustrates the impact of the mast trade (see page 180). A note in the upper right corner reads "A Large Swamp of White Pines Burnt by the Indians." In a letter Bridger wrote to the New Hampshire General Assembly in 1700, however, he exonerated the "Indians." "I prepared a great many thousand trees in order to make tar for the use of his Majesty, in the river of Piscataqua, particularly on the commons of Dover," wrote Bridger, "…yet some envious, malitious [sic] and unthinking people have felled many of said trees…Such little and litigatious [sic] actions makes me not doubt but the trees that were burnt was by design." Scorched trees were useless as masts but saleable as lumber, so a burnt forest containing regulation-size white pines could legally be harvested and milled. Bridger's map seems to document a woodland rebellion that pitted timber merchants and lumbermen against officers of the crown. The merchants wished to sell timber on the open market. The lumbermen wanted to cut and sell as much as possible. The royal officials were torn between duty to the king and accumulating personal fortunes. All parties competed for the largest trees and those closest to waterways.

The outcome of the conflict was the inevitable clear-cut, a pattern repeated throughout the Americas. By the second half of the eighteenth century all useable pines, and a high percentage of other species, had been removed from the basin. In 1700 the governor of New Hampshire, Lord Bellomont, lamented: "The wast[e]of the woods in New Hampshire has been, and still is so very great, that Mr. Bridger assures me they are forc'd to go 20 miles up into the Country to get a good mast for the use of the Navy." By 1747 another authority wrote: "The mast men are obliged to go a mile or two farther into the country every year, being almost got to the foot of the ridge of mountains."

The map on page 145 outlines the pattern of deforestation. Each zone represents about six years worth of clear-cutting at the conservative rate of one kilometer per year. A core area in zone 1 roughly corresponds to the area depicted in Bridger's map that was bereft of mast pines by 1700. From here, loggers reached the extremity of the basin by about 1750. This corresponds with the complaint in 1747 that the loggers had reached the foothills of the White Mountains (approximately the 1000-foot contour). Other sources support this assessment of deforestation rates. By the end of the period Portsmouth had grown to be the largest shipper of lumber in New England, exporting half of the 28 million board feet (8.5 million board meters) to come out of the region in 1768 (graph I). Incorporation dates for towns in the Piscataqua Basin in the seventeenth and eighteenth centuries roughly match the outward expansion of deforestation (graph II). Graph III shows the trajectory of the mast trade on the basis of British Admiralty records that only note legally exported masts—certainly an underestimate. The rapid and exponential growth of New Hampshire's population from 1650 to 1800 matches the other trends described above (graph IV).

There are no reliable eighteenth century accounts of the impacts of deforestation on sedimentation in the Piscataqua. However, we can reasonably infer the effects of rapid clearing, understory destruction, road building, and forest burning. Similar impacts have been documented at the Hubbard Brook Research Forest in New Hampshire. Plant and animal ecologies change as habitats are destroyed. With deforestation, groundwater levels decline and stream discharges "spike" after each rainfall. Raindrop impact on soil surfaces is more powerful. Faster overland flow caused by the absence of humus and roots and further accelerated along cleared roadways increases soil trapped in those efficient stilling pools. The repeated damming of all Piscataqua tributaries over the last two centuries thus trapped some of the sediment set in motion during the seventeenth and eighteenth centuries. But much of the sediment did pass over the dams and flowed downstream. Today the navigable head of the river is much further downstream than it was during the colonial era when ocean-going ships were launched in Dover, Durham, and South Berwick. Today those rivers are obstructed by silt and accessible only to shallow-draft boats. Despite the high velocity tidal flows for which the river is known, considerable sediment has accumulated in the Great Bay area. This is apparent when marine charts from the 1800s are compared to those of the present.

Rapid landscape changes accompanied colonial settlement in the Piscataqua basin. For four centuries each impact of clear-cutting and erosion followed hard on the heels of the preceding one, so that no single change acted in isolation. Instead, each disruption of the system was transformed by the next change. But evidence visible in accumulated sediment in impoundments and along the courses of smaller channels indicates early and catastrophic deforestation.

The landscape we see in the Piscataqua region today is not same as that seen by its early seventeenth century residents and settlers. In fact, the nature of the forests, the soils, and even the waterways has changed significantly, due in large part to deforestation and resultant siltation. –MB

Sources: Robert G. Albion, *Forests and Sea Power: The Timber Problems of the Royal Navy 1652–1862* (Cambridge, MA: Harvard University Press, 1926); Matthew Bampton, "From Social Conflict to Environmental Change: Colonial Forestry's Impact on New England's Piscataqua Drainage Basin" *Historical Geography* 27:193-211 (1999); William Cronon, *Changes in the Land* (New York: Hill and Wang, 1983).

Arrival of the vessel William Davenport *at Newmarket, New Hampshire, December 1906. With the Lamprey River silted in, it is impossible to imagine such a large schooner arriving in Newmarket today. Courtesy of the Portsmouth Athenaeum.*

erosion. Increased stream discharge and increased soil erosion cause an increase in sedimentation at the channel's end. These effects are exacerbated in the fine-grained, sandy, glacial sediments that are characteristic of New England's coastal plain.

Specific evidence of colonial deforestation, erosion, and siltation is hard to identify, in part because subsequent human changes to the land have been so dramatic. But some evidence remains. Most telling is the sediment in the numerous pools upstream of dams built during the eighteenth, nineteenth, and twentieth centuries. Sediment deposited into the rivers by water running off eroding lands was

DURHAM

OYSTER RIVER

OYSTER RIVER, ONE OF THE FIVE MAJOR TRIBUTARIES to Great Bay and the Piscataqua, originates in the highlands of Barrington, where a few small streams run into tiny Creek Pond, one of the river's sources. It winds through the southern corner of Barrington into Lee, where it joins another branch originating in Madbury, forming part of the Durham/Lee town line, meanwhile augmented by yet another branch running out of Wheelwright Pond in Lee, before swerving east. Picking up speed and volume, and fed by still more tiny tributaries, it cuts across the town of Durham and broadens into Mill Pond, created by a dam that supplements the natural fall line, where Valentine Hill and Thomas Beard built a sawmill in 1649. The gathered fresh waters from dozens of small tributaries now pour over the dam into the tidal estuary that forms the lower two and a half miles of the river, ending at its outlet into Little Bay at Durham Point.

While its main channel, including its brief saltwater climax, measures a mere 7.9 miles according to hydrologists, Oyster River is as historically important as any of the Piscataqua tributaries. Called the Shankhassick by Native Americans, it served as a seasonal campground and source of the shellfish that gave the river its European name. In the 1630s the river was a settlers' route into the northwestern interior of the Great Bay system, and by 1639 the beginnings of a scattered English village was discernible along its lower banks. This was "Oyster River Plantation," legally a part of the Dover settlement but containing residents who briefly bore allegiance instead to John Wheelwright's colony at Exeter. This settlement, strengthened at intervals by a dozen fortified garrison

Old Ffrost store by the dam on Newmarket Road, Durham. This building once housed the post office. Today this site is a park, with no evidence of the structure remaining. Undated photograph. Courtesy of the Milne Special Collections and Archives Department, University of New Hampshire.

houses, was the target of one of the most destructive of all the French and Indian raids during King William's War—the so-called "massacre" of July 18, 1694, during which thirteen houses were burned and ninety-four residents killed or taken prisoner to Canada.

By the time the Oyster River settlement had been accorded the status of a parish with its own ecclesiastical taxing powers in 1716, its main geographic focus had moved upstream to the fall line, at once a source of waterpower and the head of ocean navigation. There a second meetinghouse was built, quickly exceeding in importance the 1655 meetinghouse nearer the river's mouth. A church was organized in 1718, and in 1732 Oyster River Parish was incorporated as the town of Durham.

During the seventeenth and early eighteenth centuries, therefore, the river's early function as a lane for land-seeking settlers was greatly expanded. The settlement spread steadily upstream and as it achieved a measure of maturity and permanence, the river upon which it was built became more than simply a way to travel further inland; it became the settlement's main street. Gradually supplemented by a network of primitive roads, river traffic nevertheless remained for many decades the chief link between the parts of the community. The river was also Durham's highway to the Piscataqua and the sea.

Like all other Piscataqua tributaries, Oyster River's chief commercial importance during the hundred years before the American Revolution was as a conveyor of forest products from the region's wooded interior to Portsmouth for shipment to Europe or the West Indies. Like several of its neighboring towns, Durham still has a "Mast Road," over which ox teams hauled to the river's edge the giant white pines destined to become masts on British warships. There they were rolled into the water and floated downstream. The mast industry was spectacular, but far from the only, or even dominant, part of the lumber trade. Besides the major milling operation at Oyster River falls, there were smaller dams and mills on several of the upstream tributaries and on a few of the creeks feeding the saltwater end of the river as well. Some mills ground flour for the community, but others were sawmills, turning out boards for export as well as for local use. Huge loads of lumber were transported down river by gundalow, and by at least the early nineteenth century, cargos of firewood cut by upstream farmers traveled to tree-starved areas of an increasingly urbanized and clear-cut seaboard.

During the first half of the nineteenth century the river trade in forest products, carried on by schooner as well as by gundalow, was supplemented by another building material, this one a product of the river itself. Like the rest of the Great Bay system, the banks of the Oyster River yielded good quality blue clay, giving rise to its share of the several dozen brick yards (in 1951, ninety-year-old Capt. Edward Adams of Durham listed forty-three of them from memory) that lined the waters of the region. The brickyards in turn were major consumers of cordwood, thus contributing to deforestation. Because they had consumed all the available clay along the banks by the early twentieth century, the brickyards also changed the shoreline configuration of the entire estuary.

Oyster River was also a shipbuilding site. At a shipyard near the Piscataqua Bridge at the mouth of the river, Andrew Simpson built, among other vessels, two privateers during the War of 1812. A view of Durham landing about 1825 shows two schooners on the ways just below the falls. Nineteenth-century boatbuilders also constructed scores of gundalows.

Since early in the twentieth century, the river has been the site of extensive pleasure boating, including its use in recent decades by rowers of the University of New Hampshire crew, and of fishing in summer and ice fishing in winter. Just below the falls, the town of Durham maintains a public landing and park in the area once occupied by warehouses and a shipyard. Long since silted in, the river that once launched deep-sea ships is today so shallow that even eight-oared shells cannot row at low tide. Deforestation, plow-agriculture, and construction all took their toll. Less polluted than it once was, the Oyster River nevertheless looks dramatically different than it did to the first English settlers, even in its most natural stretches. –CEC

Sources: Everett S. Stackpole, Lucien Thompson, and Winthrop S. Meserve, *History of the Town of Durham* (Concord, NH: Rumford Press, 1913; Somersworth, NH: New Hampshire Publishing Co., 1973), *Durham, New Hampshire: A History, 1900-1985* (Canaan, NH: Phoenix Publishing for Durham Historic Association, 1985); Lorus and Margery Milne, *World Alive: The Natural Wonders of a New England River Valley* (Somersworth, NH: New Hampshire Publishing Co., 1977).

ADAMS POINT AND THE JACKSON ESTUARINE LABORATORY

ADAMS POINT BRINGS THE PAST AND THE FUTURE OF GREAT BAY into focus. The hardscrabble life of baymen and farmers at the point has given way to resource management and scientific research in the Jackson Estuarine Lab, now located on that site. If gundalows like the *Fanny M.*, once built here and moored in the cove, evoked the maritime heritage of the region, the research conducted in the lab today represents this estuary's future.

Pleasure gundalow Driftwood, *built by Captain Edward Adams and his son,* Cass, *ready for launching in the fall of 1950. The Adams house is in the background. Photograph by Douglas Armsden. Courtesy of Old Berwick Historical Society, South Berwick, Maine.*

Well known to dog walkers, bird watchers, and duck hunters, Adams Point is an eighty-acre promontory in the southeast corner of Durham that juts into Furber's Strait, the bottleneck separating Little Bay and Great Bay. Since 1961 this parcel of woodlands and fields has been a state-owned wildlife area, managed by the New Hampshire Fish and Game Department. They lease two of the eighty acres to UNH on a long-term basis for the Jackson Estuarine Lab.

Legendary as the saltwater farm and summer boarding house operation of the Adams family, who lived there from 1835 to 1959, Adams Point has long been meaningful to many residents and visitors for its association with natural grandeur, local heritage, and good times. During the first half of the twentieth century, locals were attracted by its grove of majestic pines (now gone), its panoramic views of the bay, and its continuum with the regional past, represented by the hospitable Captain Edward Adams and his gundalows.

The point became Adams property in 1830 when it was acquired by a born-again Methodist circuit rider from Newington named "Reformation" John Adams. A humorless and imposing patriarch, "Reformation" John built a house and raised a family here. He is buried in the family tomb overlooking Great Bay. But it was his youngest son, Joseph, and Joseph's son Edward, who made the Adams name synonymous with the heritage of Great Bay.

Joseph and his wife, Olive Esther Libby (from Berwick, Maine), farmed and operated a brickyard—two quintessential means of making a livelihood in the region during the nineteenth century. Late in the century they renovated the family house and opened a summer boardinghouse resort. Known as Adams House, it became popular, attracting boarders for decades. Tourism then was often anti-modernist, and tourists sought the supposedly invigorating environment of shore or farm. Archly romantic, even sentimental, they appreciated the bay as a sublime spot, distinctly different from suburb or city. Ironically, the "pellucid waters of Great Bay" that inspired turn-of-the-century tourists were probably more polluted by contaminants and pathogens than they are today.

Tourists kept the Adamses busy. Their grandson, Cass, later lamented that "you never could tell what those boarders were going to do next. One summer they'd be riding horses all over the neighbors' farms, and the next they'd be rowing to Newmarket and back every day, and if a fog came on you'd have to go out and hunt for 'em." Cass was not the kind of fellow to be flummoxed by a fog. He grew up messing around in boats, and his father was the foremost gundalow captain on the bay.

Born in 1860, Captain Edward H. Adams was "Reformation" John's grandson. The last builder, owner, and skipper of gundalows on the bay, Adams cherished his craft. In old age he built gundalow models, now in private collections and at the Smithsonian Institution. Earlier in his life Captain Adams built the *Fanny M.*, which he launched from the bar at Adams Point in 1886. Like the gundalow men who preceded him, he freighted bricks, lumber, cordwood, coal, and other cargoes throughout the estuary.

Fanny M. was the last of the commercial gundalows, and the only one to have an auxiliary gasoline engine. At the end of her career, in 1920, under a subsequent owner, she was abandoned in the marsh grass on Dover Point. But Captain Adams never surrendered his identity as a gundalowman, and at the age of seventy he took on a retirement project. For twenty years, beginning in 1930, he and his son built a pleasure gundalow, the *Driftwood*, which they launched on the old captain's ninetieth birthday in October of 1950.

Professor C. Floyd Jackson, a visionary marine biologist who opened a marine biological laboratory and teaching camp on Appledore Island in 1928, and who systematically studied and wrote about Great Bay, 1930. Courtesy of University of New Hampshire Media Services.

Locals flocked to the launch, propelled by nostalgic sentiment for the old skipper's dream and recognition that in an age of motor trucks and atomic bombs, *Driftwood* would be the last gundalow. Beyond the festive air suggested by bunting and flags, it was clear that Captain Adams and his gundalows had become icons of the regional past for people in Durham and Newmarket who cherished a connection to the bay.

Only nineteen years after Captain Edward Adams' death—the symbolic close of waterborne commercial traffic on the bay—his ancestral home became the site of the Jackson Estuarine Laboratory, part of the UNH Center for Marine Biology. Since its dedication in 1970, marine scientists at the lab have been in the forefront of the movement to preserve and enhance the Great Bay estuary. They have worked to mitigate and restore critical estuarine habitats such as salt marsh and eelgrass beds. They have worked on aquaculture projects, including shellfish, finfish, and seaweed aquaculture. They have worked to create models of habitat change essential to good management, and they have studied microbial pathogens and toxic compounds in the bay. Research conducted at the Jackson Lab has highlighted environmental problems and has provided the scientific data necessary for sound management, positioning the estuary for survival in the twenty-first century.

The lab was named for C. Floyd Jackson, a Marine Biology professor and dean at UNH for many decades, and author of *A Biological Survey of Great Bay, New Hampshire*, published in the war-weary year of 1944. Jackson's primary concern was not the war, but the more enduring problem of a compromised estuary. "There are 2,815 acres of potential clam-flats in the Great Bay area," he noted, "mostly non-productive due to pollution, silt, and the growth of

Spartina." A scientist with vision, he sought a governmental commission to investigate and mitigate industrial pollution in the bay. His most compelling recommendation for post-war projects, however, was that "the cities of Dover, Rochester, Farmington, Somersworth, Salmon Falls, Newmarket, and Exeter provide funds in the very near future for…installing sewage disposal plants…to reduce to a satisfactory level the bacterial count." Professor Jackson was ahead of his time.

Since then his successors at the Jackson Lab have published informative and far-reaching studies. *The Ecology of the Great Bay Estuary, New Hampshire and Maine: An Estuarine Profile and Bibliography*, edited by Dr. Frederick Short in 1992; and *A Technical Characterization of Estuarine and Coastal New Hampshire*, edited by Dr. Stephen Jones in 2000, both presented state-of-the-art scientific knowledge about the Piscataqua region. The research behind those books is as vital to the future of the bay as the gundalows were to its past.

Great Bay was, and still is, a place to make a profit, to contemplate nature, to relax, and to prove oneself. Contemporary scientists and old gundalow men have that in common. But at the end of the twentieth century, local people shifted their view of the bay in a profound way. For centuries it had been *maritime*—a site for the extraction of resources with commercial vessels. Today it is *marine*—an ecosystem in its own right worth understanding and protecting. The shift is nothing short of revolutionary, and no place reflects that change quite as profoundly as Adams Point. –WJB

On June 27, 1969, the year before the official dedication of the Jackson Estuarine Laboratory, marine science researchers from University of New Hampshire position a geological research platform in the Bay. Courtesy of the Milne Special Collections and Archives Department, University of New Hampshire.

Sources: Linnea Staples, "Age of Science Invades Historic Adams Point," *New Hampshire Sunday News* (July 26, 1970), p. 29; Evelyn Browne, "The Adamses of Adams Point," *New Hampshire Profiles* 10 (August, 1961), pp. 20-26, 40, 42; Richard E. Winslow III, *The Piscataqua Gundalow: Workhorse for a Tidal Basin Empire* (Portsmouth, NH: Portsmouth Marine Society, 1983).

RACE AND PLACE IN THE PISCATAQUA REGION

AT THE HEIGHT OF ITS SUCCESS AS A MARITIME REGION, the Piscataqua was but a tiny part of a vast Atlantic commercial system in which sailing ships and slavery were important components. The tendrils of the African slave trade reached up the rivers of this estuary. Not only did captive Africans arrive here under sail, and remain, but white people came to associate race as a natural, if awkward, part of the social landscape. Certain places in the Piscataqua are still associated with race and inscribed in racial ways, although the terms of that inscription are changing.

In 1776, when slavery was still legal in New Hampshire, the *New-Hampshire Gazette* routinely advertised slaves for sale. One was a "sprightly NEGRO FELLOW in fine health, about eighteen years of age" who was "To be SOLD for a CERTAIN TIME, or Let by the month." The slave had already "served at sea," according to his master, and was "extreme[ly] desirous of belonging to a Captain of a privateer, or going in one." Privateering might have held out the promise of status, profit, or adventure to the young black seaman; we simply do not know. In any event, during the same year that the Declaration of Independence proclaimed national freedom, the *New Hampshire Gazette* still took local slavery for granted.

PUBLISHED BY L. A. TARBELL

General Sullivan's Slave House and Monument, Durham, N. H.

Postcard from the early twentieth century. Courtesy of the Milne Special Collections and Archives Department, University of New Hampshire.

Slavery ended in the Piscataqua region soon thereafter—much earlier in New Hampshire and Maine than in most of the nation. But assumptions about black inferiority endured, even in the minds of those who knew that slavery had been morally wrong. Sometimes they were reflected in very local ways, sometimes even unconsciously. As late as 1961, people in Durham still referred casually to a point in the Oyster River by a colloquial name mired in the legacy of slavery. "We tacked across the river to Prof. C. Floyd Jackson's dock," remembered Philbrook Paine of his first sailing lesson in 1920, when his father was teaching him to handle a little boat built by Captain Edward Adams, "reached over to Nigger Point, and ran back to our landing." The name was bandied about without self-consciousness or scrutiny; it was simply a reference to a spot that had long been known as such, and still is to long-time residents of Durham. That beautiful little point can be seen today if one stands at Jackson Landing in Durham and looks across the river and upstream a bit. Ironically, were it not for the grating name, recognition of those enslaved residents likely would have been lost.

Mary P. Thompson's *Landmarks in Ancient Dover*, published in 1892,

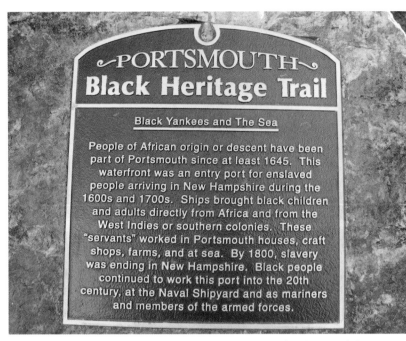

Black Heritage Trail marker in Prescott Park, Portsmouth. Photograph by W. Jeffrey Bolster, 2001. Courtesy of the photographer.

illuminates something about the point and how it got its name, explaining that "the Barhews, a Negro family of last century, owned by Deacon Jeremiah Burnham," lived there, and that "several of the Barhews were buried near 'Nigger Point.'" Thompson, like many white residents conscious of the region's history, was both uneasy with the legacy of slavery and somewhat patronizing about historic black people. Belmont and Venus Barhew had been "kidnapped in Africa," she noted disapprovingly, but one of their sons, Peter, "was of a cross grain, and required much skill in management." Kidnapping was wrong, she seems to suggest, but she also seems to suggest that Peter (despite being enslaved against all right) should have been more tractable. From this perspective, the illogic of race is revealed, as is the topic's persistent awkwardness because of that illogic.

Slightly upstream, and on the same shore in Durham, is the historic Sullivan property. During the early twentieth century, L. A. Tarbell published a postcard with two photographs taken there at the head of the Oyster River and joined them with a caption: "General Sullivan's Slave House and Monument." The juxtaposition of the photos was much more than simply a salute to Major General John Sullivan, a Revolutionary War hero who commanded the raid on Fort William and Mary in New Castle, and whose grand home is in the background. Visually, the postcard gives equal weight to the assumptions that a great American man like Sullivan would be honored after death with a granite obelisk, *and* that he was served in life by black slaves. Unconsciously or not, Tarbell was suggesting that part of the Revolutionary legacy in Durham was a legacy of black inferiority, and that the "freedom" promised by the Revolution was for whites only. Citizens in Durham not only kept slaves, but kept them in separate houses. The Sullivan slave house, however, was not on "Nigger Point." Though nearby each other, they were distinct properties with distinct residents, and each left its historic trace.

Now, at the turn of the millennium, the relationship of black people to the Piscataqua region is being redefined in public spaces. In 2000 the Portsmouth Black Heritage Trail, Inc. unveiled the first of its bronze historic site markers commemorating local African Americans. A marker on the Marcy Street waterfront in Portsmouth notes the lives and labor of black seamen. A marker at the North Church explains the custom of "Negro pews." And a marker on the South Ward Room (now The Children's Museum of Portsmouth) memorializes the first annual celebration of the Emancipation Proclamation in Portsmouth. These bronze plaques are providing new ways for residents and visitors to imagine historic black people in this traditionally "white" area, and to rethink the relationship of race and place in the Piscataqua maritime region. –WJB

Sources: Philbrook Paine, "My Bay," *New Hampshire Profiles* (August 1961); Richard E. Winslow, III, *"Wealth and Honour": Portsmouth During the Golden Age of Privateering, 1775-1815* (Portsmouth, NH: Portsmouth Marine Society, 1988); Mary P. Thompson, *Landmarks in Ancient Dover, New Hampshire* (Durham, NH: Durham Historic Association, 1965 [1892]).

THE FFROST HOUSE: CONTEMPORARY USE OF A HISTORIC BUILDING

SITUATED ON A HILL OVERLOOKING THE OYSTER RIVER and Oyster River Falls, the Three Chimneys Inn offers its visitors not only luxurious accommodations, but also a rare glimpse of the past. Dating in part from 1649, the Ffrost House is the oldest house in Durham, New Hampshire, and one of the oldest in the state. Like many old buildings it has been expanded and renovated many times.

The original building materials arrived via the Oyster River at the request of Valentine Hill, a Piscataqua entrepreneur. He built his home in 1649 and shortly thereafter established a sawmill below the falls—the first on the Oyster River. Hill understood the importance of landscape and placed the structure to his advantage: the home is situated on a rise far above the flood line, but is still quite convenient to the water. The location of Hill's home may have contributed to its survival during the 1694 Abenaki attack at Oyster River that destroyed many of the settlement's fourteen garrison houses, and killed or captured ninety-four of the settlers—fully one-third of the population.

Ownership of Hill's home passed to his descendants. During the Revolutionary War the house concealed British munitions confiscated from Fort William and Mary in New Castle. George Ffrost II, a successful merchant, purchased the home in the nineteenth century and his family used their wealth to renovate it. During the 1850s, in keeping with trends of the day, they added Italianate features to the house and barn; indeed, the barn still has its Italianate cupola. A Greek Revival porch was

Three Chimneys Inn, circa 1998, an example of adaptive re-use of a historic structure. Courtesy of Ron Peterson, Three Chimneys Inn, Durham, New Hampshire.

added to the house in the 1870s. Under the Ffrost family's ownership, the historic homestead was transformed into a gentleman's estate.

In the early 1900s the home passed to James and Margaret Pepperell (Ffrost) Sawyer, who modified the site to adhere to popular

Landing at the Falls. View of the Oyster River, Durham, circa 1823, from Sullivan's Wharf. *Ink and watercolor by Stuart Travis, 1935. The Ffrost House and the old Ffrost store figured prominently in this somewhat fanciful recreation of the Durham landing. Courtesy of Milne Special Collections and Archives Department, University of New Hampshire.*

Colonial Revival ideals. Their summer residence had extensive formal gardens that reached down to the site of the old Durham Landing, where ships had been built during the commercial era that ended about 1830. By the early twentieth century, however, Durham was a sleepy agricultural and college town, and the Oyster River had lost its commercial importance. The occasional gundalow still carried bricks or firewood, but the river was primarily a recreational resource and a scenic vista.

After the Ffrost House's early twentieth century "revival," the home and grounds reverted into substandard student housing. By the 1980s vandals and harsh weather had taken their toll on the gracious old house.

During the 1990s the Ffrost House experienced yet another "revival." Through extensive restoration and adaptive reuse, the house emerged as the Three Chimneys Inn, an upscale dining and lodging facility. While this remarkable home and its grounds are not a museum or historical society, they nonetheless have been saved for future generations because the Three Chimneys Inn's owners preserved much of the structure's historic integrity, and thus the cultural and architectural riches of the past. Saved from ruin, this historic site is once again commercially viable. –CAV

Sources: Mary P. Thompson, *Landmarks in Ancient Dover* (Durham, NH: Durham Historic Association, 1965[1892]); Historical Survey provided by the Three Chimneys Inn.

DEFEATING THE ONASSIS REFINERY

THE FIRST SIGN OF WHAT MANY SAW AS THE ULTIMATE THREAT to the sleepy bayside university town of Durham and to New Hampshire's seacoast came in October of 1973 when *Publick Occurrences*, a fledgling Newmarket-based weekly newspaper published by Phyllis Bennett and edited by Dick Levine, ran a front page story headlined "An Oil Refinery on Durham Point?" The story reported that real estate agents were quietly optioning land in Durham. By December everyone knew that oil tycoon Aristotle Onassis planned to build the world's largest oil refinery in Durham. Promoters asserted that the six-hundred-million-dollar refinery would be sufficient to supply one-third of New England's oil needs. Their plan called for 275,000 barrels of crude oil to be piped daily from a terminal at the Isles of Shoals to Concord Point in Rye, and then on to Durham. The mammoth pipeline would be partially under water, partially on land. The supertankers arriving at the Isles of Shoals actually would be larger than several of the smaller islands themselves. After refining, the oil would be piped either to a truck terminal on Interstate 95, or back to the Shoals for loading onto tankers. Plans for the refinery stipulated using six thousand gallons of fresh water per minute—more than the region's rivers could possibly provide. Engineers later reduced those estimates to fifteen hundred gallons per minute. The scheme was still so gargantuan as to be unimaginable, and yet it appeared chillingly close to becoming a reality.

A classic David and Goliath struggle emerged, pitting Aristotle Onassis, Governor Meldrim Thomson, several Texas engineering firms, delegations of publicists, and *The Union Leader* (New Hampshire's only statewide newspaper) against housewives, university professors, graduate students, a determined state legislative delegation, a tiny start-up weekly newspaper, old timers, new residents, and retirees. Most of Durham and the Seacoast rallied to preserve their towns, the islands, and the estuary, recognizing that "oil and water don't mix."

Onassis and his agents successfully acquired options to buy one-third of the land in Durham. To make their case to the public, they

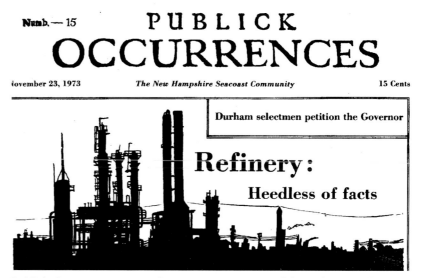

Publick Occurrences, *November 23, 1973. Courtesy of the Milne Special Collections and Archives Department, University of New Hampshire.*

hired a former president of the state senate, a former speaker of the New Hampshire House of Representatives, high-powered advertising agencies and consultants, and a former radio star. The governor courted Onassis, and *The Union Leader* enthusiastically supported the idea of a refinery in Durham. Goliath appeared to have all the advantages.

A citizens' group called SOS (for Save Our Shores) quickly formed to counter these forces, electing Durham Point housewife Nancy Sandberg as its leader. SOS raised money and consciousness. It collected petition signatures, conducted surveys, and did research. Its defiant members stood in the winter cold and stamped "Go Home Ari" in the snow as an Onassis helicopter hovered over pastures near Great Bay. Eventually thirteen SOS chapters across the state had thousands of members.

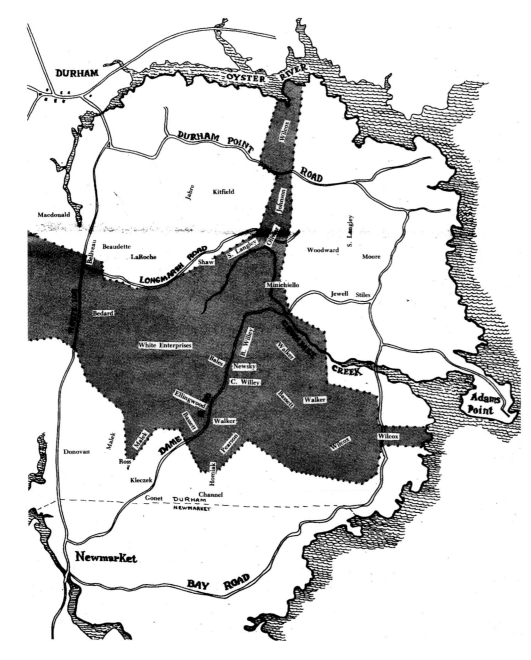

Durham's legislative delegation hung its hopes on home rule—the crusty New England belief in self-determination, and a basic tenet of New Hampshire's political philosophy since the American Revolution. A community's approval is required before a racetrack can be built or cigarettes or alcohol can be sold within a town's borders. The Durham delegation claimed an emergency situation, a necessary measure in order to introduce a bill during a year in which the New Hampshire legislature was not scheduled to enroll new legislation. Thus House Bill 18 came into being. The bill, drafted and sponsored by freshman state representative Dudley Dudley of Durham, required that a proposed refinery get approval from the community in which it was to be located before construction could begin. HB 18 was rooted in the belief that a community had the right to approve or disapprove proposals for massive changes within its bounds.

Other factors came into play as well. New Hampshire's economy was in decline. A study released with great fanfare by the state's Commissioner of Resources and Economic Development predicted the refinery would create fifteen thousand new jobs. SOS and its amateur researchers determined that new jobs would likely go to non-residents because the skills required would not be present in the local workforce. *Publick Occurences* spread the word.

With no local industry to relieve homeowners' property tax burden, Durham had one of the highest tax rates in the state. Refinery proponents claimed that

Sketch map (with landowners' names) of land on Durham Point, which agents of the Olympic Refinery had optioned for purchase. Publick Occurrences, December 21, 1973. Courtesy of the Milne Special Collections and Archives Department, University of New Hampshire.

Durham's property taxes would be reduced by 70 percent. SOS countered and *Publick Occurences* reported that only the refinery's administration building would be property-taxable. The storage tanks, machinery, and equipment would not, and tax relief might not be as great as supporters claimed.

Gas rationing was the order of the day in 1973, with a nationwide oil shortage. The Onassis team assured New Hampshire's people the refinery would supply them with an abundant flow of cheap oil. SOS learned that lines at gas stations outside refineries in Texas and New Jersey were just as long as those in New Hampshire, and that the price of gas was comparable. Again, *Publick Occurences* ran the story.

On the eve of Durham's town meeting and the legislative vote on HB 18, an eight-page unsigned pro-refinery insert appeared in each of the state's nine daily newspapers. Radio ads supported the refinery.

The town meeting in March of 1974 was the largest in Durham's history. When the votes were counted it was clear that citizens had spoken resoundingly: only 144 voted for the refinery, 1,254 against. But a victory at town meeting for the anti-refinery forces was not binding. The next day's vote in the legislature on HB 18 was the one that mattered. Representatives in Concord sensed the passion of the moment along with the threat to New Hampshire's historic tradition of local political control. In the end, the vote was 233 to 109 in favor of home rule and HB 18. David had won.

The threat of overdevelopment still looms large. No single project is likely to draw attention as the Onassis refinery did. But not until

'Just set it anywhere.'

Publick Occurrences cartoonist Bob Nilson mocked the alliance between Governor Meldrim Thompson and Aristotle Onassis, and highlighted its oily threat to the region. Courtesy of the Milne Special Collections and Archives Department, University of New Hampshire.

citizens and legislators in New Hampshire value environmental protection as dearly as they do home rule will threats to New Hampshire's landscapes and waterways subside. –DD

Sources: John M. Kingsbury, *Oil And Water: The New Hampshire Story* (Ithaca, NY: Shoals Marine Lab, 1975).

WAGON HILL FARM

ONE OF DURHAM'S MOST PICTURESQUE—and possibly most photographed—landmarks, familiar to every traveler driving north on Route 4 from Portsmouth and Newington, is a nineteenth-century farm wagon silhouetted against the sky on the crest of a roadside hill. In winter, the quiet rural scene is often enlivened by scores of brightly clad children screaming and shouting their way down the hill on sleds, toboggans, and plastic contrivances of every sort while watchful parents try to keep their own feet warm.

The wagon, placed there in the 1960s by the property's last private owner, is only the most visible feature of a 140-acre farm now publicly owned. In a bold (though not uncontested) move to preserve open space, the voters of Durham appropriated $3.1 million in July 1989 to purchase the property. With its two hundred-year-old farmhouse, hiking and cross-country skiing trails, self-conducted historical and nature tours, 6900 feet of Oyster River frontage, and a pine grove that had been one of Durham's best loved picnic areas for many decades—even before public ownership—Wagon Hill Farm is among the region's preeminent recreation and conservation areas. The historic farm is not entirely safe from the threat of development, however, because the Durham Town Council, wishing to keep its options open, did not protect it with a conservation easement. Legally, the town could sell or subdivide Wagon Hill Farm at any future time.

For more than three hundred years before 1960, Wagon Hill was a working farm. Its uses evolved from colonial- and provincial-era subsistence agriculture to prosperous diversified family farming in the nineteenth and early twentieth centuries, particularly during the ownership of four generations of the Chesley family, beginning in 1830. From then until about 1940, dairying, haying, apple growing and cider making, and the cultivation of corn, potatoes, and other vegetables variously provided a comfortable living for successive generations of farmers. Surviving evidence of the farming era, described in the self-guided

Wagon Hill Farm, Durham. Photograph by Ralph Morang, 1991. Courtesy of the photographer.

tour notes, is occasionally supplemented with demonstrations.

Only four families owned the farm before 1989, beginning with John Davis, who bought its first sixty acres from the merchant and landowner Valentine Hill in 1654 and who built a garrison house on a knoll overlooking the river. The structure was one of the few to survive the devastating 1694 French and Indian raid on the Oyster River settlement. The present house was built about 1802 by John Bickford, a merchant and ship captain who bought the farm from the last Davis family owner in 1798. This changed the orientation of the farm from river to highway, in keeping with transformations in transportation then underway.

In 1960 the lone surviving member of the Chesley family sold the farm, no longer prosperous because of changes in the economy in general and agriculture in particular, to Loring and Mary Tirrell. By agreement, the previous owner—Miss Elizabeth Chesley—lived in the house until her death in the late 1960s, after which the Tirrells moved in. They improved and maintained the property, continued to make the riverside grove available for community picnics, and put in place the wagon that was to become the farm's distinctive landmark. The wagon was once rolled down the hill by student pranksters, after which Loring chained it in place. Later it was burned by vandals and had to be replaced. After the wagon's installation, Mrs. Alma Tirrell, the owners' daughter-in-law and

Winter sledding on Wagon Hill. Photograph by Ralph Morang, 1996. Courtesy of the photographer.

a long-time town employee and community leader, gave the farm its name. It was from the Tirrell estate, following the deaths of both Loring and Mary, that the town made the purchase in 1989. The old farm with the new name connects Durham's agricultural and maritime pasts to its increasingly suburbanized present. –CEC

Sources: Everett S. Stackpole, Lucien Thompson, and Winthrop S. Meserve, *History of the Town of Durham* (Concord, NH: Rumford Press, 1913; Somersworth, NH: New Hampshire Publishing Co., 1973).

DOVER

THE MILLS IN DOVER

TEXTILE MILLS LEFT A VISIBLE MARK ON THE PISCATAQUA region in a way that pre-industrial shipyards never could. Although more than sixty years have passed since the cotton mills in Dover laid off their last worker, the giant brick buildings straddling the Cochecho River in downtown Dover still loom large in our landscape and imaginations. Initially the mills were built to take advantage of waterpower and water transportation. In their heyday, however, Dover's mills relied on steam turbines and railroads, not river power. By the time they went bankrupt, victims of an international economy that had shifted capital and production elsewhere to maximize profits, the site at Dover's First Falls had become a liability. For decades, only the abandoned husk of the industrial past remained. Today, however, the old mills have been revitalized, and while they no longer produce cotton textiles, they still define Dover's riverfront. Their epic story is a crucial piece of the Piscataqua's regional heritage.

For generations Dover was simultaneously an agricultural center with dozens of family farms and a seaport whose merchants traded internationally from an active riverfront. In 1800 Dover had about two thousand residents. By then economic infrastructure and capital had been developing throughout the region for well over 150 years, and Dover, like other strategically-placed New England towns, was about to experience an economic revolution. The industrial capitalism that transformed the town was born in the "Fish and Potatoe Club," a merchants' club that met regularly at Dame Lydia Tebbetts's tavern on Silver Street. There, with John Williams and Isaac Wendell as principals, the Dover Cotton Factory was incorporated in 1812.

Postcard view of Cochecho River and Mills in Dover, New Hampshire. Circa 1910. Courtesy of Milne Special Collections and Archives Department, University of New Hampshire.

Dover had the essentials for manufacturing cotton cloth: waterpower, humidity, pure water in local streams for bleaching, mill sites in close proximity to the sea, an ample population, and the roads and wharves that ensured effective transportation. Industrialization, however, would require not only the waterpower that sailors and timber men had known, but also the capital that previous commercial ventures had amassed.

Williams and Wendell initially sought to purchase land at the First Falls of the Cochecho River (near the present Central Ave. bridge), but owner Daniel Waldron would not sell. Their second choice was five acres on the north side of the river at Kimball's Falls, about two miles upriver, near the present-day Liberty Mutual complex. They built a three-story wooden building, and a log dam (called Horn Dam), to control the river's flow. Completed in 1815, the small factory began manufacturing cotton yarn. By 1816, with machinery surreptitiously imported from England, it began producing cotton cloth. Young women were hired to tend the looms, with male overseers.

The new factory at Kimball's Falls generated a great deal of curiosity and speculation, not only in Dover, but all over northern New England. The nervous owners whitewashed the windows to keep industrial spies in the dark. They also built homes and boarding houses at the site, now called Williamsville, and soon three hundred employees tended the mill. A few years later the Panic of 1819 bankrupted Daniel Waldron, and Williams and Wendell purchased 131 additional acres on the First Falls in downtown, raising the necessary capital from Boston investors. Downtown Dover was about to be redefined.

Elaborate Masonic ceremonies accompanied the cornerstone laying for a new mill at the downtown falls on July 4, 1821. Williams and Wendell moved their nail manufactory to Waldron's old sawmill site in town and increased their capital tenfold to $500,000. Construction of a second cotton mill began almost immediately. The Upper Factory mill continued to produce cotton cloth, but as operations grew at the First Falls, employees were moved from Williamsville into town. By 1828, most of the homes at the upper village had been physically moved into downtown Dover and Williamsville began to fade away. The old mill was used sparingly until 1849 when it was torn down to make way for the Cochecho Railroad.

Dover doubled its population between 1820 and 1830, as huge brick factories changed the skyline and the town itself. The Dover Cotton Factory's Mill No. 2 was near the current fish ladder at the Central Avenue bridge. Four stories tall, it had a wharf where gundalows unloaded iron and cotton bales. Seven hundred tons of nails were produced at Mill No. 2 in its first year, but the nail business became unprofitable and the company stopped making nails in 1828. The market for textiles, however, seemed insatiable.

The Dover Cotton Factory reorganized as the Dover Manufacturing Company in 1823, attracting more Boston investors to raise its capital to $1 million, and building Mill No. 3. During the middle of the 1820s, masons were laying sixty thousand bricks per day to build the mills. Most of the bricks came from dozens of local brickyards along the Bellamy River. Gundalows hauled cordwood to the brickyards, and carried finished bricks to the mill sites.

Mill No. 4, built in 1825, was an enormous six-story structure that ran parallel to the river for 167 feet, before turning the corner and continuing along Washington Street for another 110 feet. An L-shaped mill this massive had never been attempted in America before. Mill No. 5 was constructed the same year, adding to the Washington Street complex. Mill No. 6 later completed the mill quadrangle along Central Avenue.

There simply were not enough workers in Dover to run all the looms and spindles, so the company actively recruited farm girls from New Hampshire and southern Maine. Advertisements in area newspapers requested "50 smart, capable girls, 12-25 years of age, to whom constant employ and good encouragement will be given." By 1830 Dover boasted 112 boarding house operators, mostly widows. Strict rules assured the girls' families that they would be well cared for, physically and morally. Each girl had to join a church of her choice. At work, girls were required to give two weeks notice if leaving the job, and they had to contribute two cents a week to a sick fund. There was no unnecessary talking allowed in the factory and no "halloo"ing out open windows. Punctuality mattered, and no workers were allowed to throw waste in the river.

Mill work offered local women sociability with new friends, an opportunity for education, and an honorable way to earn a dowry. Hours were long. Head and eye injuries from flying shuttles were frequent. Light was insufficient. The noise was deafening. And as mill windows were closed to promote humidity, stuffy lint-filled air heightened the likelihood of respiratory diseases and lung infections. Still, when girls went home to their farms on vacations, they often brought back friends to join the workforce. Mill and town seemed attractive compared to life on the farm.

As brick masons worked furiously during the 1820s, the company secured water rights to Nippo Lake and Ayers Pond in Barrington, and to Bow Lake in Strafford. Without control of those tributaries, mill managers could not regulate their power source at the First Falls. Rightfully fearing that the price for land and water rights around these ponds would skyrocket if the sellers knew that the Dover Manufacturing Company was buying, the company purchased the real estate on the sly, with agents posing as individual buyers. Landowners later felt swindled when they realized what had happened, but no legal recourse was possible in that era of untamed capitalism and rampant individualism.

Calico printing operations began in the west end of Mill No. 5 in the spring of 1827. The Print Works maintained a large herd of cows on Milk Street, for in order to print richly-textured, clear colors, the fabrics had to be immersed in a "dung bath" that "set" the colors. Over thirty thousand bushels of cow manure were needed annually, and hundreds of acres of clear-cut cow pastures surrounded the mills where today there are houses, trees, and roads. Waste dye and the spent manure were flushed downstream in the river.

Worker complacency and enthusiasm did not last long. The company opened a factory store at Franklin Square, paying workers in scrip instead of cash. Managers' abuses were rampant. Prices were high, accounts were falsified, and wages delayed. Hourly rates were then lowered from fifty-eight cents a day to fifty-three cents, while quotas for each worker were raised and loom speeds increased. Joining a "combination," or union, was cause for dismissal.

On December 30, 1828, about half of the eight hundred mill girls walked out of the factory in what they called a "turn-out," or strike. They paraded around the mill quadrangle with banners, signs, and martial music. They even had artillery for show! Speakers protested conditions in the mill. The *Dover Enquirer* called the turn-out "one of the most disgusting scenes ever witnessed," and claimed the girls walked out over "some imaginary grievance." Although the job action was unsuccessful and the girls returned to work three days later without redress, this was the first strike by women in the United States. Dover's mills, and its militancy, were making history.

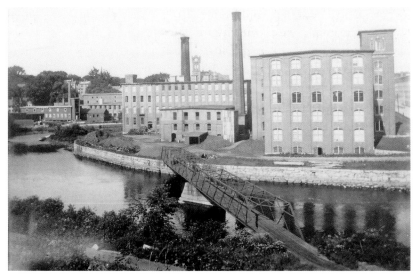

Old Coal Bridge over the Cochecho River, circa 1900. Courtesy of the Milne Special Collections and Archives Department, University of New Hampshire.

In 1840 the mills began to switch from wood fires to coal. From their inception in 1815, the factories had burned only wood, and most of the north side of Third Street was a huge wood yard. When the B&M Railroad reached Dover in 1842, coal began arriving by rail as well as in schooners. The company abandoned the wood yard, and developed large coal pockets along the Landing's riverbanks and near the railroad station. The overshot waterwheels that supplied power to the looms were replaced with steam turbines by 1850, and huge boilers were placed in the west end of Mill No. 5. Water was still crucial for producing textiles, but the river itself no longer drove the spindles and looms.

On the eve of the Civil War, 75 percent of all American cotton cloth was produced in New England. By then most workers were not farm girls, but Irish immigrants. Mill owners continued to speed up machinery and increased the number of machines tended by each worker. From the 1840s through the 1860s, wages rose only 2 percent, yet production per worker was up by 26 percent. Investors accrued vast profits.

The company's greatest production and expansion occurred between 1860 and 1895. In 1876 the company started to build a new No. 1 mill at the bend in the Cochecho River known locally as "The Beach." Now officially known as One Washington Center, it was until recently often called the "Clarostat Mill," named for the last company to occupy it fully. Several small firms have space there today. In the early 1880s, the exteriors of the mill buildings in the quadrangle were extensively renovated. Pitched rooflines with skylights were changed to flat roofs, adding more space on the top stories. Electric lights meant skylights were no longer needed.

For the most part, then, the Dover mills that remain today date from renovations in the 1880s. A new No. 2 was constructed on the site of the old nail factory, several older buildings in the quadrangle were razed, and in 1881, a new No. 3 opened with a bridge across the river to a new picker building on Main Street. The number of looms increased, and the number of spindles nearly doubled from 57,000 to about 140,000. A boiler house was built at the corner of Washington and Main Streets and two immense chimneys were constructed nearby. One still pierces the sky. Furthermore, Mills No. 2, No. 3, and No. 4 were joined to form one continuous building, improving manufacturing efficiency. Twelve hundred employees worked in the mills. In 1887 a serious fire destroyed several of the Print Works buildings, but the company turned the disaster into an opportunity, renovating interiors, adding new color plating tools, and actually expanding their product lines. By then, the boiler house was using twenty thousand tons of coal each year in forty-five boilers.

Cocheco Prints became known worldwide for their fine quality and originality of design. The Print Works developed over ten thousand different pattern designs, many of which can be seen today at the American Textile History Museum in Lowell, Massachusetts. The company was also known for their ability to "fake" materials. They still worked only with the cotton calico produced across the street, but they invented imitation wool, imitation seersucker, and satine, a shiny cloth created by heat pressure. The Print Works had machines capable of laying down twelve glorious colors onto a single piece of cloth.

Employment opportunities in both Cocheco divisions remained stable until the turn of the century, although Southern cotton mills were providing stiff competition for New England factories. In 1903 the company ventured into production of velvet. By subtly threatening to built the velvet mill elsewhere, their agent persuaded the city of Dover to deed to the company 350 feet of river frontage at the east side of the City Farm (near the present-day covered walking bridge) for free. The company also convinced city government to exempt the velvet mill (including the land, the machinery, and all raw materials) from all city property taxes for the next ten years.

Back-to-back calamities hit the company especially hard after the turn of the century. In 1906, another severe fire struck the Print Works, and the facility was unable to recover. Then in January 1907, a devastating fire destroyed Mill No. 1. Three people were killed in the blaze and the entire interior of the building was gutted. The next day, only the ice-covered brick walls remained. The company rebuilt the mill and reopened for business, but the financial repercussions were dire.

Pacific Mills of Lawrence, Massachusetts, bought the company in 1909, and the factories became known as the Cocheco Division of Pacific Mills. The printery operations were moved to Lawrence in 1913, and the velvet mill and all of the Print Works buildings in Dover's Henry Law Park were torn down by 1915. As far as the people of Dover were concerned, the company's sweetheart tax-breaks had been for naught. Production in the cloth manufacturing mills along Main, Washington, and Central diminished each year. By the eve of World War I, the majority of the workers (49 percent) were French-Canadian. The Irish contingent had dropped to 13 percent and Greek immigrants made up 10 percent of the factory population. Another 20 percent simply listed themselves as American. There was a brief upturn in production during World War I when the company made fabric for military uniforms and blankets. But business declined further after the war.

The weakened company could not survive the Great Depression. After 121 years of industrial textile production in Dover, all operations at the Cocheco Mills ceased in 1937. The eerie stillness of the abandoned mills signaled an end to the industrialization and immigration that had defined the city. For several years all was quiet in the mills but

Cocheco Arts Festival. Photograph by Ralph Morang, 1991. Courtesy of the photographer.

from interior walls to expose the historic brick. Sheetrock, glass, and doors defined new office space. Windows were replaced, attractive new entrances were constructed, copper flashing was added at the rooflines, and an outdoor courtyard, suitable for concert performances, was built in front of Mill No. 2 on Central Avenue. Liberty Mutual Insurance Company became the first major tenant. After decades of decay, Dover presented a new face to the world.

Perched above the Cochecho River, and invoking a history that stretches back through generations to French-Canadian, Greek, and Irish immigrants, to girls fresh off the farm tending new looms, to sinewy brick layers, to visionary industrialists, and to cantankerous gundalow skippers, the massive mills are a monument to the people who called this place home. And what of the river itself? Once the inspiration and source of power for those mills, it was diminished by the dams and buildings that straddled it. Today the river is just an ornament as it splashes through the courtyard on its way to the sea. –CCB

the river itself. In 1940 the city of Dover—the sole bidder—bought the mills at auction for $54,000. The city leased portions of the buildings to smaller companies during the 1940s and 1950s, and eventually sold portions of them to Eastern Air Devices, Miller Shoe, and Clarostat. But by 1970 the historic brick buildings had fallen into serious disrepair, and many people considered the Cocheco Mills an eyesore.

The turning point came in 1984, when Tim Pearson and Joseph Sawtelle formed the Dover Mills Partnership. Determined to gentrify and revitalize the mills, they purchased the entire complex. Their contractors chemically washed the exteriors, and sandblasted layers of paint

Sources: Robert A. Whitehouse, ed., *Historical Notebooks*, vols. 1 and 1A: *The Mills of Dover.* (Unpublished manuscripts donated to Dover Public Library, 1987); Diane L. Fagan Affleck, "Printed Cottons in Victorian America: Cocheco Manufacturing Company, Dover, New Hampshire," *Surface Design Journal* (Winter 1984); Richard M. Candee, "The 'Great Factory' at Dover, New Hampshire: The Dover Manufacturing Company Print Works, 1825," *Old Time New England* (Summer/Fall, 1975).

BUD MCINTOSH: PISCATAQUA BOATBUILDER

His obituary in December of 1992 read: "David C. 'Bud' McIntosh, boat builder and designer, died Friday in Wentworth-Douglas Hospital in Dover, after a brief illness. He was born in 1907 and was a lifelong resident of Dover. A graduate of Dover High School, he attended Dartmouth College and did post-graduate work at Harvard University in English. In 1931 he established a small boat yard on the Bellamy River near Sawyers Mills, and moved in 1935 to a site on the Piscataqua side of Dover Point. There he devoted the rest of his life to designing and building boats."

There could have been much more. Bud built over seventy substantial boats, not counting the seventy-five or so skiffs and little sloops he started with in 1931. He designed about half of those large yawls, cutters, and schooners. Among famous yacht designers who consulted with Bud were Sam Crocker and Waldo Howland, the founder of the Concordia Company. Howard Chapelle, who researched the Piscataqua River gundalows for the WPA in the early 1930s and later was curator at the Smithsonian Institution, used to visit Bud for information and insight.

Bud McIntosh was a crucial figure to the Piscataqua River Gundalow Project when in 1978 the group organized to build a reproduction of Captain Edward Adams's gundalow, *Fanny M.* He was present at that first meeting, and while others there were experts in fundraising and public relations, Bud had brought along a couple of powerful, soft-spoken woodsmen who knew where to find the big trees that were needed for timbers. Bud always knew what was really important.

In the March 1983 issue of *WoodenBoat* magazine, Peter H. Spectre published an interview with Bud: "I grew up on a sort of gentleman's farm with five or six acres under cultivation. I was supposed to learn the virtues of hard work at an early age. My father got a Guernsey cow for me when I was seven and I had to milk that cow twice a day and take care of it. By the time I had escaped to college I had six registered Guernseys that I was looking after. That may be partly why I love boats so much.

"My real interest in building boats came after my father bought an island out in Great Bay when he got interested in duck hunting. From then on I spent all the time I could building boats to get out to that island, building something to go shoot ducks out of. Before then I had a passion for boats themselves. It was completely irrational. I felt any body of water should have me on it, floating in something.

"My justification for seeing the boat builder as an artist can be stated simply this way: A sailboat is undoubtedly the most beautiful thing man has ever made, and this one that I'm building is undoubtedly the most beautiful boat that was ever made, therefore I am creating the most beautiful thing that has ever been created. What more can you ask of an occupation? It's a ridiculous concept, but it's pretty close to the truth as far as I'm concerned."

Bud's importance to the Gundalow Project extended well beyond his technical expertise. He had known old Captain Adams fairly well—he had even helped the Captain build his workboat, the "Baby Gundalow," in the carriage shed at Adams Point in 1930—so he was a direct link with the last of the gundalow skippers.

Ned McIntosh, Bud's brother, wrote from his boat at Great Guana Cay in the Bahamas: "In 1938 Bud took on the job of building a thirty-foot sloop for my sister Peggy, and Babe, her classmate at Smith College, who was to become Bud's wife. We spent a couple of weeks setting it up, framing, etc., then Bud had to go away for a week, so Harold Roberts and I spent five days planking her, a fairly satisfactory job I thought. Bud returned, took one look, and shouted, 'That's not planked! That's just boarded up!' He was a perfectionist at planking. Fifty-five years and three hurricanes later, *Mickey Finn* still doesn't leak.

"Babe's father brought his beautiful little varnished, copper riveted clinker dinghy up to Bud's to store for the winter. His parting words were, 'Please don't take care of it as if it were your own!'

"Bud and I both learned to sail on Great Bay from Adams Point, and Captain Adams was our great mentor. One of Bud's favorite sayings by the old captain was "No boat is finished 'til it's sunk, and then some damn fool will get her up again."

Gordon H. Swift—"Swifty" to his friends, and also to many who heard Bud talk about him, built boats for and with Bud for thirteen years. "Not often does an employer and his wife become the best friends an employee has," wrote Swifty. "I went to Bud McIntosh as a neophyte in boat building at which time he took me on and gave me two month's trial. Five years later I accomplished what I thought was a great day by putting two strakes all around on a 39-foot cutter. I made the remark that I guessed I was a boat builder. After a very pregnant pause Bud said he believed in the English system of apprenticeship that lasted seven years.

"Master Boat Builder." Painting of Bud McIntosh by John W. Hatch, 1985. Courtesy of Strawbery Banke Museum.

"I recall a young fellow that came into the shop looking for work. He said he could get work as a carpenter but he didn't have any tools, whereupon Bud spent the next three hours constructing a beautiful toolbox and then put in all the duplicate tools he had until the young man had a collection of tools I envied.

"Once the federal government got involved in the McIntosh Boat Shop in the form of the IRS. Bud called to me and asked if I knew of the whereabouts of 'the shingle.' Being innocent of the purpose of the shingle I replied I had no idea. The poor unsuspecting agent said, 'What shingle are you referring to?' Bud replied, 'Well you've got to keep your records on something.' In less than an hour the agent said it wasn't worth it and left."

Herb Smith has built seven Bud McIntosh-designed boats (three named *Appledore*) and sailed two of them around the world. "In 1971 when I went to ask Bud if he would build my first 48-foot *Appledore* he was sixty-three years old and suggested that I build it myself. I couldn't imagine doing that but Bud could—he encouraged me and promised to come over to my construction site and show me how. He told me that a boat builder was just a glorified carpenter. Bud never discouraged, he was an inspiration to me as I'm sure he has been to all that visited his shop. He never held back in giving his knowledge on boat building, which probably accounts for all the younger boat builders in New Hampshire and southern Maine.

"Bud's genius was in easy-to-build designs, beautiful flat runs in the bilges, superb, honest construction details, and patient, congenial communications with the novice. Bud once told me that if it goes together easy, without a lot of plank steaming, it will probably sail easy. The 43-foot waterline *Appledore III* may lend credence to this theory with a two-thousand-mile passage in ten days. But Bud was not designing for speed. His main concern seemed to be for seaworthiness, and to me that was the essence of yacht design. If it's not safe, how can it be good?"

"In his later years, Bud was the master, who, like in art, could only proceed further in his expression through the release of his knowledge to an apprentice."

Paul Rollins was one of the gifted young boat builders who learned from Bud. "When I first showed interest in the trade and persisted through some initial projects, Bud passed me small jobs that were distracting him from his main focus. Sooner than I expected he had me building a 36-foot lobster boat hull for the Andersons and two vivid images emerge from that project eighteen years ago: I'd lost a big iron planking dog that is used to wedge planks tightly together. I had searched for what was probably an hour and a half, even raked up the shop and was pretty discouraged when Bud walked up whistling just a bit so as not to startle you when he came up. I described my frustrating situation (he'd lent me the tool and you can't buy 'em in hardware stores.) He walked directly to where the tool was snuggled up by the stem and pulled it out. At the time it was a miracle.

"The other occurrence involved driving bronze nails into oak. I'd spent quite a lot of time driving nails, having worked on a house framing crew. There were no pneumatic guns in those days, so when I couldn't drive nails into holes drilled as Bud instructed I figured it couldn't be done. He must have given me the wrong drill size. He happened to check up on me though, and I saw him scowl at my suggestion and then grab the tools. He drilled a string of holes down underneath, in the middle of the garboard, then (at age sixty-seven, mind you) lying on his back in the gravel drove a handful of those nails and never a missed blow, then set them with a punch, no fuss. A teacher's demonstration of a powerful, focused human will. Attitude."

Bob Eger is another young boat builder who sought Bud's advice. He worked for three years on the crew building the gundalow *Captain Edward Adams*. "On a number of occasions during the building of the *Edward Adams* I visited Bud for his counsel on how something should be done. We would discuss the situation and talk about different ways to go about it. In the end he would ask me what I planned on doing and then nod his approval. Whether he would have done it the same way I didn't know, but if I was to be the builder then it would be my decision. He never once told me how I should do something or how he would do it. It was this expression of confidence in my abilities and decisions that was the essence of his inspiration to myself and many others who visited his shop on the river."

Michael Gowell is the Executive Officer of the *Captain Edward Adams* and likes to row traditional boats. "I remember Bud being interested in my small adventures in my dory. He said one of his best memories was when he was in high school and built a 16-foot dory. He launched into Great Bay and cruised to mid-coast Maine. 'I stuck a compass in the bunghole of a water cask,' he said, 'and navigated by the length of the seaweed and an Esso road map.'

"On a visit to Bud's shop in 1976 I was getting advice for improving the arrangement of tholepins in my dory. During our conversation I made some reference to the legendary maritime historian Howard Chapelle and was surprised to hear Bud refer to him as 'Chappie.' It seems that years ago Bud had been commissioned by Chapelle to build a sailboat for the great man's personal use, and upon launching Bud hadn't been too impressed with Chappie's sailing skills. 'But the real problem with Chappie,' said Bud, 'was that every time he found an old boat on the beach he figured it must have been the best one of its type and he would take off the lines and put them in a book. A lot of times those boats were on the beach for a damn good reason.'"

Bud was recognized posthumously by the presentation of the W.P. Stephens award at Mystic Seaport "in recognition of a significant and enduring contribution to the history, preservation, progress, understanding, and appreciation of American yachting and boating." –MG

Sources: Excerpted from *The Piscataqua Current: The Newsletter of the Piscataqua Gundalow Project.* Vol. XV (Spring, 1993), with permission.

ROLLINSFORD

FRESH CREEK AND SLIGO LANDING

SLIGO IS A DISTRICT OF ROLLINSFORD, one of the earliest settled in that town. It is bordered on the west by Fresh Creek, a tidal inlet that flows into the Cochecho River, on the east by the tidal portion of the Salmon Falls River, and on the north by Route 4, also known as Portland Avenue. At various times, Sligo's economy has been primarily agricultural, or maritime, or industrial. Traces of each remain. Sligo not only had access to the sea, but was also a Yankee farmer's paradise. "The soil is naturally fertile and productive," raved the *History of Rockingham and Strafford Counties* published in 1882, "and along the Salmon Falls River and by the shores of Fresh Creek the grass and other vegetation grow with something like a tropical luxuriance. The Best Farms are in this locality." Sligo's historic connection to the sea is considerably diminished today but it remains a fertile agricultural region, with much of its land significantly protected for the future by conservation easements.

The Stackpole mansion along the Salmon Falls River in the Sligo district of Rollinsford. Photograph by Peter Michaud, 1995. Courtesy of the photographer.

Settlement of the area began in the 1630s when grants sliced up available land along the riverbanks. In 1652 mill privileges were granted for Fresh Creek. A sawmill was soon producing lumber for local use and for export. By the end of the seventeenth century the area sup-ported a garrison house, several mills, and many successful farms, as well as shipyards and active wharves.

In 1700 a road was laid out in response to the growing population, thereby connecting the Sligo area with the larger town of Dover. Meanwhile, the Salmon Falls River was active with boat building,

Stackpole's landing and warehouse, Rollinsford, New Hampshire. The Stackpole mansion is visible in the background; the Humphrey Chadbourne site is across the river. Apparently built during the early eighteenth century, this overhanging warehouse was a tangible reminder of Rollinsford's connection to seafaring commerce. It was demolished about 1900, to the dismay of Sarah Orne Jewett and others interested in historic preservation. Undated photograph. Courtesy of Old Berwick Historical Society, South Berwick, Maine.

During the nineteenth century, corporations purchased water rights in the area and demolished saw and gristmills to make way for large brick multi-floored factories. Tillage became less remunerative, and fertile farmland was converted into pasture—first for sheep, later for dairy cows. In fact, the rolling pastures began to resemble the green hills of Sligo's namesake in Ireland. As shipping declined in the Piscataqua region, the shipyards and wharves disappeared from the riverbanks, and the area became less commercial. Nature reclaimed land that had been developed. By the end of the nineteenth century, responding to a rumor that Captain Kidd had buried treasure in the "Indian Hills" that overlook Fresh Creek, locals armed with shovels and picnic lunches embarked on leisurely treasure hunts. Except for their stories, they came home empty-handed.

wharves, and warehouses, and the rolling Sligo hills were actively farmed. Gundalows plied Fresh Creek during the eighteenth and nineteenth centuries. Fresh Creek also supported six salt hay beds that were harvested as supplemental feed for cattle. Some residents prospered, and by the second half of the eighteenth century the Stackpole family, one of the longest-settled in the area, was able to build a fine Georgian mansion along the banks of the Salmon Falls River. It still stands, and is visible by car or by boat.

As the twentieth century dawned, the Sligo area was a provincial landscape that reflected what some residents thought of as New Hampshire's proud colonial past. Evidence of old wharves and shipyards existed along the riverbanks. One eighteenth-century warehouse similar to the Sheafe warehouse in Portsmouth still perched on the Salmon Falls shore in a state of picturesque decay. Among the fields and hills sat a variety of houses, from vernacular capes and farmhouses

The Stackpole house, built circa 1710, not to be confused with the Stackpole's Georgian mansion. This house was moved from its original location near the mansion to a site further downstream about 1830. Photograph circa 1920. Courtesy of Peter Michaud.

to the grand Georgian mansion of the Stackpoles. It was a powerfully evocative landscape, at once historic and natural.

During the 1920s much of the land in Sligo, along with the Stackpole mansion, was purchased by Dr. Robert Morris of Boston. A successful orthopedic surgeon, Dr. Morris wanted a gentleman's farm and summer retreat. Here he found deep roots and an intriguing history. His family renovated and decorated the house in the Colonial Revival style then popular. While some features were restored and care was taken to preserve the central hall and stair, many changes were made to accommodate a twentieth-century lifestyle. The result was a large comfortable summer home with the integrity of antiquity, surrounded by land that Dr. Morris farmed. During the 1930s the finished house was featured in an issue of *House Beautiful*. Had the Colonial

Revival not generated interest in such historic properties, Sligo likely would have been subsequently subdivided, and its valuable green space compromised.

Today the Sligo area of Rollinsford is a mix of rich heritage and active use. Open pasture along the river is bisected with lines of trees and shrubs that run perpendicular to the river, marking some of the original property lines of the 1600s. The road laid out in 1700, now called the Newichanwannock Trail, is still a country dirt byway. Used for both agrarian and recreational purposes, it winds its way from Dover to the heart of the Sligo area. The "Indian Hills" are still actively hayed, but are no longer the scene of Saturday picnics and treasure hunts. The salt hay beds on Fresh Creek have been drowned out by Route 103's man-made causeway over the creek, yet further up the banks evidence of early mills remains. The eighteenth-century warehouse is gone, but the Stackpoles's Georgian mansion is as sturdy as ever. In its shadow is an active dairy farm, one of the few still located on the banks of a tidal river in the Piscataqua region.

Dr. Morris's descendents have thoughtfully protected much of the area with conservation easements, and there are plans for more easements in the future. This stewardship will preserve the rich and fertile hills, and ensure that Sligo's green grass will continue to grow with "a tropical luxuriance." –PM

Sources: Alfred Catalfo, Jr., *The History of Rollinsford, New Hampshire: 1623-1973* (Somersworth, NH: New Hampshire Printers, 1973); Ruth Emerson and Florence Philpott Greenaway, *Rollinsford's Heritage 1623-1976* (South Berwick, Maine: Chronicle Print Shop, 1976); Duane Hamilton Hurd, *History of Rockingham and Strafford Counties, New Hampshire, with Biographical Sketches of Many of Its Pioneers and Prominent Men* (Philadelphia: J. W. Lewis & Co., 1882).

SOUTH BERWICK

FIRST PEOPLE: NATIVE AMERICANS IN THE PISCATAQUA REGION

THE HUMAN HISTORY OF THE PISCATAQUA REGION begins with Native American occupation some 11,000 years ago. Though not widely recorded in texts, Native American history has been preserved through oral tradition and in archaeological sites along the region's rivers and estuaries. Archaeologists are only beginning to understand the complex and dynamic Native American past—long neglected in favor of Euro-American history—while archaeological sites are rapidly being lost to development.

Hunter-gatherers for most of their history, Native Americans had a keen understanding of the distribution of natural resources. The first people of the Piscataqua used the distinctive Paleo-Indian stone tool technology found across North America between 11,500 and 10,000 years ago. A site on a ridge overlooking the Piscataqua in Eliot, Maine, testifies to the presence of people who specialized in hunting caribou and other large mammals. These early inhabitants traveled or had ties to other groups far to the north, as their tools were made of volcanic stones from the Munsungen Lake region of Maine, some 155 miles distant.

Their descendants inhabited the Piscataqua region throughout the Archaic period (8000-1000 B.C.), generally seen as a time of "settling in" and adapting to local environments. Some sites on the smaller rivers emptying into Great Bay have been radiocarbon-dated from 8,600 years ago, and comparably early sites were likely present on the coast before being obliterated by rising sea levels. By 5,000 years ago, coastal people had developed specialized maritime economies, hunting swordfish and

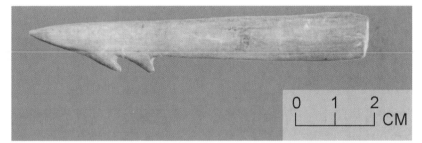

Bone harpoon point, Hunt's Island Site, Seabrook, New Hampshire. Photograph by Mark Greenly. Courtesy of the University of New Hampshire Department of Anthropology.

other deep-water species. In the interior, the economy was based on a wide variety of plants, mammals, fish, and reptiles. Small bands of people followed regular patterns of seasonal movement, repeatedly occupying favored sites for thousands of years.

Archaic period tools were crafted from locally or regionally available stone, but artifact styles are similar to those found throughout the Northeast, including finely made stone rods, gouges, and adzes, and a wide variety of flaked stone points, knives, and scrapers. The symmetry and polish of many of these tools reflect an attention to aesthetic as well as functional detail; combined with evidence from human skeletons indicating a well-nourished population, this indicates a stable economy that afforded significant leisure time. At the end of this period, artifact styles reflective of a new, possibly intrusive culture

Spear and Arrow Points from the Hunt's Island Site, Seabrook, New Hampshire. a) Brewerton Eared-Notched Point, 2000-3000 BC; b) Small Stem Point, 2000 BC-AD 1000; c) Meadowood Point, 1000-100 BC; d, e, f) Jack's Reef Corner-Notched Points, AD 400-600; g) Levant Point, AD 800-1500; h) un-typed, undated point. Photograph by Mark Greenly. Courtesy of the University of New Hampshire Department of Anthropology.

appear, coinciding with the disappearance of the specialized maritime cultures.

The Woodland period, beginning roughly by 1000 B.C., is dated by the appearance of ceramics. Styles of ceramics and projectile points change throughout this period, mirroring changes throughout the Northeast. A period of intensive long-distance interaction occurred between 400 A.D. and 800 A.D., indicated by exotic, lustrous jasper originating from the Mid-Atlantic region that appeared on sites in Seabrook and Durham. Native peoples maintained their traditional broad-based hunting and gathering economy, only beginning to incorporate cultivation of maize, beans, and squash by 800 A.D., when the evidence for long-distance interaction disappears from the archaeological record. Unlike other areas of eastern North America where large earthen mounds and stratified societies are associated with the Woodland period, the people of the Piscataqua region neither built mounds nor abandoned their traditional egalitarianism.

By the time of the earliest European settlements in 1623, native societies had already been transformed by European contact, as an epidemic in the years 1616-1619 produced 90 percent mortality among coastal populations. Survivors of the epidemic coalesced to form new communities at a time when intensifying trade with Europeans and trade-related warfare contributed to additional disruption of traditional culture. As a result, the "tribal" names recorded by Europeans during the seventeenth century may not be reliable indicators of pre-contact social organization.

Who were the Native Americans of the Piscataqua region? Anthropologists have incorporated them into one or another large cultural grouping, such as the Massachusett, Pawtucket, and Penacook. Three "tribal" territories were described in the Piscataqua region: the Newichawannock, in the upper Piscataqua drainage; the Piscataqua, on the east bank of the Piscataqua River; and the Winnacunnet, in the Hampton/Seabrook area. Following the epidemic of 1616-1619, many of the survivors of these groups gathered at Dover, where they were known as the Cocheco Indians. A smallpox epidemic in 1633 killed many of the remaining native people in this area.

The archaeological record of the contact period shows rapid cultural change in the face of disease and European encroachment, but also ongoing resistance to the process of acculturation. European goods were incorporated into native cultural contexts; brass kettles, for instance, were routinely cut into triangular arrow points that were copies of the stone points being used on the eve of contact. Native ceramics were made with a high degree of decorative elaboration and technological sophistication that intensified during the early decades of European contact.

The history of Native Americans continues. In the face of catastrophic population decline, the loss of traditional culture, and oppression by the conquering society, Native Americans maintained a sense of identity and community even as much of their culture was lost or driven underground. Descendants of the Piscataqua region's original inhabitants have enjoyed increasing visibility in recent years, and gather annually at powwows in York, Durham, and elsewhere throughout their ancestral homeland. –RGG

Sources: Victoria Bunker, "New Hampshire's Prehistoric Settlement and Culture Chronology." *The New Hampshire Archeologist* 33/34: 20-28 (1994); Brian Robinson and Charles Bolian, "A Preliminary Report on the Rocks Road Site (Seabrook Station): A Late Archaic to Contact Period Occupation in Seabrook, New Hampshire." *The New Hampshire Archeologist* 28 (1): 19-51 (1987); Dean Snow, *The Archaeology of New England* (New York: Academic Press, 1980).

Ceramic Artifacts from the Hunt's Island site, Seabrook, New Hampshire. a) Fabric-impressed Vinette I Ceramic Sherd, 1000 BC-AD 1; b) Pseudo-scallop shell Stamped Ceramic Sherd, AD 1-400; c) Dentate/Punctate Ceramic Sherd, AD 400-800; d) Punctate Rim Sherd, undated; e) Cord-Wrapped Stick Impressed Ceramic Sherd, AD 800-1200. Photograph by Mark Greenly. Courtesy of University of New Hampshire Department of Anthropology.

THE GREAT WORKS RIVER AND HUMPHREY CHADBOURNE

EUROPEANS ARRIVED IN THE PISCATAQUA REGION looking not only for rich fishing grounds and fertile farmland, but also for falling waters that could power machinery. Waterfalls on streams that were small enough to harness but sufficiently robust to drive a mill were central to their vision of a "new England." One of the very first sawmills in New England rose on the Great Works River, which flows into the Salmon Falls River in South Berwick, Maine.

In 1634 John Mason, the Proprietor of New Hampshire, sent a crew of English carpenters to the Piscataqua; there they constructed a sawmill and a gristmill on the river Native Americans called Assabumbedock. Mason realized that both of these mills were essential for a successful colony: the gristmill would turn wheat into flour allowing settlers to feed themselves, and houses could only be built once a sawmill turned prime timber into lumber. Further,

Archeological excavation at the Chadbourne site in South Berwick, Maine. Photograph by Emerson W. Baker, 1997. Courtesy of the photographer.

lumber would soon prove to be the region's crucial export. Mason's mills operated for only a few years; in 1651, however, the town of Kittery granted Richard Leader the right to erect a sawmill on the Assabumbedock River. His complex occupied four hundred acres on both sides of the river and featured nineteen saws running at once. Locals called Leader's impressive operation "Great Works," and soon the waterway became known as the Great Works River. Down river from

Leader at the lower falls, William Chadbourne and his son Humphrey erected their mill in the 1650s. The prosperous sawmill—combined with his work as a merchant—would quickly make Humphrey and Lucy Chadbourne among the wealthiest residents in New England.

Archaeologists have excavated the remains of the Chadbourne homestead, yielding insight into the lives of the earliest European settlers of the Piscataqua. The Chadbournes initially built a modest home; over time they added to it, creating an impressive mansion that was surrounded by barns and outbuildings. Nails and windows were costly in early New England, but the Chadbourne house was built with thousands of nails, much fancy hardware, and many windows. The parlor, the finest room of the house, featured a massive brick fireplace and plastered walls. At the time, plastering was a new fashion in England and was found in very few New England homes. The Great Works River was not only an industrial site; it was also a refined one.

Over 30,000 artifacts have been found at the Chadbourne site including a range of tools—from axes and adzes to hoes and hammers. Many artifacts reflect the daily activities of preparing and consuming food. Numerous knives and spoons have been recovered, as have fragments of fine dinner plates imported from England, France, and Portugal. Analysis of the thousands of bones found in the Chadbournes's garbage indicates a rich and varied diet that included livestock, wild animals, seafood, and wild fowl. Artifacts from the Chadbourne site are on exhibit at the Old Berwick Historical Society's Counting House Museum.

The Chadbourne exhibit includes Native American artifacts that suggest the site was occupied on several occasions over the past three to four thousand years. In prehistoric times Native Americans built birch bark canoes and used the Great Works and other rivers as their highways. The headwaters of the Great Works are close to the Mousam River in Sanford; by traveling up the Great Works, natives could gain access to the Mousam and other interior waterways. The river was an important source of food as well—a place to harvest the abundance of salmon and sturgeon migrating up stream.

During the seventeenth century, Sagamore Rowls and his Pennacook people planted corn along the lower shores of the river. In 1643 Rowls sold the old planting ground and hundreds of acres to Humphrey Chadbourne, who ran a trading post in addition to his sawmill. Years later other natives regretted such sales. In 1690, during King William's War, a combined force of Native Americans and French allies raided South Berwick and burned most of it, including Chadbourne's homestead and mill.

After the war the Chadbournes rebuilt their mill. Over time the series of falls on the river were developed for sawmills and other indus-

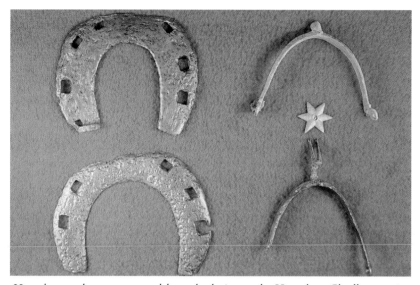

Horseshoes and spurs excavated by archeologists at the Humphrey Chadbourne site. The embossed brass spur (upper right) is particularly fancy. The horseshoe in the upper left was found in a doorway, and probably had been hung over the door as counter-magic. Photograph by Emerson W. Baker, 2001. Courtesy of the photographer.

tries. Larger dams created bigger millponds and more waterpower. In the nineteenth century a plaster mill, a sawmill, and a gristmill operated at the lower falls and the Newichawannock Company made wool at the upper falls. Though this company went out of business in the 1940s, its dam and several of its large wooden buildings still stand as a reminder of the industrial past of the river.

The old mills are now quiet, so people in South Berwick cannot help but see the river differently. Today it is tranquil and clean, and but for the dams, almost "natural." Yet here on the site of the Great Works River rose one of English America's first industrial complexes. –EWB

Sources: Chadbourne Site Exhibit (South Berwick, Maine: Counting House Museum, permanent exhibit opened in 2000); Wilbur D. Spencer, *Pioneers on Maine Rivers* (Baltimore: Genealogical Publishing Co., Inc., 1973[1930]). Everett Stackpole, *Old Kittery and Her Families* (Lewiston, Maine: *Lewiston Journal*, 1903).

HAMILTON HOUSE

SOUTH BERWICK ONCE SENT ITS SONS TO SEA. During the American Revolution, Jonathan Hamilton of South Berwick went privateering and amassed a fortune. With peace he purchased thirty acres of land along the eastern shore of the Salmon Falls River from Woodbury Langdon. There, on a high bluff, Hamilton built a Georgian-style mansion in 1785 that, he boasted, would be a "finer house than Tilly Haggin's," the present-day Sarah Orne Jewett house. Indeed it was. Despite the assumptions of many contemporary visitors, however, Hamilton had not built a gentleman's country retreat; this sea captain's house was designed to survey a sea captain's commercial empire.

The grand house faced downriver toward the sea from which the money flowed. Directly in front of it was a natural depression in the riverbed known as Hobb's Hole, deep enough for launching a ship, and one of the few upriver areas sufficiently deep for a ship at low tide. During Hamilton's time, the shoreline around Hobb's Hole was crowded with active shipyards and wharves, many of which were located on his property. Until the commercial depression associated with the War of 1812, this was one of the most active spots on the river, and Hamilton's mansion did not sit in splendid isolation as it does today. No zoning ordinances separated residential from commercial sites, and Hamilton (along with other merchants of his era) thought it quite appropriate that his aristocratic home sit like a crown above his shipyards and wharves.

The bottom fell out of the regional maritime economy in the early nineteenth century. Piscataqua shippers never recovered from President Jefferson's embargo on American shipping in 1807 and the war with Britain from 1812 to 1815. The Hamilton family, like other mercantile families of the age, lost their wealth and sold their lordly home in 1811. By 1840 a family named Goodwin lived there, grazing sheep on the thirty acres. The shipbuilding and river traffic were virtually moribund; no sailors, caulkers, or shipwrights looked up the hill at the house as they trudged to work, and the old wharves slowly collapsed.

By the end of the nineteenth century, the house and grounds were in a dilapidated state. At the encouragement of Sarah Orne Jewett, whose writing was central to the Colonial Revival, a wealthy Bostonian named Emily Tyson and her stepdaughter Elise purchased the house as a summer home in 1898. The two women redecorated Hamilton House in the Colonial Revival style and designed a landscape that reflected their romanticized interpretation of the past. The Tyson women spent summers there, entertaining guests from Boston and the surrounding area.

In 1949 Elise Tyson Vaughan gave the house and gardens to the Society for the Preservation of New England Antiquities (SPNEA), and donated the wooded bridle paths to the state of Maine in memory of her husband. Vaughan Woods, now a public park, is open year round. The Hamilton House is open to the public June 1 through October 15. As a fine example of Colonial Revival style, it conveys how families like the Tysons sought to perpetuate memories of the heyday of Piscataqua shipping, when wealthy mercantile families built monumental homes, and local rivers were their highways to the world. –PM

Hamilton House, South Berwick, Maine. Photograph by David Bohl, 1983. Courtesy of the Society for the Preservation of New England Antiquities.

Sources: Marie Donahue, "Hamilton House on the Piscataqua," *Down East* (1975).

ELIOT

MASTING ON THE PISCATAQUA, 1641–1815

LOGGING TRUCKS LOADED WITH WHITE PINE are a familiar sight in the Piscataqua region, but pine today is relatively small, and of no consequence to international politics. During the seventeenth and eighteenth centuries, however, struggles over Piscataqua pine spilled much blood and treasure. Ultimately human harvesting diminished stocks of what had been the largest tree in New Hampshire's forest. When axmen reconnoitered the colonial forest for mast trees, individual specimens of white pine, *Pinus strobus*, grew over 250 feet tall and measured more than six feet in diameter at breast height. No better tree existed for the masts of square-rigged sailing ships.

Shipwrights were masting English ships with Piscataqua pines as early as 1641, and by mid-century masting operations were underway on every tributary. There were three mast coves along the main river, and another near the head of Spruce Creek in nearby Kittery. Felling mast pines and getting them out of the forest required special tools, considerable experience, and the collaboration of many men and oxen. First, woodsmen prepared a cushioning bed from smaller saplings so that the huge pine would not break when it struck the ground. Then a path was cleared from the stump to a mast road, or to a stream sufficiently deepened by small dams to carry the great log to navigable water. After axmen felled and limbed the tree, it was cut to length and hauled to water on great wheels (in the summer) or on sledges (in the winter) drawn by as many as thirty-two teams of oxen. Down river where ocean-going vessels could anchor, the masts were hauled out in a mast yard, covered by a shed roof, squared, and then eight-sided. Ships later carried them to England or to a New England shipyard.

Difficult though masting was, ten shiploads of masts left the Piscataqua annually for England by 1671. During the Anglo-Dutch wars the Royal Navy came to depend on Piscataqua masts for its greatest ships. The region was England's "strategic naval reserve;" without its steady supply of masts the Royal Navy would have been immobilized after any large battle. During the second Anglo-Dutch War, in 1666, Samuel Pepys noted that the British Navy had been virtually saved by the arrival of mast ships from the Piscataqua. New Hampshire regained its independence from Massachusetts in 1679 in part because the Crown distrusted Massachusetts' republican tendencies, and did not want to leave the Massachusetts Bay Colony in control of crucial Piscataqua mast stands.

Knowing how crucial mast pines were to the Royal Navy, the French in Canada armed and encouraged their Indian allies to attack masting centers during every Anglo-French conflict. Nearly every town on the Piscataqua and its tributaries was attacked at least once, and some suffered casualties repeatedly between 1675 and 1763. At Oyster River (now Durham), Dover, Berwick, and nearby York, the settlers were virtually wiped out in surprise attacks and massacres. In 1700 Jonathan Bridger, the King's forester, made a map of the Piscataqua showing the forest reserves and a "large Swamp of White Pine Burnt by the Indians."

Nearly every autumn from the 1660s until the 1760s, one or more mast ships arrived in the Piscataqua, often anchoring in the pool near Little Harbor. Carrying up to twenty cannon and sixty or more crew, these were the largest ships to enter the Piscataqua in their day, and the most heavily armed, for hostile navies regularly patrolled Atlantic

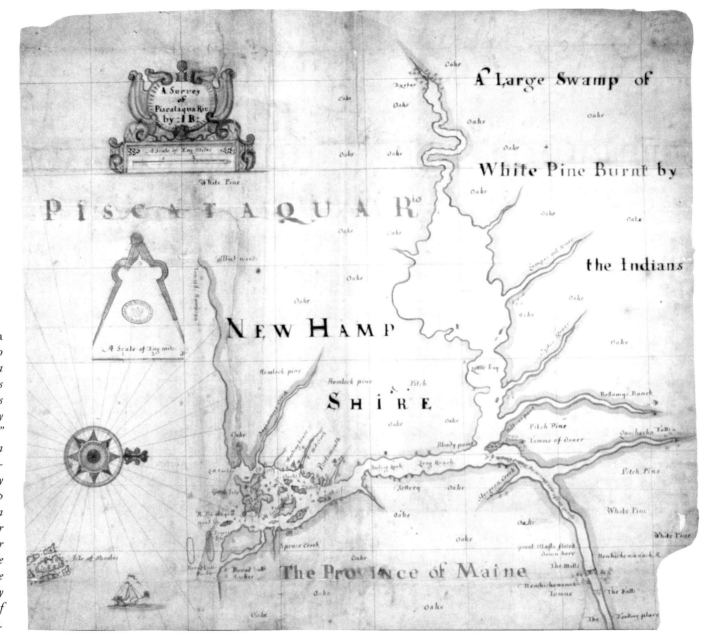

A Survey of Piscataqua River, *attributed to Jonathan Bridger, circa 1700. Native Americans attacked masting operations at times, but this map may misrepresent who "burnt" the pine woods. Historian Faith Harrington has suggested that the fire probably was set by colonists to stop Jonathan Bridger from enforcing the King's timber laws, and that Bridger blamed the Indians to hide his poor relations with the colonists. No one really knows. Courtesy of Portsmouth Athenaeum.*

waters looking for mast ships. It may have been easier to protect masts on the high seas than in the forests, for while mast pines were legally property of the Crown, local foresters regularly harvested pine to feed the sixty-odd sawmills on the Piscataqua. Those mills, with no political loyalties, served a wide international market. The Surveyor General of the King's Woods and Admiralty subcontractors with mast contracts were not the only ones to profit from the pines.

As early as 1665 observers complained that mast pines were getting scarce in the Piscataqua basin, and that sawdust from the mills was clogging the rivers and jeopardizing the salmon population. No doubt this was partly true, but the Piscataqua provided a steady supply of masts right up to the American Revolution, and over thirty Piscataqua masts and spars appeared on the cargo manifest of a ship bound to India from Portsmouth as late as 1802. The mast harvests during the seventeenth and eighteenth centuries depleted, but did not eradicate, the supply of good white pine around the Piscataqua.

With the sheep craze in the early nineteenth century, however, local farmers began to clear their woodlots for pasture, and large stands of pine virtually disappeared from southern New Hampshire. Thereafter, Piscataqua shipbuilders were forced to import their masts from Maine, which still possessed large, untouched stands of pine. Today, as a result of the historic harvests of giant pines, there may be fewer pines in the Piscataqua basin that have the genetic potential to match trees that for two centuries supplied the mast industry. –WBL

Sources: Robert G. Albion, *Forests and Sea Power* (Cambridge, MA: Harvard University Press, 1926); W. B. Leavenworth, "The Ship in the Forest" (PhD dissertation, University of New Hampshire, 1999); *Calendar of State Papers, Colonial Series*, vols. 1-43 (London: HM Stationery Office, 1860; Kraus Reprint, 1964).

The "Paul Bunyan Tree," a 250-year-old white pine in the University of New Hampshire's College Woods, formerly Ben Thompson's woodlot, 1925. Courtesy of the Milne Special Collections and Archives Department, University of New Hampshire.

LONG REACH AND THE NARROWS

"LONG REACH" FIRST APPEARED ON A map more than three hundred years ago, referring to the distinctive section of the Piscataqua River between Eliot, Maine, and Newington, New Hampshire. Vessels used the favorable prevailing winds to sail on an easy "reach" (where the wind is more or less across the beam) through this mile-long straight section of an otherwise quirky and challenging river. "Long Reach" is not named as such on modern charts, but many local boatmen still use that term. The most striking aspect of Long Reach today is the contrast between the eastern and western shores. The New Hampshire side is heavily industrialized, marked by the tall, steaming stacks of two large power plants, and the tank farms and deep-water terminals of several bulk storage facilities. The Maine side remains heavily forested, rural and residential.

Long Reach, with industrial development on the New Hampshire shore, and a wooded residential landscape on the Maine shore. Photograph courtesy of Fred Short, Jackson Estuarine Laboratory.

Newington got its industrial start in the summer of 1917. The L.H. Shattuck Company signed a contract that year with the U.S. Shipping Board Emergency Fleet Corporation to build thirty identical 280-foot wooden transports for the Great War. The Shattuck Shipyard covered fifty acres of the upper Newington shore, and within one a year employed thousands of men and women working at a break-neck pace. In May of 1918, sixty men framed an entire ship in just three and a half days. Two months later, on the Fourth of July, the Shattuck Shipyard managed the first triple launch in the nation's history. Productivity on this scale demanded a tremendous volume of raw materials. The shipyard's first lumber order required forty-five million feet of Georgia pine. Lumber arrived initially by tug and barge, and then by rail. The infrastructure for that wartime industry—landings for the barges, straight roads for heavy trucks, and railroad spurs—was the foundation of today's industrial Newington.

Current industry continues to use the same rail line. The same straight roads have gained more lanes and asphalt and now lead nicely to Interstate 95. And today, oil tankers berth just upstream from where the Shattuck Company built the last of the Piscataqua's wooden ships.

Meanwhile, on the opposite shore, Eliot developed in its characteristic way because of another shipyard, and because of political decisions made in the state capitol at Augusta. The Portsmouth Naval Shipyard in Kittery also hired workers for the war effort, and Eliot appealed to many as a quiet place to live. Local citizens' preferences, however, do not always determine the nature of industrial development. The state of Maine, with its long and deeply figured coastline, channeled economic resources for industrial port development elsewhere, and Eliot remained residential. Eliot itself had once been renowned for shipbuilding, but the business dried up before industrialized shipbuilding transformed Long Reach.

The Hanscom Shipyard in Eliot built seven clipper ships, although just one gained notoriety. In 1851 Samuel Hanscom built an extreme clipper designed by his brother, Isaiah, a genius who could design and loft a ship before he was twenty-one years old. Initially the ship's name was to have been "Sarah Cowles," but when the Swedish singer Jenny Lind (known as the "Nightingale") performed in Eliot, the inspired owners christened the vessel in Lind's honor. *Nightingale* made fast passages to Australia and China. Later a slaver, she was captured off the African coast, and subsequently leased by the navy. Freighting lumber, *Nightingale* ended her days on the wild Norwegian coast in 1893. *Nightingale's* radical beauty and her long and

Clipper ship Nightingale *built in Eliot in 1851. Print by Currier and Ives. Private collection.*

checkered life earned her what one admirer called a "niche in the halls of maritime immortality." Today she appears as an emblem of a particular cultural moment at the crossroads of the traditional and the modern, a moment when a Piscataqua-built cargo ship named for a singer could be employed as a slaver.

In 1890, while *Nightingale* still sailed, a large hotel rose on what had been the Hanscom Shipyard. The grand hotel, overlooking Long Reach and the bucolic Newington shore, became known as Green-Acre-on-the-Piscataqua. The poet John Greenleaf Whittier actually suggested the name. A few years later, due to the vision of Eliot resident Sarah Jane Farmer, the hotel began hosting conferences on the comparative study of religion. "I realized how much more receptive the mind and heart would be if the body were in such a cool and healthy environment," Farmer wrote after attending a lecture in Boston during the sweltering summer of 1892. The conferences grew to include spiritual leaders of diverse philosophies from all over the world, and the hotel gradually evolved into the present Green Acre Baha'i School. Sarah Farmer's vision endures, although the view on Long Reach has changed.

Downstream from Long Reach is another section of the river with a local name. Known to old-timers as "The Narrows," or occasionally as "the palisades," it is one stretch of the Piscataqua dominated by bluffs. Where Interstate 95 reaches across the river from New Hampshire to Maine, the highway towers above land that was once part of the vast Atlantic Corporation, a shipyard that built nine steel transport ships during World War I. One hundred yards south of the bridge, where the launching ways lay in 1919, a gypsum plant and bulk-storage facility now occupy Freeman's Point. Just upriver of the bridge, also on the New Hampshire side, is Atlantic Heights, a development built to house the shipyard's workers. Architect Walter Kilham designed that industrial community, one of the nation's first, to resemble an English village. Pressured by the war, builders completed it in one year.

Across the Narrows from Atlantic Heights lurked one of the Piscataqua's most threatening dangers to navigation—Boiling Rock. Just beneath the surface on the Maine side, where the river bends abruptly and then broadens into Long Reach, lay a ledge barely deep enough, even at high tide, for vessels to pass safely. The ebb tide seethed around the rock. An adage aboard downbound vessels from upriver ports held that one "was half way to Boston" once securely past Boiling Rock. With the savoir-faire of a bygone era, gundalow skippers and coasting captains treated all hands to a dram at the Rock. Early in the twentieth century, however, the toasts to Boiling Rock ended abruptly when the ledge was dynamited to allow deep-draft ships safe access to the budding industrial facilities in Newington.

Times change. Conventions change. Names change. The National Transportation Safety Board today would not condone professional mariners drinking on the job. But the practice was common years ago, as were references to places on the Piscataqua now virtually forgotten, such as "Long Reach" and "The Narrows." –NBB

Sources: Richard M. Candee, *Atlantic Heights: A World War I Shipbuilders' Community* (Portsmouth, NH: Peter E. Randall, for the Portsmouth Marine Society, 1985); Anne G. Atkinson, Robert Atkinson, Rosanne Buzzell, Richard Grover, Diane Iverson, Robert H. Stockman, Burton W.F. Trafton, Jr., *Green Acre on the Piscataqua* (Eliot, Maine: Green Acre Baha'i School Council, 1991)

The Green Acre Inn and "Sunrise Camp," circa 1895. Overflow guests from the hotel stayed in the tent village during summer conferences held at Green Acre. The clipper ship Nightingale was built and launched on this site in 1851. Today the Eliot boat launching ramp is about where the three cows are standing, and the Green Acre Inn, now home of the Green Acre Baha'i School, still stands atop the knoll. Courtesy of the Eliot Baha'i Archives.

KITTERY

ROCK REST: AFRICAN AMERICANS VACATIONING BY THE SEA

ROCK REST IN KITTERY POINT, MAINE, was one of several guesthouses north of Martha's Vineyard that catered to African American "summer people" prior to 1960. These black-owned and operated establishments were known to be safe and comfortable vacation retreats at a time when black tourists were denied access to other hotels and restaurants. Enterprising families along the New Hampshire and Maine coasts converted or added rooms to their homes to accommodate vacationers, usually for one or two weeks. Others simply welcomed overnight travelers into their homes upon recommendation from an acquaintance who didn't have extra space.

Clayton Sinclair and Hazel Colbert, two such homeowners, met through a mutual friend in Portsmouth in 1927. Both had accompanied their employers from New York City to their summer homes in York, Maine;

African Americans vacationing in the Piscataqua Region. Undated photograph. Courtesy of Valerie Cunningham.

Mrs. Sinclair and guest, Kittery, Maine. Undated photograph. Courtesy of Valerie Cunningham.

1950s, a visiting couple could enjoy comfortable accommodations plus a hearty breakfast and sumptuous dinner.

Rock Rest felt like home. The small dining room usually could welcome one more at the table. If not, the sun porch could accommodate two card tables, each set with one of Hazel's embroidered (for breakfast) or crocheted (for dinner) tablecloths, and a floral centerpiece from her garden. The menu included homemade breads and jams, Clayton's homegrown vegetables, Southern cooking (in the style later called "soul food"), lobster dinner on Sunday, and rich desserts.

No advertising beyond word-of-mouth was needed to find summer guesthouses like Rock Rest. Chauffeurs and maids and children's nurses who spent summers in New England with their white employers knew where they would be welcome. And once a satisfied visitor returned home, the news spread quickly and far. Day trips from Rock Rest included the usual attractions of sightseeing, swimming, clam bakes, picnics, and attending Sunday church services at the black church in Portsmouth, People's Baptist Church. Lasting friendships formed as the same travelers returned year after year, perennially welcomed to the few black residences in the Piscataqua region. –VC

Sources: Valerie Cunningham, "Oral History Interviews With African American Elders of New Hampshire and Maine Seacoast" (Unpublished, 1991); Valerie Cunningham and Maureen Reardon, "Rock Rest: Memories of Summer in Maine" (Lecture and exhibit, 15th Annual Seacoast Black Heritage Festival, 1999).

Clayton as a chauffeur and Hazel as a lady's maid. The year after they met and married, the Sinclairs decided not to return to New York. They bought a small, dilapidated house (she called it "a shack") with a few acres of land on Route 103 in Kittery Point. Although Hazel protested the purchase, Clay promised to improve it before she would have to set foot inside; they moved in a year later, new floors, plumbing, and electricity finally installed. Thereafter, repairs and improvements never ended. Word spread about the Sinclairs's place in Maine: friends and friends of friends soon called to spend a few summer days at what would become known as Rock Rest, a guesthouse for African American vacationers.

Mrs. Sinclair had in the meantime established a reputation as a caterer, cooking and serving everything from private family meals to formal affairs for wealthy white summer people and elite Seacoast residents. She realized that she could combine her hospitality and culinary skills by offering a night's lodging and two home cooked meals to post-war travelers. For a weekly rate of $40 per week in the early

FORT MCCLARY (PEPPERRELL'S FORT)

FORT MCCLARY WAS BUILT AS THE RESULT OF A TAX and boundary dispute between the colony of New Hampshire and the settlers of the territory of Maine. In a controversy that still resonates today, New Hampshire sought to tax Maine settlers for the use of the Piscataqua River. In 1715, Massachusetts, which had jurisdiction over the territory of Maine at the time, ordered that the fort be built to support the settlers' assertion of their right to use the river.

The fort was first named Pepperrell's Fort after the most prominent family in the town of Kittery. But the Pepperrell family remained loyal to the King at the time of the Revolutionary War and American patriots renamed the fort in honor of Major Andrew McClary of the First New Hampshire Regiment who was killed in the Battle of Bunker Hill, June 17, 1775.

Located on opposite sides of the Piscataqua River, Fort McClary and Fort Constitution were well situated to provide formidable crossfire to defend Portsmouth Harbor's entrance. Both forts were fortified with cannon against possible British invasion during both the Revolutionary War and the War of 1812. At Fort McClary, a distinctive hexagonal blockhouse was built at this time and it became the characteristic distinguishing feature of the fort. Extensive improvements were undertaken during the Civil War to create massive granite walls. But significant improvements in naval artillery soon made masonry forts obsolete, and construction at Fort McClary (as at Fort Constitution) stopped abruptly.

The site was fortified again in 1898 as part of the Endicott Board's coastal defense plan. Under this plan, Fort McClary was considered an inner harbor fort to protect the city of Portsmouth and the Portsmouth Naval Shipyard from naval assault. In response to the improved range of naval artillery, however, outer harbor forts were built or refortified with new guns to repel naval assaults at greater distances from the harbor. By the end of World War I, the outer forts

Fort McClary. Photograph by Ralph Morang, 1997. Courtesy of the photographer.

carried the burden of coastal defense and Fort McClary was relegated to a minor supporting role.

Today, Fort McClary is open to the public as one of the Maine State Park Historical Sites. Visitors can see the blockhouse, explore the granite masonry fortifications, and, from a perch on one of the granite blocks strewn about the site, enjoy a view of Pepperrell Cove and the mouth of Portsmouth Harbor. –TCM

Sources: Ray Bearse, ed. *Maine, A Guide to the Vacation State* (Boston: Houghton Mifflin Co., 1969 [1937]); Barbara Clayton and Kathleen Whitley, *Historic Coastal New England* (Old Saybrook, CT: Globe Pequot Press, 1995).

FORT FOSTER

FEW PLACES IN THE UNITED STATES HAVE AS MANY FORTS per square mile as the mouth of the Piscataqua. The Spanish-American War woke Americans up to the dismal condition of their coastal defenses at the end of the nineteenth century. As a result of this realization, Fort Foster was built on Gerrish Island, across the mouth of the Piscataqua River from Fort Stark.

The Endicott Board, evaluating coastal defense for President Grover Cleveland, reported in 1886 that Forts Constitution, McClary, and Sullivan were in a dilapidated condition and could do little to defend against an enemy fleet shelling Portsmouth. The report pointed out that with current naval artillery advances, an enemy could anchor outside Gerrish Island and, at a distance of less than four miles, easily shell both the Portsmouth Naval Shipyard and the city.

Built on the threshold of the Piscataqua River and the Atlantic Ocean, Fort Foster was fortified with three 10-inch guns. Their 8-mile range extended the harbor's defensive perimeter well into the open ocean. Following recommendations by the Endicott Board, the fort was built with dispersed batteries, unlike earlier masonry forts like Fort Constitution and Fort McClary, which had walled enclosures. Reinforced earth and concrete berms surrounded the batteries. The forward parapets were up to forty-five feet thick. Recessed in deep wells on "disappearing carriages," the guns could retract into the well after firing. When viewed from an approaching ship, these gun emplacements were very low on the horizon and difficult to see. They were an effective countermeasure to the new naval artillery of the day.

The importance of submerged mines in naval warfare was forcefully demonstrated during the Russo-Japanese War of 1904-05. The lesson was not lost on coastal defense planners and by 1906, mining capacity between Fort Foster and Fort Constitution had been established. For a brief time, the coastal defenses employed at Fort Foster had a recognized superiority over the naval artillery that threatened them. In the years leading up to World War I, however, rapid advances

World war II observation tower at Fort Foster, Kittery, Maine. December 1999. Photograph by Thomas C. Mansfield, 1999. Courtesy of the photographer.

in naval artillery turned the tables once again. Previously, naval guns had a limited range, and were restricted to flat trajectory firing. By the end of World War I, naval gunnery had greatly improved accuracy and was capable of delivering high trajectory "plunging fire." At that point, the embankments could no longer protect Fort Foster's Battery. Within twenty years of construction, it had become obsolete.

Fort Foster entered World War II essentially unimproved from its post-World War I condition. In January of 1942, however, more land was purchased for construction of a covered "casemate," or bunker, known as Battery 205, which was to be armed with two modern 6-inch guns. By the time the casemate was ready to receive the guns, the threat to Portsmouth had greatly diminished, and the guns were diverted to areas with more pressing needs. The long history of Portsmouth's coastal defense, rightfully perceived as a necessity, nevertheless could be summed up as "much ado about nothing."

The primary strength of Fort Foster during World War II was its mine capacity. Three strings of mines ran between Fort Foster and Fort Constitution; the outermost two strings were controlled from Fort Foster. The M4 mines on these strings rested on the harbor floor. When fully loaded they weighed 5,000 pounds, making a formidable explosion when detonated. The mines were supplemented with a submarine net that ran from Fort Foster on the north to Fort Stark on the south. The crib piers that supported the net from Gerrish Island to Wood Island are still in place and are often mistaken for the pilings of an old bridge.

After World War II, Fort Foster was decommissioned and turned over to the town of Kittery, Maine, as a municipal park. Today the park comprises eighty-eight acres fronting both the ocean and the harbor. Its beaches, playground, ball field and many scenic picnic areas seem far removed from the threat of attack by sea. But for centuries—until quite recently, really—coastal dwellers could not help but see the ocean as a highway for enemies. Thus the sheer number of coastal fortifications, including Fort Foster, has become one of the hallmarks of the Piscataqua maritime region. –TCM

Sources: Howard S. Crosby, Wendy W. Lull, and Richard T. MacIntyre, *Footprints In Time* (Bath, Great Britain: Alan Sutton Ltd., 1994); The Thoresen Group, *State Coastal Properties Project* (Concord: New Hampshire Office of State Planning, June 1983).

Looking seaward from Fort Foster. The cribs that supported anti-submarine nets during World War II are visible behind the pier. In the distance lies Fort Stark, in New Castle. Photograph by Thomas C. Mansfield, 1999. Courtesy of the photographer.

PEPPERRELL COVE

PEPPERRELL COVE IS DEFINED BY THE curving shoreline of Kittery Point and protected by Fishing Island (originally Tavistock Island). This island is a delightful place to land a small boat for a picnic, bearing in mind that it is privately owned and must be left in pristine condition. If you stand on this island and look landward, you see Capt. Simeon's Galley, (formerly a chandlery) and Frisbees Supermarket ("North America's oldest family-owned store"). Perhaps teacher Oliver L. Frisbee stood here in 1896 as he composed his annual oration for the Island and Harbor (schools) Alumni Association and reflected the imperialism of his times in saying "I hope the time will come when there will be only air enough between the Isthmus of Panama and the Northern Pole to float one flag, the Stars and Stripes, over six hundred million American citizens."

A view of Kittery, Maine, showing Pepperrell House, Whaleback light, Fishing Island, Pepperrell's Tomb, circa 1885. Courtesy of the Society for the Preservation of New England Antiquities.

Looking landward, the long red rambling house on the high point of land to the northeast is the Bray House. It has been much added to over the years but the central section dates to 1662, making it the oldest surviving dwelling house in the state of Maine. It was built by John Bray, a shipwright who migrated from Plymouth, England. Bray established a very successful shipyard in Pepperrell Cove.

West of Bray House stands the large, brown William Pepperrell House. It is the only remaining trace of the once extensive Pepperrell estate that included stores, warehouses, a shipyard, gardens, a deer park and the inevitable blockhouse for defense against marauding Indians. A young fisherman from the Isles of Shoals, William Pepperrell was an industrious entrepreneur who specialized in making "dunfish," slowly

Pen and ink drawing of Sir William Pepperrell, from Samuel Adams Drake, Nooks and Corners of the New England Coast, *1875. Courtesy of the Milne Special Collections and Archives Department, University of New Hampshire.*

cured cod that brought three times the price of ordinary dried cod among the epicures of Europe. He bought land on Kittery Point in 1662, the same year Bray built his house, and presumably had both business and social contacts with Bray over the next several decades. In 1680 William married Bray's daughter, "fair Margary," and was given an acre adjacent to Bray's house on which to erect a house. Pepperrell became a very successful merchant and eventually was joined by his son (also William) who proved equally successful. The younger William Pepperrell helped to finance and recruit a force of New England men who launched a devastating raid on the French fort at Louisbourg, in 1745. This action helped to end King George's War and in recognition of his leadership, the English king appointed him baronet Sir William Pepperrell. He prospered mightily and when he died in 1759, he was said to own more shipping capacity than any other man in North America.

Tradition holds that the small gray building at the water's edge in front of the Pepperrell house is a surviving counting house from the Pepperrell enterprises. During the nineteenth century the Bellamy family resided in the Pepperrell house, and the waterfront outbuilding became the personal workshop of John Haley Bellamy, one of the most gifted woodcarvers in the history of American craftsmen. Known for elaborate panels, and his signature flat-backed eagle wall-carvings, Bellamy also carved elegant catheads and sternboards that adorned U.S. Navy vessels. His most famous piece was the stunning figurehead for the wooden steam-sloop *USS Lancaster.* Carved in 1880 during the

Kittery Point, Maine from New England Calendar *for 1947. Private collection.*

vessel's overhaul at the Portsmouth Naval Shipyard, the 3,200-pound wooden eagle had upraised wings spanning eighteen feet. This magnificent gold-leafed sculpture has been a major attraction at the Mariners' Museum in Newport News, Virginia, for seventy years.

Bellamy was regularly visited in his waterfront workshop by William Dean Howells, prominent author and editor of the *Atlantic Monthly* during the 1870s, and a fellow resident of Kittery Point. Howells sometimes brought other visitors whom he thought would appreciate Bellamy, including Mark Twain and Winslow Homer. Thus as the Colonial Revival focused national attention on the Piscataqua's heritage and antiquities, some of the nation's most influential writers, artists, and carvers gazed onto Pepperrell Cove.

Coasting schooners often sought temporary sanctuary in Pepperrell Cove during the late nineteenth century, waiting for a favorable breeze, or what skippers referred to as "a chance along." Today population pressures in New Hampshire and Maine have turned it into a crowded mooring field, full of pleasure boats and lobster boats, even though it is an open bight, and rather exposed to the ocean. Strong southerlies like those which precede a hurricane occasionally drive boats into one another and on to the rocks, reminding residents of the fury mariners have always faced seaward of the Piscataqua. –MG

Sources: Byron Fairchild, *Messrs. William Pepperrell: Merchants at Piscataqua* (Ithaca, NY: Cornell University Press, 1954); John Eldridge Frost, *Colonial Village*, 2nd ed. (Kittery, Maine: Kittery Historical Society, 1980); *The Island and Harbor Echo*, vol. IV, no. 1, January 1897 (school alumni publication; Archives of Rice Library, Kittery, Maine); Interviews with Joseph W. P. Frost, March and June 2001.

Pen and ink drawing of the Sir William Pepperrell House, from Samuel Adams Drake, Nooks and Corners of the New England Coast, *1875. Courtesy of the Milne Special Collections and Archives Department, University of New Hampshire.*

HENDERSON'S POINT

Henderson's Point from Seavey's Island, looking toward Peirce and Shapleigh Islands, circa 1902. Extending approximately five hundred feet into the Piscataqua River's main channel, this sharp bend was nicknamed "Pull-and-be-Damned Point." The powerful current wrapping around it could slow steam-powered tugs to a crawl. The cove to the left of the white house was a popular landing for the wherries used to ferry men to and from work at the Portsmouth Naval Shipyard. The oarsmen that taxied around the point did so with a fair current, or risked never making it in the intended direction. The point has not existed since 1905. Courtesy of Portsmouth Athenaeum.

HUMANS HAVE ALWAYS AFFECTED THE PISCATAQUA LANDSCAPE. Algonquian peoples systematically burned the forest. Europeans then felled trees, cleared fields, dammed rivers, filled inlets, and ultimately erased significant features of the landscape. The removal of Henderson's Point between 1902 and 1905 is a vivid example of the careening industrial momentum of the age and pure can-do spirit.

Since the destruction of Henderson's Point, improved understanding of the consequences of ecological tinkering has changed the way we think about altering the natural landscape. Yet contemporary manipulation of this landscape continues. While the Piscataqua River's hard bottom and swift current means that the naturally deep channel is mostly self-dredging, persistent trouble spots require regular deepening to ensure ships' safety.

The Port Authority sponsors much of the dredging on the coastline and rivers that compose the Piscataqua estuary. They must now satisfy state and federal requirements, provide tests and surveys, and consider abutters and environmental interests before even one bucket of bottom is disturbed. –NBB

The removal of Henderson's Point occurred in several stages, and ultimately took three years of excavation and blasting. The semi-watertight wooden cofferdam held back enough of the river so that the brave gangs in the pit could dig and drill. The cofferdam and excavation shown here were probably photographed from Peirce Island, circa 1905. Courtesy of Strawbery Banke Museum.

Inside the cofferdam, circa 1905. Nine men carry a drill section. Fifty tons of dynamite was rammed into deep holes drilled both vertically and horizontally into the rock ledge. Courtesy of Strawbery Banke Museum.

The Big Blast, July 22, 1905. Some reports claimed the explosion was the largest in the country; others claimed it to be the largest in the world. Special trains ran to and from Boston for the event. Among the eighteen thousand spectators were dignitaries, captains of both ships and industry, and engineers from around the nation and abroad. Photograph by C. S. Gurney. (Note that someone defaced the lower right portion of this glass-plate negative. They scratched out "Copyright 1905 by C. S. Gurney.") Courtesy of Strawbery Banke Museum.

The Aftermath. The tug Portsmouth *and numerous small craft crowd in for a look at the aftermath, and to collect fish and firewood. The bit of ledge remaining (right-center of river and photo) was blown up in a second blast with little fanfare. The underwater remains of Henderson's Point can be seen in Color Plate V. Courtesy of Strawbery Banke Museum.*

SEAPOINT BEACH AND THE RACHEL CARSON NATIONAL WILDLIFE REFUGE

SO POWERFUL WAS THE INFAMOUS NO-NAME STORM of Halloween 1991 that its huge waves rearranged almost a third of the promontory at Seapoint Beach, flinging huge rocks over the barrier beach into the adjacent marsh and leaving a debris field where none existed before, the stupendous slurry resounding for miles. Although Seapoint recovered most of its beachfront, the truncated spit only seems to presage the time when another Perfect Storm will finish the job, when Seapoint Beach will go the way of its neighbor, Crescent Beach, and bury most of its sand under berms of stones deposited by an unimpeded ocean. Until that happens, however, Seapoint stands as a singular strand in southern Maine, more Down East than Gold Coast, a sunbather's delight in the dog days of summer and a beachcomber's lark in the neap tides of spring and fall, a gently sloping crescent of white sand (often wrack-strewn) that delivers up the frigid Atlantic Ocean in classic Maine fashion. Indeed, the setting is the way life should be on this coast, an extensive marsh system protected by the circumference of the curving beach, the wetlands affording a grand proscenium to an upland edge buffering a relatively untouched forest. Save for a scattering of houses near the shore, Cutts Island presents an anomaly for the Vacationland visitor, for it remains relatively pristine, an enclave of natural habitats that comprise the Atlantic barrier-beach ecosystem in all its northern-ended glory. Here the beach, marsh, upland edge, and forest function in unison, an interlacing "wetland" almost ten thousand years old.

Gerrish Island Bridge, Chauncey Creek, Kittery, Maine, 1885. Courtesy of the Society for the Preservation of New England Antiquities.

Natural history is the history of record here, and so it is no surprise to find the name Rachel Carson attached to it. Fully two-thirds of Cutts Island is a national wildlife refuge, dedicated to her memory in 1970. Indeed, starting here with the Brave Boat Harbor Division, The Rachel Carson National Wildlife Refuge extends in stepping stone fashion all the way up the southern Maine coast, comprising ten divisions in all. Of those, the 565 acres of Brave Boat Harbor is the least disturbed of all the wetlands in southern Maine. Indeed of all the divisions this one is most evocative of the woman and her writing. One can trek through the splendid mixed forest dense with pine, oak, maple, birch, and ash, emerging at the site of the old trestle, with its wonderful view of the marsh and the broad tidal inlet. That surf-guarded channel brings the sea directly into the sluiceways of the marsh. Here, at the very beginning of Maine, one can find a seascape remarkable for its quiet beauty and plenitude. As if it came from the pen of Rachel Carson herself, this stirring location, so distant from the vacationland onslaught just a few miles away, invites reverie and contemplation, the "thoughts of all the birds and other creatures and all the loveliness that is in nature."

Rachel Carson National Wildlife Refuge, 2001. Photograph by Peter E. Randall. Courtesy of the photographer.

The denizens of Cutts Island, aside from the few humans, number in the thousands. Among the terrestrial mammals are white-tailed deer in voracious numbers, red and gray fox, coyotes and raccoons and skunks, snowshoe hares and fishers, pine voles and gray squirrels and eastern chipmunks, shorttail shrews and masked shrews and meadow voles, meadow jumping mice and Gapper's red-black vole, mink and short and long-tailed weasels. Harbor seals frequent the channel, and the occasional stray moose lumbers into the Reserve. American black ducks, red-breasted mergansers, buffleheads, common goldeneyes, mallards, and Canadian geese share the skies overhead with the least tern and roseate tern, osprey and peregrine falcon and bald eagle, and another 250 species making use of the Atlantic Flyway. On the upland edge smooth cordgrass, Olney's bulrush, alkali bulrush, switch grass, and narrow leaf cattail dominate, while in the flood plain of the marsh itself saltmeadow cordgrass (*Spartina alterniflora*) and seashore saltgrass (*Spartina patens*) divide the nutrient spoils, the saltgrass giving rise to saltwater farming—the predominant human activity on this island until the late nineteenth century.

Human history has been kind to Cutts Island. Originally part of the huge seventeenth century Champernowne land-grant, its history remained uneventful through the nineteenth century, with the Cutts family and the Raynes family owning the island between them. Although trees were felled for farm needs, including pasturage and firewood, a rejuvenated forest now remains, unlogged. The marshes

Seapoint Beach, 2001. Photograph by Peter E. Randall. Courtesy of the photographer.

the stretch leading down to the beach. A road was built along the edge of the beach itself, leading to the point, and a short-lived chowder house and hot-dog stand eventually followed. During Prohibition, rumrunners came ashore here, and in World War II patrols from the nearby Coastal Artillery Unit walked the beach, enforcing the black-out. The town closed that littoral road in the late 1950s, and the great nor'easter of 1978 made that closure permanent. During the last two decades Seapoint has become a desirable place to live year-round, and several large houses have been built on land once owned by Rosamund Thaxter, grand-daughter of Celia Thaxter, the renowned Isles of Shoals poet.

That Cutts Island could remain a naturalist's wonder and an environ-mentalist's trophy owes in no small measure to that other presiding spirit, William Francis Raynes, saltwater farmer extraordinaire, whose love for

that, yielding their bounty of salt hay over the centuries (as fecund as the richest Iowa cornfield) have become fallow once again, are pre-served by the Rachel Carson Refuge on the northeast side of the island and by zoning and private ownership on the southern exposure where Chauncey Creek meanders in oxbow fashion toward extinction just shy of Seapoint Beach.

Seapoint Beach itself supported a small arts colony at the end of the nineteenth century, an offshoot of the renowned colony on Appledore Island (visible from the rocks on the promontory). At the beginning of the twentieth century rusticators built summer cabins on

this island was only exceeded by his generosity in deeding much of his property to the Rachel Carson Refuge. Without his abiding resistance to developmental pressures, Cutts Island would be just another exclu-sive address. That it belongs to the Rachel Carson Refuge instead is a tribute to the man; Brave Boat Harbor would not be what it is with-out his prosaic bravery. –RWA

Sources: Robert Andersen, "Driving New England's Historic Coast," *The New York Times* (July 23, 1989); Robert Andersen, "Savoring Maine's Unspoiled Nature," *The New York Times* (July 7, 1991).

The John Thaxter house, Cutts Island, Kittery Point. Better known as Champernowne Farm, this house overlooking Seapoint Beach was built by the son of poet Celia Thaxter, about 1890. The site was first built upon circa 1640, by Captain Francis Champernowne, a nephew of Sir Fernando Gorges; then again in 1773 by the Cutts family. Photograph by Douglas Armsden, circa 1950. Courtesy of the photographer.

YORK

YORK RIVER, THE JOHN HANCOCK WAREHOUSE, AND MARSHALL STORE

THE THREE PRIMARY BUILDINGS IN THIS IMAGE still stand today, clear evidence of the past in the present. George A. Marshall built the store, at left, in 1870, after buying the land from Alexander Dennett three years before. The store was the "last word" when built. The large cellar door (partially obscured by stacked wood) opened directly onto the wharf and was wide enough for the hogsheads of Barbados molasses that filled the jugs "for all of York and part of Kittery and Elliot [sic]." George's daughter Katherine took over the business in 1905 and ran it as a general store until closing in the late 1930s. The Marshall Store shipped kidney beans to buyers in Washington DC, and sent salt-fish to customers in Iowa. For customers closer to home the

York River, the John Hancock Warehouse, and the George A. Marshall Store, circa 1890. Hancock's warehouse is the dark, two-story building near the water. Marshall's store is the white, three-story building to the left. Courtesy of Old York Historical Society.

store carried everything from groceries to hardware to sou'westers and coal.

The two schooners at the Marshall wharf are probably delivering goods for the store. Coasting schooners were the trucks of the late nineteenth century, as common then as eighteen-wheelers are today. Schooners brought coal to the store from Perth Amboy, New Jersey, and often continued downeast to Stonington, Maine, for return cargoes of paving granite. The Marshalls had a steam hoist for unloading coal, but it still took three days or more. Once the schooner crews unloaded the cargoes, they were occasionally paid off in York. This could lead to days of celebration, which raised eyebrows (and occasionally fists) of the local populace. Rude behavior by transient sailors was rarely welcome, even in maritime towns.

The warehouse in the center of the photo has a longer and perhaps more romantic history. John Hancock acquired half interest in the warehouse from Daniel Bragdon about 1780. Opinions vary as to whether the acquisition was a simple sale or mortgage foreclosure, but it is agreed that Hancock shared ownership with Joseph Tucker. It is also uncertain whether Hancock ever actually visited York or if he enlisted a local agent for his business arrangements.

John Hancock was the first to sign the Declaration of Independence, his legendary flowing signature large enough for the King to read without his spectacles. He is also known for his vast wealth. Hancock had wharves and warehouses all along the Northeast coast, as well as vessels to shelter and transport his goods. The reason for Hancock's interest in a small warehouse in York, Maine, may have to do with the building's seclusion. A booklet published in 1968 by the Society for the Preservation of Historic Landmarks in York County indicates, "The surreptitious storage of tea and other contraband in riverside storehouses was a common practice. Although he paid legal duty on Madeira wine, it was well known that [Hancock] paid no taxes where he considered them unjust." Ebenezer Hancock, John's brother and heir, sold his inherited interest in the York warehouse and wharf back to Joseph Tucker. The property was passed down through generations until it was purchased for preservation by the Newcomen Society in 1954.

The Samuel Lindsay House (circa 1793) sits upon the knoll at right. Samuel Lindsay was a mariner and ship's captain, and the son of a local tavern keeper; the frontage road still bears their family name. This Georgian-style home was nearly a century old when this image was made, and it is still a private residence today.

The couple rowing the elegant Whitehall-type pulling boat in the foreground could have no better conditions. The emblem on the pulling boat's bow indicates that it was from a livery in York Harbor and that this was pure recreation. A century ago recreational rowing was the equivalent of today's kayak craze. Rowing a Whitehall boat in dress clothes, an activity of leisured middle- or upper-class people, was understood as something quite distinct from the necessity of rowing a dory for work. The flat calm on this day assured smooth rowing, dry clothes, and security for the elaborate headwear. Some clues in the photo suggest it was taken on a falling tide with a light ebb current. Look at the height of the water and the attitude of the outboard schooner's dory, which is being pulled by the tide to the right, downstream. With those conditions, the women rowing were assured a quick trip back to the livery by starting out against the current.

Both the Marshall Store and the Hancock Warehouse are now maintained by the Old York Historical Society, whose site and properties connect visitors with York's maritime heritage. –NBB

Sources: Magazine Section, Lewiston Journal, Lewiston, Maine. May 4, 1940; York Maine, Then and Now, A Pictorial Documentation. Old Gaol Museum Committee and the Old York Historical and Improvement Society. (Somersworth, NH, New England History Press, 1976); John Hancock, His Wharf and Warehouse, (Society for the Preservation of Historic Landmarks in York County, Inc., 1968).

SEWALL'S BRIDGE AND THE ELIZABETH PERKINS HOUSE

Just upriver from the Marshall Store and Hancock Warehouse, a ferry operated from sometime in the seventeenth century to about 1754. At low tide one can still see the stumpy pilings on the mud flats that mark the site of that ferry. But in 1754 Samuel Sewall, an engineer, housewright, and cabinetmaker, began the construction of a pile-driven drawbridge of his own design adjacent to the ferry. Sewall's bridge has carried traffic across the river since that time. The bridge, the first of its type in America, was restored and reconstructed in the 1930s as an alternative to a planned concrete replacement. The bronze tablet commemorating the bridge's status as a National Engineering Landmark sits at its north end. Sewall's bridge is historic in more than ways than one: in 1775, sixty-one York patriots marched over this bridge to join the battles of Lexington and Concord.

The large set of red buildings on the south bank of the river after Sewall's Bridge is the Elizabeth Perkins property of the Old York Historical Society. The main part of the house dates from the 1730s, and parts of its rear wing are purported to have been built in 1686. The dramatically gabled outline and large bulk of the river side of the house date from renovations and enlargements during the 1920s. Today the property is restored to 1951, the last year Miss Elizabeth Perkins, one of the founders and a major benefactress of the Old York Historical Society, was in summer residence. The house

Sewall's Bridge looking upriver towards Perkins house, circa 1900. Photograph by Elizabeth Bishop Perkins, nitrate negative. Courtesy of the Old York Historical Society.

is open to the public and displays a notable and wide-ranging collection of American, European, and Oriental fine and decorative arts. The

View of York River and Elizabeth Perkins' Native American statue, circa 1938-1940. Courtesy of Old York Historical Society.

boathouse adjacent to the bridge, the location of the annual summer lecture series, was added to the property in 1935.

The point of land upriver from the boathouse is actually the remains of an eighteenth century wharf. Today it is surveyed by the "Perkins Indian," a carved wooden figure placed by Miss Perkins, ostensibly in homage to the original inhabitants of the town of York. Its annual appearance on the riverbank in early June signals the beginning of the summer social season in York. The local landmark remains in place until Columbus Day Weekend, when the great summer homes were traditionally closed. Summering in York, a trend started during the Colonial Revival, has been a custom for some people for more than a century. The summer residents venerated traditions, including the Perkins Indian, because they suggested continuity, even though summering—like so many other activities along Piscataqua waters—has stayed much the same even as it has changed over time. –TBJ

Sources: George Ernst, *New England Miniature: A History of York, Maine* (Freeport, Maine: The Bond-Wheelwright Company, 1961); Sarah L. Giffen and Kevin D. Murphy, *"A Noble and Dignified Stream": The Piscataqua Region in the Colonial Revival, 1860-1930* (York, Maine: The Old York Historical Society, 1992); Charles Edward Banks, *History of York, Maine.* Vols. I & II. (Portsmouth, NH: Peter E. Randall, 1990 [1931-1935]).

"Up River"

Just beyond the Perkins House are the manicured lawns of the York Country Club, the site of the large Norton Brick Yard in the nineteenth century. Further upstream, the river bends to reveal a large rock at low tide thought to resemble the profile of a ram's head; this rock gave its name to an adjacent farm on the south bank. The yellow farmhouse on the rise surveys this domain, now protected for perpetuity under conservation easements.

Up river from the golf course just before the Route 1 Bridge and I-95 double spans is the gleaming white façade of "River House," the Breckinridge-Patterson estate. Built by a daughter of rubber magnate B. F. Goodrich, the house and grounds were presented to Bowdoin College in the 1970s and are now known as the Breckinridge Public Affairs Center. Near the riverbank the columned "gymnasium" and pergola sit at the edge of the largest round in-ground saltwater swimming pool in New England, if not America.

Passing under the I-95 spans, the next point of land on the right is the site of Sir Ferdinando Gorges's manor house, built in 1641. Gorges was the founder of York, but this property, now privately owned, is not accessible to the public.

Further on is Scotland Bridge, another ancient river crossing. Beyond, in an area of sinuous turns meandering through salt marshes that typify the York River's upstream reaches, one can glimpse the McIntire Garrison House. This gray-shingled building with its massive center chimney and medieval overhangs is one of Maine's oldest documented buildings, dating from 1707. The McIntire Garrison is still privately owned by descendents of its builder. They have preserved not only the building, but also the aura of openness that settlers knew by donating conservation easements on the surrounding land. –TBJ

The McIntire Garrison, built in 1707, is one of the oldest buildings in Maine. Photograph by Henry A. Harding, circa 1975. Courtesy of the Old York Historical Society.

Sources: George Ernst, *New England Miniature: A History of York, Maine* (Freeport, Maine: The Bond-Wheelwright Company, 1961); Sarah L. Giffen and Kevin D. Murphy, "*A Noble and Dignified Stream*": *The Piscataqua Region in the Colonial Revival, 1860-1930* (York, Maine: The Old York Historical Society, 1992); Charles Edward Banks, *History of York, Maine.* Vols. I & II. (Portsmouth, NH: Peter E. Randall, 1990 [1931-1935]).

The upper reaches of the York River from the McIntire Garrison. This watery landscape is protected by conservation easements. Photograph by Henry A. Harding, circa 1975. Courtesy of the Old York Historical Society.

THE SAYWARD-WHEELER HOUSE

THE SAYWARD-WHEELER HOUSE, situated on the banks of the York River, overlooks the harbor and a small fishing fleet. In 1718, when the house was built, an active fleet of sloops and schooners from York sailed the eastern seaboard and to Caribbean ports. The Sayward family, which owned the house by 1730, was among York's earliest mill builders. Had it not been for their ability to harness mill streams and the sea itself, the Saywards would not have prospered, and it is unlikely that their imposing home would have been spared from what Sarah Orne Jewett later called the "destroying left arm of progress." The Sayward House is an extraordinary artifact, an example not only of colonial craftsmanship, but of the values that prevailed in this region for centuries.

Most people in colonial New England worked the land, but the possibility for profit was much greater in milling and maritime commerce. The Saywards tried it all. Henry Sayward's mills in York burned down in 1669, but he rebuilt there and acquired other mills as far north as Wells and North Yarmouth. Henry nevertheless died a poor man in 1679, his properties mortgaged. His descendant Joseph Sayward, however, in partnership with Johnson Harmon, gave permission to the New Mill Company for the construction of a dam, and erection and operation of a saw and gristmill at Barrell Mill Pond in York in 1725-26. Sayward and Harmon then owned the land to the east and west of the pond. But Joseph Sayward, like Henry before him, also experienced serious financial difficulties.

In 1732 Joseph's son Jonathan bought what is now known as the Sayward-Wheeler house from his father, as well as many of the remaining mill shares. Jonathan moved into the house with his new wife and expanded his business ventures by investing in small shipments of

Lantern slide of the Sayward-Wheeler House, by Elizabeth Bishop Perkins. Courtesy of Old York Historical Society.

goods to Nova Scotia and the West Indies. With previous experience as a deckhand, he began to sail as captain of his own coasting vessels. This included regular trips to the Isles of Shoals, Portsmouth, and Boston, as well as to more remote destinations. A man-on-the-make with poise and presence, Jonathan Sayward received a commission from Governor Shirley in 1745 to command a small ship, the *Sea Flower*, in the attack on Fortress Louisbourg. Under the command of Kittery's William Pepperrell, a contingent of colonials from the Piscataqua region conquered the famous French fortress in Nova Scotia. Although the victory was short-lived, Sayward and others returned with booty, as well as with a sense of military valor.

By 1764 Jonathan Sayward had become a leading citizen, a Justice of the Peace, a deacon in the Congregational Church, a representative to the Massachusetts General Court, and a very wealthy man. In addition to his ocean-going vessels and imposing house in the harbor, he owned six farms in York, many woodlots, and five hundred acres of unimproved land. In 1760 Sarah Sayward, Jonathan's only daughter, married Nathaniel Barrell, the son of a wealthy Boston merchant. Barrell was then doing business in Portsmouth. It may have been on this occasion that the parlor of the house on the York River was updated with the latest Georgian details, such as fluted pilasters flanking new mantels and paneled walls.

Most of the Saywards' privileges ended abruptly, however, during the political crisis that foreshadowed the American Revolution. The Townsend Revenue Act of 1767 prompted the Massachusetts General Court (i.e., the legislature) to issue a circular letter to other colonies inviting them to boycott British goods. The British ministry demanded that the Massachusetts legislature rescind the letter or face punishment. Sayward was one of the few representatives, and the only one from the province of Maine, who voted to rescind. As a "rescinder," Sayward lost the confidence of his townsmen, and for years thereafter his poignant diary entries reveal his inner conflict with what he considered the madness of the revolutionaries.

Once one of the wealthiest self-made men in New England, and then a distrusted Tory, Jonathan Sayward died in 1797. He left the family house to his eldest grandson, Jonathan Sayward Barrell. Subsequently Barrell's two elderly unmarried sisters lived there and showed the house—largely unchanged since their grandfather's day—to visitors as early as 1860. Like many other old families in the region who had once had assets, but who did not shift them into textile mills or other investments, the Barrell sisters lived quite modestly, despite their genteel surroundings. As Victorian ladies conscious of their heritage, they looked to the past.

At the turn of the twentieth century Elizabeth Cheever Wheeler, a direct descendant of Jonathan Sayward, purchased the house. As a child she had visited the Barrell sisters. Wheeler desired not only an exclusive summer retreat from the hustle and bustle of modern life, but a slice of colonial maritime history and family history as well. The Wheelers summered there for years, and several generations developed fond memories of time spent at the old Sayward House. In the early 1970s their family generously donated the house, its contents, the land, and an endowment for its upkeep to SPNEA (the Society for the Preservation of New England Antiquities).

Today the Sayward-Wheeler House is an extraordinary example of architectural and cultural preservation. For nearly two hundred years after Jonathan Sayward's death, the house's inhabitants viewed him and his era as a legacy worth preserving. Thus the best parlor, overlooking a porch and the glorious riverfront, still contains chairs from 1760 with original upholstery. Engravings of George III and members of the English nobility, as well as Sayward's commission from Royal Governor Shirley, adorn the walls. Trophies from the expedition to Louisbourg are on display, as are an extraordinary set of Chinese export plates that Nathaniel Barrell purchased in England between 1760 and 1763, while establishing business contacts in London and Bristol. The house is a monument not only to early York's maritime trade and to the refinement of its British colonial squirearchy, but to subsequent generations' veneration of that past.

Although the adjacent Barrell Pond is no longer part of the property and the water-driven mills have long gone, the site remains evocative of the time when the Piscataqua was primarily a maritime region. The bridge (formerly the Boston and Maine Railroad bridge) leading south on Route 103 brings one past the pond, now separated by the "wiggly bridge" from a sheltered tongue of land that is a delightful nature reserve. Walking along the path, which was possibly a Native trail, and which has been used as a shortcut since the first English and Scottish settlers arrived in York, one reaches Sewell Bridge, leading across the York River from Lindsay Road to the Old York Historical Society's Perkins House. This section of York, one of its oldest, has changed less over time than any other and is protected by covenants to keep it that way. –USW

Sources: Charles Edward Banks, *History of York, Maine.* Vols. I & II. (Baltimore: Regional Pub. Co., 1967 [1931-1935]); Kirk J. Upton, "The Loss of Trade, The Scorn of Abjects, The Slight of Friends: The Life of Jonathan Sayward, A Maine Merchant and Loyalist, Based on His Diary," (Master's thesis, University of New Hampshire, 1992); Richard C. Nylander, "The Jonathan Sayward House, York, Maine," *Antiques* (September 1979).

York's History of Land Conservation

Drifting in a canoe on the upper reaches of the York River, perhaps on Smelt Brook as the tide has turned toward the sea, is beautiful and peaceful. At times there are no houses in sight and centuries are erased. The narrow river curves around on itself, enclosing high tide ponds filled with wading birds. Salt marsh is everywhere. Hawks patrol on duty. Kingfishers perch on tree branches preparing to dive. Timelessness prevails.

Population pressures on southwestern Maine, however, mean that unless towns like York confront head-on the implications of growth, this environment will be compromised or irrevocably lost. Fortunately the York Land Trust and the York Rivers Association recognize the urgency of protecting water quality, wildlife habitat, and a distinctive landscape of forest, field, and marsh. Growth is inevitable, but it need not be recklessly destructive of the York we have known.

The York River rises almost entirely in the town of York. Feeder streams in Eliot are important to the upper reaches of the river, which has had a history of abundant smelt, herring, and flounder populations. And as a healthy estuary, the York River contributes significantly to the productivity of the Gulf of Maine. The river and its tributaries have served residents for hundreds of years: middens along the riverbanks attest to the abundant shellfish that sustained Native American populations in the summer, and settlers' sawmills, gristmills, and brickyards took advantage of the flowing streams. Before the construction of bridges, travel by boat was routine. During the twentieth century, as the human population expanded, the river became a playground, used especially for recre-

View of York River, circa 1893. Photograph collection of Marvin Breckinridge Patterson. Courtesy of Old York Historical Society.

ational fishing and boating. Beautiful views and a sense of serenity and timelessness attracted homeowners. While some wise landowners kept their properties intact for years, residential development on the river and subdivision of farms and forest progressed rapidly. This trend recently inspired a movement to inform residents, boaters, and town planners about the river's extraordinary value. Now residents are giving back to the river.

In 1994 the growing need for education about the York River and land conservation in its watershed inspired Carol Donnelly to invite the Radcliffe Seminars Landscape Design Program to study the river. Led by John Furlong, a group of graduate students spent six months studying the natural and cultural environment of the York River. Their report examined the potential for continued growth and its impact on the local environment. From this emerged a master plan (available at the York Public Library) that outlined plausible conservation and preservation alternatives.

At the conclusion of the Radcliffe study, the York Rivers Association was created to raise awareness about the river. A series of well-attended lectures on the river's past, present, and future followed, while a series of newsletters entitled "Sharing the Lifeline" were published and distributed to five thousand households as an insert in *The York Weekly*. In the summer of 2000, more than one hundred people participated in the York River Survey in kayaks and canoes and on foot, and a brochure on good boating practices and local history was produced to encourage stewardship of the river. The York Harbor Master and the National Park Service Rivers, Trails, and Conservation Assistance Program have partnered with the York Rivers Association in these accomplishments.

When efforts to deepen appreciation of the York River began in 1994, few residents were aware that an organization—the York Land Trust, formed in 1987—existed to help property owners conserve their land. The Trust owns land and secures, holds, and monitors easements in the Yorks, Cape Neddick, Ogunquit, Wells, and South Berwick. Easements, legal restrictions a property owner may place on privately held land, become part of the deed; when the land changes hands, new owners are bound by the terms of the easement. Typical conservation easements prohibit subdivision or new construction.

Genuine excitement about the possibilities of conserving land in the York River watershed inspired the Trust's Board of Directors to increase its activities and outreach. The board expanded its membership and focused on providing information to homeowners about land preservation options available through the York Land Trust and other organizations such as the Maine Coast Heritage Trust. Preserving the York River became a top priority.

By early 2000, the York Land Trust had become the permanent steward of 840 acres, including picturesque river lands such as the thirty-six-acre field and salt marsh on Route 91 owned by Mary McIntire Davis. This beautiful field with its beloved view of the York River will never be developed. The Fuller family has donated an easement on Southside Road called Ram's Head Farm River Land, which includes thirty-nine acres of field, forest, and pine plantation with extensive river frontage. This historic property has a view treasured by residents and visitors alike. A similar easement exists on the farm owned by Marion Fuller Brown across Southside Road. Other public-spirited landowners along the river are in the final stages of negotiating easements with the York Land Trust, thus preventing thousands of feet of river frontage from further development and protecting water quality, wildlife habitat, and river views.

A century ago York residents taken with the Colonial Revival movement struggled to preserve old homes and buildings. Today another generation of stewards is working to preserve York's land and waters. Without these dedicated conservationists and the continuation of their efforts, the York we have known could be lost. –HW

Sources: Charles Edward Banks, *History of York, Maine*. Vols. I & II. (Baltimore, Regional Publishing Company, 1967 [1931-1935]); *York River Watershed Study* (Radcliffe Graduate School of Landscape Design Environmental Studies, 1995); interviews with Marion Fuller Brown, Lynn Eaton, and Carol Donnelly, 2000.

EPILOGUE

SUSTAINING A SENSE OF PLACE

THIS BOOK HAS INVITED YOU TO CONNECT with the Piscataqua maritime region in light of its past, and future, as an estuary, and to use maritime history and environmental conservation to forge meaningful links with place. Whether you are a visitor, a newcomer, or a tenth-generation resident with deep family roots, consciousness of local history and nature can be cultivated. An informed awareness of our surroundings connects each of us to place, to the historical continuums and natural systems to which we belong, and, indeed, to the mysteries of our humanity.

Surroundings obviously trigger discernable physiological and psychological responses. Anyone who has had night descend on a mountainside when they have blundered alone far from the well-marked trail, or has taken a wrong turn in the run-down waterfront of a strange city, has felt a visceral response to place. Alternatively, some places, whether human-built or wild, are richly nourishing. They prompt enthusiastic affirmation, or inspire a quiet calm. Such surroundings, observes Tony Hiss, in *The Experience of Place*, make us feel connected and complete, more human, and more resourceful. Those places are worth savoring, celebrating, and preserving. They are also worth understanding. The Piscataqua maritime region is rich in such sites.

All of us benefit from the fact that people still use this estuary without overwhelming it. In fact, the Piscataqua's hallmark has long

A street scene from New Castle in the 1920s. Photograph by Paul Rubens Frost. Courtesy of the Portsmouth Athenaeum.

been the presence of human heritage and nonhuman nature as a backdrop for ongoing human occupation. It is neither entirely "wild," nor "civilized," and somehow the balance seems reassuring. Much of the quiet charm and profound satisfaction that people find here originates in a landscape that is simultaneously historic and natural. Ice fishermen, historic house guides, real estate agents, recreational boaters, and every artist who has ever been moved by a glimpse of local waters knows that magic. Now, in the face of intense developmental pressure, the challenge is to make residents and visitors aware of the Piscataqua's fragility.

Consciously cultivating a sense of place defined by the estuary's maritime heritage and its ecological diversity will provide bearings for concerned residents as they try to sustain a viable Piscataqua. Gertrude Stein once quipped about Oakland, California, that when you get there, there isn't any "there" there. How impoverished would life be, for visitors and residents alike, if the Piscataqua lost what had been characteristic of the region for centuries? Savoring the Piscataqua's historical inheritance and preserving its natural environments is one way to keep the soul of this special place intact, thereby nourishing ourselves and future generations. –WJB

Source: Tony Hiss, *The Experience of Place* (NY: Vintage Books, 1990).

A kayaker paddles past the historic Sheafe Warehouse in Portsmouth. Photograph by Ralph Morang, 2001. Courtesy of the photographer.

New Castle, near Pest Island looking toward the causeway. Photograph by Davis Brothers, circa 1900. Courtesy of Portsmouth Athenaeum.